DIARIES
of an
ADIRONDACK BOY
1890–1901

The Years When "School Didn't Keep"

SCHROON-NORTH HUDSON HISTORICAL SOCIETY, INC.
from the Diaries of Walter J. S. Whitney

Graphics North
Jay, NY

Printed in the United States of America
09 08 06   5 4 3 2 1

Library of Congress Control Number: 2004105234

Bibliography: p. 351

Diaries of an Adirondack Boy 1890–1901
Schroon North Hudson Historical Society
    The personal diaries of a young Schroon Lake boy kept from
    1890 through 1901, just before his early death.

ISBN 0-9643452-3-4

Book Design, Cover Design, and
Special Diary Photographics: Nadine McLaughlin

Printed on 70# Accent® Opaque, Warm White, Smooth finish
paper proudly produced at International Paper's Ticonderoga mill
from working Adirondack forests, managed responsibly in accordance
with the principles of the *Sustainable Forestry Initiative®* (SFIsm).

Published by Graphics North
PO Box 218, Jay, New York 12941, USA

A picture of Walter Whitney's home taken in later years

When the name that I write here
is dim on the page
And the leaves of your album
are yellow with age,
Still think of me kindly,
and do not forget,
That wherever I am,
I remember you yet.

CONTENTS

1890 – Walter's first diary 18

1891 – Farming 38

1892 – Transportation 62

1893 – Industry 86

1894 – Churches 116

1895 – Medicine 146

1896 – Schools 180

1897 – Taylor's Hotel 208

1898 – Year of the missing diary 239

1899 – Home on the farm 240

1900 – At the turn of the century 276

1901 – Fairs 306

Epilogue 335

Two extra note books 337

Family Names 340

Genealogy 341

Family Album 343

Credits 351

Mrs. Maxim's headstone in the South Schroon Cemetery

PREFACE

THE Schroon-North Hudson Historical Society was started when Jack Richards met in his home with a small group of interested people in 1972. In 1976 the Society received its permanent charter from the University of the State of New York. From the very beginning the By Laws of the Society had as its objectives "to amplify, enhance and foster interest in the history of the towns of Schroon and North Hudson..."

It is in the spirit of furthering these goals that brought our Society to the decision to publish these diaries, because they preserve the first-hand experiences of a boy who grew up in South Schroon before the turn of the century.

Virginia Deming Baumgartner donated these diaries to the Society. She apparently found the box containing the diaries in her house when she bought it. If it were not for her thoughtfulness, we would not be reading them today.

The committee who worked with these diaries to ready them for publication found that each reading revealed more and more information. The writer does not elaborate as a novelist would, but gives short, terse statements devoid of emotion, such as, "Mrs. Maxim burned today and so she died."

In other places, a statement is repeated day after day. We felt this, although repetitious, gives the reader an understanding of how much time certain activities took in those days. In late winter, tapping trees and boiling sap for maple products consumed the better parts of February, March and April. Planting started in May. Haying took place in June, July, and August. The fall was for harvesting and preserving. Logging took place in the winter months.

The names of people mentioned by Walter in his day-to-day activities give substance to the names on the grave stones in the South Schroon cemetery. These were people who interacted with one another, and many are the ancestors of you who are reading this book.

The Society feels we would not be fulfilling our mission statement if we did not put these diaries into a form which is accessible to all.

Betty M.Osolin, *President*
Schroon-North Hudson Historical Society, Inc.

Winter Scene, Schroon Lake, N.Y.

ACKNOWLEDGEMENTS

The Schroon-North Hudson Historical Society wishes to thank the following persons for their invaluable assistance with the Whitney Diaries.

Without them it would not have been possible to get this project off the ground.

We are indebted to Joseph Swinyer, who called our attention to this valuable resource in our collection. He was the first to suggest that the Society might want to publish the diaries some day. Joy Cook took on the momentous task of typing the text verbatim from the original diaries. Clara Connell then checked the originals with the typed copy. Ann Breen Metcalfe contributed her knowledge, research, and encouragement to the effort. Virginia Fish, Charlotte Rowe, Lucille Roblee, Ruthede Burke, Don Hale, Jack Burke, Merrett Hulst, Mr. and Mrs. Hal Bloom, and Eleanor Jenks all contributed information related to the life of Walter Whitney. A special thanks to Fred Danz, who gave a sizable donation to the project. Bob Borquist and John Osolin made the pen and ink sketches which are scattered throughout the text. Brenda Borquist did the research and composed the paragraphs at the beginning of each year, which put Walter's diaries into the context of the world at that time. Dick Newell was responsible for introducing us to Nadine McLaughlin, who has been much more than just a publisher and designer of this book. She has been our mentor, patient advisor, and friend.

We are grateful to the Diary Committee: Chairperson Rita Burdick, Joan Mohrmann, Brenda Borquist, and Betty Osolin. They spent many hours planning, researching, and editing to bring the diary to its final form. The Committee is especially grateful to the Board of the Schroon-North Hudson Historical Society, which stood behind the project.

A very special thanks to Betty Osolin, whose love of history, whose firm belief in the importance of preserving the past, and whose vision and enthusiasm for this project was the impetus that engaged all of the people connected with this publication and brought the project to its fruition.

Thank you one and all for your assistance.

*Many great minds refer to the past
as a beacon for the future.
With the sincere desire
to preserve the past
for the children of tomorrow,
the Historical Society invites you
to enjoy the entries
WALTER J. S. WHITNEY
penned in his diaries
as his mark on humanity.*

INTRODUCTION

The Historical Society of Schroon and North Hudson takes pride in introducing you to Walter J. S. Whitney, a local historic figure.

Walter Whitney was born in South Schroon on March 24, 1882. He lived with his parents, Lewis and Marion Whitney, a few miles south of Schroon Lake village on what was then the south end of Charley Hill Road. He died at age 19 on January 9, 1902. In his short life and limited worldly experience, he was a student, musician, a scholar, and a teacher. His travels extended as far south as Chestertown, and as far north as Crown Point. His days as a young boy were dotted with the usual homespun activities of domestic chores, "getting lessons," going to church, planting, harvesting, sugaring, and playing with his cat.

What makes his name so special today is the legacy he leaves to all of us through the diary entries he wrote from 1890–1901. In spite of his short life and inexperience, his diligent entries transport us back in time, give us a look at our cultural heritage, and provide us with the point of view of a young boy growing up during the Gilded Age in a small Adirondack community.

Each entry portrays the security in the mutual give and take of small community life. Each one demonstrates how this 19th century life was comfortably and confidently settled amidst the events, the progress, and the sophistication of the rest of the world.

DIARIES
of an
ADIRONDACK BOY
1890–1901

The **1890 diary,** *Walter's first, has a lovely tan genuine-leather cover stamped with an artistic design, but the overall condition of this volume is poorer than most of the others. The age-yellowed, blue-lined pages have come away from the binding in one loose section; and the boy's entries end abruptly at the bottom of the last page with the one for December 11. There is, however, a single larger sheet of paper folded carefully and tucked inside the book. This has all the missing entries for 1890 written on both sides.*

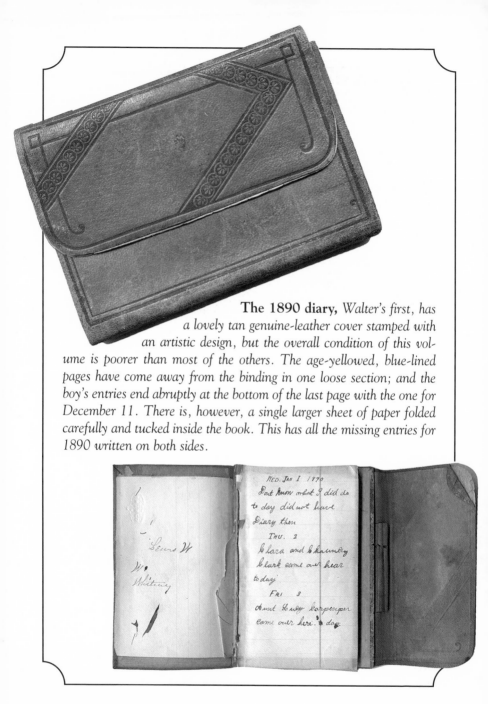

Tapping maple trees

The 1890 era was the beginning of the age of technology. The onset of electricity drove industry out of the home and into the factories where 12-hour shifts needed workers to keep the machines running, and there would soon be plenty of people to do that. On December 31, 1890, Ellis Island opened as the United States immigration depot, and the Great White Way lured people from England, Ireland, and Europe; and the melting pot bubbled.

Tenement and rooming houses of New York City were crowded, yet a refuge to the new factory workers and gold to the landlords. They came into the harbor in the bowels of the great ships, while the upper decks glittered with the finery of the real estate barons, the oil speculators, and the railroad entrepreneurs. They were the *nouveaux riches*, the American aristocracy, the American "Royals" on their return from the social season in London and Paris.

These aristocrats sometimes made their way to the Adirondack Mountains and the newly found social environment of the Leland House and the Windsor Hotel. They brought with them the immigrants who sidestepped factory employment and found themselves in service in the great mansions and townhouses of New York City. They came as maids, butlers, and footmen; and though they came to work, they, too, reaped the benefits of mountain air, water, and sky, as well as the homegrown products these elements produced, one of which was maple syrup.

Sugaring was an important domestic industry in the Schroon Lake area. Not only adults but children participated in the production of maple syrup. Walter Whitney, in his direct language, records his responsibilities in the process. The Whitneys of South Schroon were industrious about this product, and the fruits of their labor no doubt sweetened the breakfast tables and pleased the palates of many of those guests at the grand hotels.

MAKING MAPLE SYRUP

Production of maple syrup and sugar required a grove of maple trees (sugar bush) and the freezing nights and thawing days that come during early spring in the Adirondacks. The trees were tapped and the sap was collected in buckets. To be rendered into syrup, it had to be boiled to a proper consistency. Walter's use of the word "peaking" may refer to the control of the temperature of boiling sap. The liquid, having reached its peak, could not be allowed to get any hotter.

The arches that Walter watched his father build refer to the area where wood was stacked in an arch-like configuration for the boiling of the sap.

A special treat for adults and children was to fill a bowl with snow and pour the freshly-made syrup on it. The snow cooled and hardened the syrup, turning it into soft candy. Some people ate the syrup and followed that with pickles from brine, alternating the sweet and sour flavors until their bellies were full.

(*This diary for 1890 has no introductory pages or title to designate the author: Walter J.S. Whitney. There is a scrawled name: Lewis W. Whitney.*)

Wednesday, January 1, 1890
Don't know what I did do today. Did not have Diary then.

January 2
Clara and Chauncey Clark came over hear today.

January 3
Aunt Lucy Carpenter came over here today.

January 4
Aunt Lucy brought me a drawing slate. I drew almost all day.

$$2 \times 2 =$$
$$6 \times 6 =$$
$$10 \times 10 =$$

January 5
Got a good lesson. Did not go to Sunday School.

January 6
Don't know what I did do. Did not have Diary then.

January 7
Don't know what I did do.

January 8
Aunt L.A. is sick with Grip. I helped take the loom down.

January 9
Clara Clark came over hear today to color carpet rags.

January 10
Don't know what I did do.

January 11
Don't know what I did do.

January 12
Got a good lesson. Did not go to Sunday School.

January 13
Don't know what I did do.

January 14
Learned to multiply.

January 15
Took tacks out of the carpet.

January 16
Learned the multiplication table 5's.

January 17
I learned the 4's today.

January 18
I went up to Grandma's. Learned 6's coming home. Uncle Jim learned them to me.

January 19
Went up to Grand ma's.

January 20
Got 7's today.

January 21
Aunt Lib came over today.

January 22
Went up to Grand ma's.

21

Thought I froze my
ears going up.
January 23
Did not do much of any-
thing today.
Read a piece in my third
reader.
January 24
Made a wooden watch but
would not run.
January 25
Went up to Grand ma's.
January 26
Went to Sunday School.
January 27
Went to P.O. with Pa in
snow storm.
January 28
Half sick. Pa and Ma went
to Pottersville to have teeth
pulled.
January 29
Half sick Ma and I both.
January 30
I am better. So is Ma.
January 31
Wrote a letter to Grand
ma Culver.

Saturday, February 1, 1890
Did not do much of any-
thing but bother women.
February 2
Went to Sunday School.
February 3
Made a map of N. Y.

February 4
Went up on hill where Pa
was cutting wood.
February 5
The wind has blown and
it has been so icy I rather
stay in the house than go
out and slip down and
bump my crown.
February 6
Went up on hill where Pa
was cutting wood and
brought down big saw.
February 7
Had tooth pulled. Went up
and helped Pa saw up log
with cross cut saw.
February 8
It has been so squally I
have not gone outdoors
much.
Made Uncle Henry a map
of N. Y.
February 9
Went to Sunday School
with Pa.
Ma had teeth ache so she
could not go.
February 10
Made a set of dominoes. Pa

and Ma
went to
have
Ma's
tooth pulled.
February 11
Drew Grand ma Culver's

house. Pa went to town. I helped do the barn chores. Grand ma was down.

February 12

Wrote a letter to Arthur Floyed.

February 13

I have got a little cold in my head.
Wrote a letter to Henry Carpenter.

February 14

Got cold yet blowed my nose a good deal.
Made a little writing book.

February 15

All got cold. Did not do much of anything.

February 16

Had to much cold to go to Sunday School.

February 17

Did not do much of anything. Helped Ma wipe the dishes.

February 18

Did not do much of anything.

February 19

Went outdoors and tried the snow. Read 4 pieces in 3 readers.

February 20

Pa, Ma and I went up to Grand ma's. It has snowed and blowed and drifted some.

February 21

I shoveled a road to hog pen. Read 6 pieces in my 3 readers.

February 22

Went up on hill where Pa was cutting wood.
Got through my reader.

February 23

Went to Sunday School.

February 24

Grand ma was down. I commenced reading through my reader.

February 25

Went over on hill and helped Pa cut up a log with cross cut saw.

February 26

Went up to Grand ma's. Grand ma Whitney went down to Uncle Jim Whitney's. So I helped Ma wipe the dishes.

February 27

Went over on hill where Pa was cutting wood.
Found some gum.

February 28

Went over on hill. Got a letter from Arthur Floyed.

Saturday, March 1, 1890

Went over on hill and helped Pa saw up a log. Grand ma and Uncle

Jim came down.

March 2

Went to Sunday School with a wagon.

March 3

Helped do the chores. Charley Foster worked for Pa.

March 4

Went over on hill. Glen Foster came over with some buckets for Pa to fix. I helped him unload them.

March 5

Went over on hill. Pa and Ma went down to South Schroon. I stayed at home.

March 6

It has been so stormy I have not gone outdoors much. Read 3 pieces.

March 7

Helped Pa do the chores. Weighed my cat and Brahma hen. The cat weighed 5 pounds and hen 6 pounds.

March 8

Went over to Abel Walker's with Pa.

March 9

Went to Sunday School. Clara Clark and two preachers stayed to supper.

March 10

Gathered up eggs all day. Jim Allen give Pa a pickerel which weighed 5 pound and 14 oz.

March 11

Went over to Granger's for Ma. I helped do the chores.

March 12

Helped Pa . Got letter from Aunt Lucy and Henry Carpenter.

March 13

Tagged Pa around all day. Corded up a little wood for Uncle Henry. Chauncey Clark came over.

March 14

Went down to saw mill with Uncle Jim. Corded up some wood for Uncle Henry.

March 15

Helped Pa make a wire door out to barn. Read two pieces in my reader.

March 16

Went to Sunday School.

March 17

Went up to Grand ma's. Pa went to village. Grand ma Whitney got home.

March 18

Uncle Bish's folks came over. Emory Whitney's

24

folks came up. I played with May.

March 19
Pa's been gone all day. I stayed in the house most all day.

March 20
Went up to Grand ma's. Thurmey Warren came up to play with me.

March 21
Visited with Lewis and Martha Richardson this afternoon.

March 22
Helped Pa fix buckets. Went down to Jim Whitney's a visiting. Came home in the rain.

March 23
Went to Sunday School.

March 24
Arthur Granger came over here with his goal. I played with him.

March 25
Helped fix buckets. It has snowed some.

March 26
Helped get the buckets into the sugar works.

March 27
Did not do much of anything. Read 3 pieces in my 3th reader.

March 28
I have got a little cold in my head. Uncle Jim made me a saw boy. Stayed in the house.

March 29
Did not do much of anything. Had such a cold.

March 30
Ma and I had to much cold to go to Sunday School.

March 31
Had to much cold to go outdoors any. Stayed in the house all day.

Tuesday, April 1. 1890
Have not been outdoors today so I did stay in the house.

April 2
Went outdoors today. Ma went to So. Schroon. I stayed at home.

April 3
Went down in to the sugar works, sugared off for the first time today. Henry Carpenter came over.

April 4
Did not do much of anything but eat sugar. Sugared off 100 Lbs..

April 5
Went down in to the sugar works and up on Schneider.

April 6
Went to Sunday School. Went into a higher class today.

April 7
Went down in sugar works. Eat enough sugar to make woman jaw.

April 8
Been down in sugar works all forenoon. Got two twin lambs. First ones.

April 9
Helped Pa clean out colts' stable. Got another pair of twins.

April 10
Pa went to village. I stayed in house all day.

April 11
Went up to Grand ma's. Henry Carpenter gave me a knife.

April 12
Aunt Lib came down here today. I played with Eddy. Went down and got sheep up to barn.

April 13
Went to Sunday School. Aunt Lib and Eddy is here tonight.

April 14
Been up to school to see how I liked it.

April 15
Went to school, business commenced today.

April 16
Felt kindy old this morning so I did not get to school.

April 17
Went to school. Got dismissed and came home alone to help Pa.

April 18
Went to school. Pa was up to Grand ma's and came home with me.

April 19
School don't keep Saturday. Stayed at home. Went to So. Schroon with Pa.

April 20
Went up to Grand ma's. Did not go to Sunday School.

April 21
Went to school. Old cat had kittens. Aunt Lib and Eddy came down this afternoon. Eddy and I went and got sheep.

April 22
Went to school.

April 23
Went to school.

April 24
Went to village. Pa got me a knife and a new pen stalk.

April 25

Did not go to school. Eddy and I went down in sugar works.

April 26

Went up to Grand ma's. Uncle Jim Floyed came over after Aunt Lib.

April 27

Rained all day, so did not go to Sunday School.

April 28

Did not go to school. Fixed up my playhouse. Chas. Foster been here this afternoon.

April 29

Went to school.

April 30

Went to school.

Thursday, May 1, 1890

Did not go to school. My head ached about all day. All teased for me to go to school but at night glad I didn't go.

May 2

Went to school. Arbor Day today. Spoke my first piece today. Surprised myself to see how good I spoke it.

May 3

Pa went to village, he got me a slate pencil like lead one only slate pencil.

Corded up some wood.

May 4

Went to School.

May 5

Did not go to school. School don't keep today.

May 6

School did not keep today. Stayed in the house all day. Uncle Jim came down with his colt.

May 7

Went up to School house but teacher did not come. Stayed at school house till about noon then came home.

May 8

Did not go to School. Helped Pa sit out a little apple tree.

May 9

Went to School.

May 10

Rained today. Uncle Jim, Grand ma, and Mrs. Elizabeth Tripp has been down here today.

May 11

Went to Sunday School. After we got home, Pa and I went up to Grand ma's. She give me some onions.

May 12

Went to School. Nell has

got a colt, found it this morning. Jersey had a calf.

May 13
Went to School. Rained so I stayed till school was out.
Uncle Jim came up after me then came home.

May 14
Went to School. Pa went to village.

May 15
Went to School. Ma went to Grand ma's with me.

May 16
Went to School. Did not feel very well so got dismissed and came home.

May 17
Made 5 or 6 whistles. Pa was half sick all day. Dr. Griswold stopped here to see Pa.
Uncle J. Henry worked here all day.

May 18
Did not go to Sunday School.
Went to P.O. afoot and alone. Pa gave me 5 cents for going down.

May 19
Did not go to School for it rained.

May 20
Did not go to School.

May 21
Went to School.

May 22
Did not go to School.

May 23
Went to School. Got me a new lead pencle. brought all my books home to study next week.

May 24
Grand ma and Uncle Henry was down to dinner. Went to Grangers.

May 25
Went to Sunday School. Uncle Jim gave me a new pen stalk.

May 26
Ciphered about through Addition. Made a little water wheel.

May 27
Grand ma and Uncle Jim and Henry was down.
Dropped some corn.

May 28
Dropped corn till got sick of it.

May 29
About all I done today was to drop sweet corn. Sit around and see Pa work, went down and got cows.

May 30
Went to Decoration. Eat dinner at the Town Hall.

28

May 31
Pa went to village. Made a
little gun.

Sunday, June 1, 1890
Went to Sunday School.
June 2
Went to School.
June 3
Went to School.
June 4
Did not go to School.
June 5
Went to School.
June 6
Went to School. Dropped a
few beans after I got home.
June 7
Dropped beans in corn
field.
Cut some hens toes off to
keep from scratching up
corn.
June 8
Went to Sunday School
with Pa. Ma did not go.
June 9
Went to School.
June 10
Went to School. Teacher
came down home with me.
Talked around till bed
time.
June 11
Went to School. Teacher
went up with me.

June 12
Went to School.
June 13
Did not go to School.
Rode a horse to cultivate
potatoes and sweet corn.
June 14
Pa and Uncle Henry went
to village. Got me a tablet
and spelling book.
June 15
Went to Sunday School.
June 16
Went to School.
June 17
Went to School.
June 18
Went to School.
June 19
Went to School.
June 20
Went to School.
June 21
Uncle Jim and I went
fishing. We got 11.
June 22
Went to Sunday School.
June 23
Went to School.
June 24
Went to School.
June 25
Went to School.
June 26
Did not go to School. Wed
onions and got 10¢.
Rode horse to cultivate

corn for nothing.

June 27

Went to School.

June 28

Went a berrying.

June 29

Went to School.

June 30

Went to School.

Tuesday, July 1, 1890

Went to School.

July 2

Went to School.

July 3

Did not go to School.

July 4

School did not keep today.
Stayed at home all day.
Went up to Grand ma's.

July 5

Wed out 2 beds in garden.
Got ten cents for it. Rode
horse to cultivate out potatoes.

July 6

Went to Sunday School.

July 7

Went to School.

July 8

Went to School.

July 9

Went to School.

July 10

Went to village.

July 11

Went to Mill Brook.

July 12

At Mill Brook.

July 13

At same place.

July 14

Came home today.

July 15

Did not go to School.

July 16

Went to School. School is
out for good. Tahehe.

July 17

Got lessons all that I do
to School just as good too.
Spread hay. Burnt fallow.

July 18

Got lessons.

July 19

Got lessons.

July 20

Went to Sunday School.

July 21

Got lessons. After supper.
Uncle Jim, Pa, and I
went to fallow. Did not
get home until dark.

July 22

Got lessons.

July 23

Got lessons. Got our

haying done.

July 24

Got lessons. Went up to Grand ma's.

July 25

Got lessons. Went up to John Ford's after supper.

July 26

Got lessons.

July 27

Went to Sunday School.

July 28

Got lessons. Went up to Grand ma's.
Went over to Granger's.
Made a little boat.

July 29

Went up to Grand ma's. Did not get lessons.

July 30

Got lessons for yesterday and today.

July 31

Got lessons.

Friday, August 1, 1890

Got lessons. Went up to Grand ma's. Went to Granger's.

August 2

Got lessons. Set wood chuck trap. Pulled weeds.

August 3

Went to Sunday School.

August 4

Went over to Uncle Jim's and Henry's fallow.
Did not get lessons.

August 5

Got lessons for yesterday and today.

August 6

Got lessons. Picked peas.

August 7

Went to village. Got me a hat, shoes and paints. Did not get lessons.

August 8

Got lessons for yesterday and today.

August 9

Got lessons. Went up to Grand ma's.

August 10

Went to Sunday School.

August 11

Got lessons.

August 12

Did not get lessons. Went a fishing, did not get anything.

August 13

Did not get lessons. Pa is half sick.

August 14

(no entry)

August 15

Stayed at home all day.

August 16

Went to Agnes Rickert's funeral.

August 17

Got lessons. Went up to

Grand ma's. Stayed all day.

August 18
Did not get all lessons. Pa is sick.

August 19
Did not get lessons.

August 20
Did not get lessons.

August 21
Did not get lessons.

August 22
Stayed at home. Pa and Ma went to Pottersville. Did not get lessons.

August 23
Went to funeral. Did not get lessons.

August 24
Went to Sunday School.

August 25
Got part of lessons. Went to Mash Pond.

August 26
Went over to Mash Pond. Did not get lessons.

August 27
Picked some berrys. Did not get lessons.

August 28
Rainy day did not do much of anything.

August 29
Went to village. Got me some boots.

August 30
Went up to Grand ma's.

Uncle Jim Whitney and wife have been up today.

August 31
Went to Camp meeting all day.

———

Monday, September 1, 1890
Went to village.

September 2
Went to Jeb Taylor's with Pa. Made a kite.

September 3
Pulled weeds.
Went over to Granger's.

September 4
Went up to School, did not go.
Helped Pa sit out strawberry plants.

September 5
Went up to Grand ma's.
Played with a girl.

September 6
Played with a girl. Play with a girl a good deal lately seems to me.

September 7
Went to Sunday School.

September 8
Went to School.

September 9
Did not go to School. Raised cain.

September 10,
Went up to School. Had a head ache and came home.

September 11
Did not go to School.
Rain day.
September 12
        Rainy day.
Made a jacklantern.

September 13
(no entry)
September 14
Rainy day.
September 15
Went over to Granger's.
Did not go to Sunday
School.
September 16
Went to School.
September 17
Went to School.
September 18
Went to School.
September 19
Went to School.
September 20
Helped Pa thresh.
September 21
Went down to South
Schroon but did not have
any Sunday School.
Went up on hill to meet-
ing.

September 22
Went to School. Ma was
up to Grand ma's to come
home with me. Pa got a
bottle of ink.
September 23
Went to School. Ma was
up to Grand ma's.
Stayed up there till about
dark. Went down and got
cows.
September 24
Went to School. Helped
Ma cover up tomatoes.
September 25
Picked up about 25 bushel
of potatoes. Sent down to
fair and got 17 pears.
September 26
Rainy day. Husked corn.
September 27
Husked corn most all the
forenoon.
Uncle Bish and Aunt
Lucy came over.
September 28
Went up to Grand ma's
all day.
September 29
Went to School.
September 30
Went to School.

Wednesday, October 1, 1890
Threshed here, did not go to
School.

October 2

Went to village. Got me a new suit of cloths.

October 3

Went up to Grand ma's.

October 4

Fixed sign board. Took tacks out of carpet.

October 5

Went to Sunday School.

October 6

Had distemper so I could not go to School.

October 7

Rainy day did not go to School.

October 8

Went to School. "Pop" drew in pumpkins. Had 300 and more too. 12 squashes.

October 9

Went to School.

October 10

Went to School.

October 11

Went up to Grand ma's.

October 12

Went to Sunday School.

October 13

Went to School.

October 14

Went to School.

October 15

Went to School. Teacher came down with me and stayed all night.

October 16

Went to School.

October 17

Went to School. Helped draw stone after I got home from school.

October 18

Gathered apples. Stub came over.

October 19

Rainy day. Did not go to Sunday School.

October 20

Went to School.

October 21

Went to School. Pa went to village and got me a thing.

October 22

Went to School.

October 23

Went to School.

October 24

Went to School. Snowed today.

October 25

Went to South Schroon with Uncle Jim Made some ink. Grand ma was down.

October 26

Went to Sunday School.

October 27

Went to School.

October 28

Went to School.

October 29

Went to School.

October 30
Went to School.
October 31
(no entry)

Friday, November 1, 1890
Went to School.
November 2
Went to P.O.
November 3
Went to Sunday School.
November 4
Did not go to School.
November 5
Did not go to School. Had a cold.
November 6
Did not go to School.
November 7
Stayed in the house.
November 8
Pa fixed or took down chimney.
I went up on the house a lot.
November 9
See Pa build chimney.
November 10
Did not go to Sunday School.
November 11
Did not go to School.
November 12
Went to School.
November 13
Went to School.

November 14
Went to School. Got scared out of year's growth.
November 15
Went to School.
November 16
Went to Mill Brook.
November 17
At Mill Brook.
November 18
At Mill Brook.
November 19
At Mill Brook. Came home.
November 20
Went to Chester.
November 21
Came home.
November 22
Did not go to School.
November 23
Stayed at home all day.
November 24
Did not go to Sunday School.
November 25
Did not go to School.
November 26
Had a cold so could not go to School, layed on the lounge all day.
November 27
Good deal better. Mary Whitney and Laura Sherman came up. Butchered.
November 28
Better yet. Grand ma and

Uncle Jim came down.
November 29
Went out doors. Did not
do much of anything.
November 30
Did not go out doors.

Sunday, December 1, 1890
Did not go out doors.
December 2
Did not go out doors.
December 3
Did not go out doors.
Uncle Jim went up to
School and got my
books.
December 4
Got lessons. Did not go
out doors. Snowed all day.
December 5
Got lessons. Did not go
out doors.
December 6
Got lessons. Did go out-
doors.
December 7
Did not go out doors. Got
lessons.
December 8
Did not go out doors. Pa
went to Sunday School
with colts.
December 9
Got lessons.
December 10
Got lessons.

December 11
Went outdoors. Got lessons.

*(This diary ends here with pages
missing and no conclusions as to
what happened to them. However,
one additional loose sheet of larger
paper was found carefully folded and
tucked inside the Diary. Here are
those entries for all the remaining
days of 1890):*

December 12
Got lessons. Went down to
the barn.
December 13
Got lessons. Ma got my
pants done.
December 14
Did not go.
December 15
Made a road from fence
back of house to barn.
December 16
Got lessons. Dipped can-
dles little ones about 3 in.
long.
December 17
Did not get lessons. (Went
up to Grandma's.)
December 18
Got lessons.
December 19
Got lessons.
December 20
Got lessons.

December 21
Went to Sunday School.
Got Christmas present.
December 22
Got lessons. Made map of
New York.

December 23
Got lessons.
Stayed in the house
all day.
December 24
Chan wove and I grubled
all the way.
December 25
Got lessons. Stayed to
home all day.
December 26
Got lessons. Snowed about
all day.
December 27
Got lessons. Went to
South Schroon with
Uncle Jim.
December 28
It was so cold did not go
to Sunday School.
December 29
Got lessons. Went up to
Grand ma's.
December 30
Got lessons. Drew map of

Maine and N. H.
December 31
Got lessons. Aunt Lib
came over.

————

Good bye Old Year

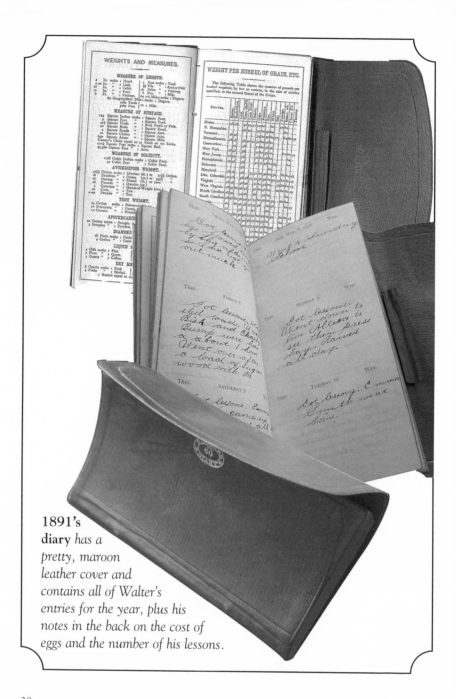

1891's diary has a pretty, maroon leather cover and contains all of Walter's entries for the year, plus his notes in the back on the cost of eggs and the number of his lessons.

The farm at Taylor's-on-Schroon

1891 arrived with a bang but closed with an idea that would become a source of leisure and recreation.

The news of a mine explosion in Mt. Pleasant, Pennsylvania, may never have reached the gossip columns of South Schroon, but the fact that 109 people perished remains a significant piece of mining culture and United States history.

The Dalton gang, immortalized in 1957 at Frontier Town in North Hudson, may not have been a South Schroon household phrase either, but its members made a lot of noise in this country's first train robbery. The great blizzard of 1891, acknowledged by Walter Whitney on February 8, brought things to a temporary standstill, while a West Virginia wedding permanently ended the famous 20-year feud between the Hatfields and the McCoys.

Communication progress continued. The telephone, though common in many small towns, would not arrive in South Schroon for a few more years; but the connection between London and Paris, in April of 1891, penetrated ancient barriers and drew the world a little closer together. Edison patented the motion picture camera; and the Empire State Express train made record time from New York City to Buffalo, 436 miles, in 7 hours and 6 minutes.

The need and the novelty of mechanization set the country and the world spinning with inventions. James Naismith, however, had a different slant on life, which diverted from the mechanized world to that of leisure and recreation. In December of 1891, he created the game of basketball. Our subject, Walter Whitney, refers to playing ball a good deal in September of 1891; but he would not know the game of basketball. His life was involved with school, church, and chores; and games and recreation seemed to stem from his own resource and creativity and only when time allowed. However, his Christmas stocking of 1891 did contain a game of challenge for leisure time and was accompanied by a very peculiar item, with connection to a boy's recreation: Tom Sawyer style.

FARMING

Farm life required hard work. After the fields were cleared of trees, stumps and rocks had to be removed. Teams attached to a plow were used for clearing and plowing. Grindstones, moistened with water, were used to keep scythes, axes, and other blades sharp. The farm animals ate oats and barley raised by the farmers.

People came to the Adirondacks in the late 1700s as pioneers from New England to farm and establish their own independence. Some came from the coastal areas so their children would not go to sea. The fertile plain of the Champlain Valley was the impetus for the migration to New York, but settlers were pushed west into the mountains when the fertile land was sold by New York to rich developers from New York City.

The first thing a pioneer had to do was to build a shelter, crude as it may be. Then it was imperative to clear the land, so crops could be planted. Settlers joined in logging bees; and once the trees were felled, the logs were burned. The potash product rendered from the burning was sold in Vermont and New Hampshire and was used for soap making as well as explosives. A ton of potash would yield $200-$300, enough to afford the necessities of pioneering for awhile.

Plowing between the rocks and stumps was possible with handmade tools, because the virgin soil was porous and easily managed. It was necessary after many years of use, however, for heavier equipment to be used to cultivate the hard, overworked soil. By the 1840s, over 25,000 John Deere and Joel Norse machines had been sold to achieve appropriate soil conditions for crop planting.

The usual livestock included cattle, hogs, and oxen. Oxen, if affordable, were valuable animals. They were slow, being able to plow only half an acre a day, while the horse could plow two acres in the same amount of time; but oxen were far less susceptible to disease than the horse and were more able to forage when food supplies were short.

Pioneers usually cared for small herds of animals of a dozen or less. Larger herds would have sacrificed many to long frigid winters, food shortages, and attacks from wild predators. Sheep were brought into the territory only after bounty was placed on wolves.

Fences were built to keep livestock out of crop areas. Animals were allowed to roam free and were identified by ear markings. Livestock owners were penalized and assessed for any damage done to crops or fences.

Harvesting prior to the 19th century had not changed for thousands of years. The development of the reaping machine helped the farmer enormously. The work that traditionally took 19 days to complete took only one day by 1860 using a reaper that would reap, cut, and bind the grain. Corn shellers, winnowing and threshing machines continued to make farming in the Adirondacks easier and more profitable.

In the Schroon Lake area at the turn of the century many of the local farms supplied local residents and the grand hotels with the freshest produce. Eleanor Knox Jenks and Clara Swan Connell report that their families delivered eggs and milk to Taylor's and fresh flowers to the Leland House. Walter and his father often delivered to Schroon Lake, chickens, fresh eggs, vegetables, maple syrup, and even the farm product of fragrant, homemade soaps.

Courtesy of Essex County Historical Society

January 1, 1891
Got lessons. Aunt Lib came down from Grand ma's. Played with Eddy and Howard.

January 2
Did not get lessons. Played with Eddy and Howard.

January 3
Got lessons for yesterday and today.

January 4
Went to Sunday School.

January 5
Got lessons. Will Culver was up to Grandma's. Uncle Jim came down after Ma and I so we went up.

January 6
Got lessons. Will Culver came down and went away about 2 p.m.

January 7
Got lessons. Made a little sled about 13 inches long and 9 wide. Stayed to home while Pa and Ma went to South Schroon.

January 8
Got lessons. Pa was drawing wood or logs for Richardson boys. I went with Pa in the afternoon one load.

January 9
Got lessons.
Done chores some.

January 10
Got lessons. Stayed home all day.

January 11
Went to Sunday School. Got caught in the rain.

January 12
Got lessons. Went up on hill with Pa after a load of wood. It is icy a little.

January. 13
Got lessons. Went up on hill with Pa.

January 14
Got lessons. Went up on hill with Pa. Ma went up to Grand ma's. I stayed at home.

January 15
Got lessons. Drawed in some wood.
Fussed around quite a lot but not worth writing down.

January 16
Got lessons. Uncle Bish and Aunt Lucy came over. They and Ma and I went up to Grand ma's. Came home afoot. Got two Almanacs up to Grand ma's.

January 17
Got lessons. Ma reviewed me. Made a blood blister on my finger. Stayed in the house all day except when I went out to do chores and bring in wood.

January 18
Went to Sunday School. Snowed most all day.

January 19
Got lessons. Went up to Grandma's. Went up on hill with Pa.

January 20
Got lessons. Done chores. Went over back of Granger's with Pa after a load of wood for Jim Allen.

January 21
Got lessons. Made a run-way for the cat so when she came in she had to come out and come back once or twice. Stayed to home all day. Took the cat doings down again.

January 22
Got lessons. Snowed some in morning. Then commenced to rain and rained all day.
Uncle Jim was down most the forenoon.

January 23
Got lessons. Went down to P.O. with Uncle Jim, had a lot of fun.

January 24
Got lessons.

January 25
Went to Sunday School.

January 26
Got lessons. Went to village with Pa with a load of wood. Pa made me a skipper.

January 27
Got lessons. Mrs. M. Burbank and Mrs. E. Tripp was here. Slid down hill quite a lot on my skipper.

January 28
Did not get lessons because I had a cold. My head felt bad. Pa went to Pottersville and Dr. Griswold sent me up an Almanac.
Stayed in house all day.

January 29
Got lessons for yesterday and today. Did not go outdoors.

January 30
Got lessons. Stayed in house.

January 31
Got lessons. Grand ma was down. Dipped little candles 16 of them about 2 inches and a $1/2$ long. Stayed in the house all day.

Good bye January.

———

Sunday, February 1, 1891
Did not go to Sunday
School Ma I or Pa. Ma
and I had a cold and Pa
thought he could not get
back time to do the chores.
Went outdoors.

February 2
Got lessons. Went outdoors
1/2 of a hour.

February 3
Got lessons. Addie Allen
came up here.

February 4
Got lessons. Weighed my
cat. He weighed 6 pounds
and 13 ounces. Got a lamb
the first one. Pa give it to
me I would take care of it.

February 5
Got lessons.

February 6
Got lessons. Done chores.

February 7
Got lessons. Uncle Bish
and Aunt Lucy came over.

February 8
Did not go to Sunday
School for it snowed so.
Grand ma was down.
Uncle Bish's folks went
home.

February 9
Got lessons. Made Ma a

cook book and wrote recipes.

February 10
Got lessons. Done chores.
Had some cold and cough.
I did not go outdoors
only doing chores and
bringing in wood.

February 11
Got lessons. Cut off a little
wool from sheepskin. I
washed it, picked and card-
ed it and Aunt L. spun it.
Had a knot before, doubled
and twisted. Made a little
boat.

February 12
Got lessons. Mr. and Mrs.
Russell came here.

February 13
Got lessons. Been
over to Granger's
Ma and I. Pa went
to village- Pa
got me some
cough medicine.

February 14
Got lessons. Pretty cold.

February 15
Did not go to Sunday
School for I had a cough.
Grandma was down.
Stayed to home while Pa
and Ma went to Sunday
School.

February 16
Got lessons. Stayed in
house all day. When I

stay in the house I do not do enough or what I do do is not worth writing down.

February 17

Got lessons. Stayed in house. Made a knife, fork spoon.

February 18

Got lessons. Cyrus Kittenback was here a few minutes towards night. Uncle Jim was here about 3/4 of the day to help doctor Bessie. Pa went to village.

February 19

Got lessons. Did not go outdoors. Pa found Bessie dead this morning. Grand ma and Uncle Henry went to Mill Brook.

February 20

Got lessons. Did not go outdoors. Grand ma and Uncle Henry came home from Mill Brook. Aunt Lib sent me a dried herring.

February 21

Did not get lessons. Went down to David Hall's a visiting all day. Pa, I and Ma come down. Pa stayed till noon then went up to caucus.

February 22

Did not go to Sunday School. Pa and Ma went and I stayed at home.

February 23

Got lessons for Saturday and today. Went outdoors. Got through my Geography first time I have been through it. Made a one horse gig out of a spool, pins and sticks.

February 24

Got lessons. Went down in sugar works to help move the buckets from one side of sugar house to other. Been outdoors quite a lot today.

February 25

Got lessons. Made Grand ma Culver a thing to scour knives on. Rained about all day it was so icy when I came from barn I stiped down.

February 26

Got lessons. Went up to Grand ma's about all day.

February 27

Got lessons. Made Grand ma Culver a bosom board and me a snow shovel. The blade was about 3 in. long. Pa went to village.

February 28

Got lessons. Put a patch on Uncle Henry's rubber.

Pa and I had a boss slid over beyond lower barn. Snowed some this afternoon.

Sunday March 1, 1891
Did not go to Sunday School. Pa and Ma went. Grand ma came down.

March 2
Got lessons. It was so cold I stayed in the house more than I generally do.

March 3
Got lessons. Pa went up to Town Meeting. Ma went down to Uncle Jim Whitney a visiting. I stayed to home. Pa got me some pants.

March 4
Got lessons for yesterday and today. Snowed all day. Ma has been making me some nice pants.

March 5
Got lessons. It has blowed awfully this afternoon so I did not go out much.

March 6
Got lessons. Shoveled roads. Uncle Bish and Charley Bump were here about 1 hour. Went over after a load of sugar wood with Pa.

March 7
Got lessons. Emma Smith came up visited around all day.

March 8
Went to Sunday School.

March 9
Got lessons. Went down to Jim Allen to see them press hay. Rained all day.

March 10
Got lessons. Emma Smith went home.

March 11
Did not get lessons. Went up to Grand ma's. Uncle Jim and I went to the P.O.

March 12
Got lessons for yesterday and today. Pa tapped two trees and had some molasses for supper.

March 13
Got lessons. Uncle Jim came down after Ma and I to go up and see Uncle Henry. Went up and stayed all night.

March 14
Stayed up at Grand ma's till about noon. Pa was up and brought Ma and I home. Got lessons.

March 15
Did not go to Sunday School. Went up to Grand ma's.

March 16
Got lessons. Made a little
burning iron. Went up to
Grand ma's and stayed
all night.
March 17
Came down from
Grandma's about 10:30.
Got lessons.
March 18
Got lessons. Tapped 3
trees.
March 19
Got lessons. Abel Walker
and I went down to see
them press hay. Abel and
I done chores alone at
night.
March 20
Got lessons. Uncle Jim
come. I did chores at
night. He stayed down
and I slept with him.
Dr. G. came up to see Pa.
Ma's birthday.
March 21
Got lessons. Uncle Jim
and I done chores.
March 22
Did not go to Sunday
School for Pa was sick.
Uncle Jim, Floyd, Aunt
Lib and the children come
over.
March 23
Got lessons.
Dr. G. come up.

March 24
Did not get lessons. My
birthday 9 years old.
Did not go outdoors.

March 25
Did not get lessons.
Grand ma was down. Pa
and I made Grand ma a
thing to take pies out of the
oven with.
March 26
Got lessons for Tuesday
and today.
March 27
Did not get lessons. Got
up this morning and
found myself sick. Dr. G.
came up to see me.
Grand ma. Uncle Jim
and Uncle Henry stayed
all night.
March 28
Did not get lessons. Little
better. When I am sick I
don't do much.
March 29
Did not go to Sunday
School.
March 30
Got lessons. Strung up 16

spools on some twine. Commenced boiling in sugar works, going to boil all night.

March 31

Got lessons. Sugared off today first. Fussed with my spools some. Good bye March.

Wednesday, April 1, 1891

Got lessons. Sugared off 3 times.

April 2

Got lessons. Eat sugar.

April 3

Got lessons. Uncle Jim and Henry was down. Snowed today.

April 4

Got lessons. Pretty cold at night.

April 5

Did not go to Sunday School. Pa and Ma went with Uncle Henry.

April 6

Did not get lessons. Maime Allen was up about all day. I played with her.

April 7

Got lessons for yesterday and today.

April 8

Got lessons. Ma went up to Grand ma. I stayed at home. Helped Ma wipe the supper dishes. Pa went to the village.

April 9

Got lesson. Went down in sugar works.

April 10

Got lessons. Went down in sugar works. Tinkered up my little cart. Went over to fallow with Pa after sap.

April 11

Got lessons. Went in sugar works. Rained today.

April 12

Did not go to Sunday School. Went up to Grand ma's.

April 13

Got lessons. Went in sugar camp. Pa and I went up on Schneders emptying water out of the buckets.

April 14

Got lessons. At night helped Pa get sheep.

April 15

Did not get lessons. Aunt Lib and the children came down.

April 16

Did not get lessons.

April 17

Did not get lessons.

April 18
Did not get lessons. Aunt Lib and the children went home.

April 19
Did not go to Sunday School.

April 20
Got lessons. Caught a wood chuck but he got away getting him out.

April 21
Got lessons. Caught a wood chuck.

April 22
Did not get lessons. Maimie Allen was up. I put up a swing.

April 23
Got lessons for yesterday and today. I put up a rope.

April 24
Got lessons. Went up to Grand ma's for a few minutes.

April 25
Did not get lessons. Claud Smith came up and I played with him.

April 26
Went to Sunday School.

April 27
Helped Pa draw manure. Pa grafted a little after supper.

April 28
Went to school.

April 29
Went to school.

April 30
Got to school. Went down to Uncle Jim Whitney's and stayed all night.

Friday, May 1, 1891
Went to school.

May 2
Went to village.

May 3
Did not go to Sunday School.

May 4
Went to school.

May 5
Went to school.

May 6
Went to school.

May 7
Went to school.

May 8
Went to school. Arbor Day.

May 9
Planted me some taters in my garden.

May 10
Went to Sunday School.

May 11
Went to school. Set out a bed of onions in my garden.

May 12
Went to school.

May 13
Went to school.
May 14
Went to school. Went to
So. Schroon after supper.
May 15
Went to school.
May 16
Rained all day.
May 17
Went to Sunday School.
May 18
Pa and I was to fallow
all p.m..
May 19
Planted Chans taters for
25 cents. Daddle
Whitney got home.
May 20
Dropped taters about all day.
May 21
Did not do much.
May 22
I went down to So.
Schroon with Pa.
May 23
Went to Grand ma's.
May 24
Did not go to Sunday
School.
May 25
Went to school.
May 26
Went up to Grand ma's.
School did not keep.
May 27
Went to school.

May 28
Went to village.
May 29
Went to school. Aunt
Lucy and Uncle Bish
came over.
May 30
Hurt my left foot in
morning and limped all
the rest of day.
May 31
Did not go to Sunday
School.

Monday, June 1, 1891
Did not go to school. Pa
and I worked in garden
about all day and went
down to So. Schroon.
June 2
Went to school.
June 3
Did not go to school.
Went to village with
Uncle Jim.
June 4
Did not go to school.
June 5
Went to school.
June 6
Went to Mill Brook.
June 7
At Mill Brook.
June 8
Came home from Mill
Brook.

June 9
Went to school.
June 10
Went to school.
June 11
Went to school.
June 12
Did not go to school.
June 13
Done every thing.
June 14
Did not go to Sunday
School.
June 15
Did not go to school.
June 16
Did not go to school.
June 17
Went to school.
June 18
Went to school.
June 19
Did not go to school.
June 20
Pa, Uncle Jim, Henry and
I took the boat over to
Mash Pond. Caught 50
bullheads.
June 21
Pa and I went to
Sunday School afoot.
June 22
Did not go to
school. Uncle Jim,
Frank Granger
and Pa went to Mash
Pond a fishing. Got 5

pickerels and 29 bullheads.
June 23
Went to school.
June 24
Went to school.
June 25
Went to school.
June 26
Did not go to school.
June 27
Half sick.
June 28
Did not go to Sunday School.
June 29
Did not go to school.
June 30
Went to school.

———

Wednesday, July 1, 1891
Went a berrying.
July 2
Did not go to school.
July 3
Went to school.
July 4
Rained some.
July 5
Did not go to Sunday
School.
July 6
Did not go to school.
Done 100 examples.
July 7
Went to school.
July 8
Went to school.

July 9
Did not go to school.
July 10
Went to school.
July 11
Helped clean out cellar.
Went to Mash Pond
fishing.
July 12
Went to Sunday School.
July 13
Did not go to school.
July 14
Went to school.
July 15
Went to school.
July 16
Went to school.
July 17
Went to picnic.
July 18
Helped draw hay.
July 19
Did not go.
July 20
Got lessons.
July 21
Got lessons.
July 22
Got lessons.
July 23
Got lessons.
July 24
Did not get lessons.
July 25
Did not do much of any-
thing. Uncle Henry

brought me some nuts.
July 26
Went to Sunday School.
July 27
Got lessons. Picked berries
for Ma.
July 28
Played with Edward
Gifford Ford.
July 29
Pa and I went over to
Mash Pond fishing. I
caught 2 pickerel and 6
bullheads. Pa 1 bullhead
and 2 pickerel.
July 30
Got lessons.
July 31
Got lessons.

Saturday, August 1, 1891
Helped rake hay.
August 2
Went to Sunday School.
August 3
Did not get lessons.
August 4
Did not get lessons.
August 5
Did not get lessons.
August 6
Got lessons.
August 7
Got lessons.
August 8
Went to So. Schroon.

August 9
Went to Sunday School.
August 10
Did not get lessons.
August 11
Got part of lessons.
August 12
Got part of lessons.
August 13
Did not get lessons.
August 14
Did not get lessons.
August 15
Grand ma Culver was down.
August 16
Did not go to Sunday School.
August 17
Had visitors.
August 18
Had visitors.
August 19
Stayed at home. Put cards in scrap book.
August 20
Went fishing. Got 48 bullheads and 1 pumpkin skin.
August 21
Rained.
August 22
Uncle Sam and Uncle Jim W. came up.
August 23
Went to Sunday School and meeting.

August 24
Rained wide. Teased Pa to go fishing.
August 25
Been to Grand ma's. Picked berries.
August 26
Watched Pa and Frank Granger sow oats. Went berrying.
August 27
Stayed at home. Pa went fishing.
August 28
Went to village Pa, Ma, Grand ma and I. Got pictures taken.
August 29
Pa and Frank got in oats. Raked after.
August 30
Went to Sunday School.
August 31
Picked up taters. Went fishing.

Tuesday, September 1. 1891
Went to school.
September 2
Went to school.
September 3
Went to school.
September 4
Went to school.
September 5
Went to village.

September 6
Did not go to Sunday School.

September 7
Ma was sick. Did not go to school. Pa was here.

September 8
Did not go to school.

September 9
Went to school.

September 10
Went to school.

September 11
Went to school. Pa and Uncle Jim went to village with his Nell and Pa's Cinder. They got me a new Arithmetic and Geography.

September 12
Picked up stone some.

September 13
Did not go to Sunday School.

September 14
Went to school.

September 15
Went to school.

September 16
Went to school.

September 17
Went to school.

September 18
Went to school.

September 19
Played ball a good deal. Ciphered some.

September 20
Did not go to school. Went to Grand ma's.

September 21
Went to school.

September 22
Went to school.

September 23
Did not go to school. Pa, Uncle Jim and Henry, Fred Parsons, Rob Granger and Mr. Granger killed a deer.

September 24
Went to school.

September 25
Did not go to school. Helped Pa a lot.

September 26
Stayed at home.

September 27
Went to Sunday School Convention on Charley Hill.

September 28
Stayed at home to help work.

September 29
Stayed at home to help work.

September 30
Stayed at home.

_____

Thursday, October 1, 1891
Went to Mill Brook.
October 2
At Mill Brook.
October 3
Came home.
October 4
Stayed at home.
October 5
Stayed to home.
October 6
Did not go to school.
Helped Pa husk corn.
October 7
Did not go to school. Ma
sick.
October 8
Stayed at home.
October 9
Went to Grand ma's and
to So Schroon with Uncle
Jim. Doctor was here.
October 10
Went to So. Schroon with
Uncle Jim.
October 11
Did not go to Sunday
School.
October 12
Helped Pa draw pumpkins.
Uncle Bish and Aunt
Lucy came over. Helped Pa
gather apples.

Commenced getting
lessons in my new
Arithmetic.
October 13
Got lessons. Arthur
Granger and I went and
got some beechnuts. Went
to fallow with Pa and
Uncle Billy. Went to
Grangers twice.
Sold Aunt Lucy my
onions for 15 cents.
Picked up taters. Grand
ma has been down.
October 14
Did not get lessons.
Picked up taters all day.
Slept in lounge all
evening. I expected my
new card table but did not
get it.
Guess I worked pretty
hard.
October 15
Did not get lessons. Picked
up potatoes until 3 p.m.
Got potatoes dug.
October 16
Did not get lessons. Went
to Lant Silvermain with
Pa.
Got my card table.
October 17
Got lessons. Herb Howe
came here about noon.
October 18
Went to S. S.

October 19
Got lessons. Grand ma
came down. Pa went to
Mill Brook.
October 20
Went to So. Schroon. Got
lessons.
October 21
Got lessons. Went to So.
Schroon.
October 22
Was down in woods about
all day watching Pa and
Uncle Henry dig hole for
arch.
Got lessons. Snowed little
in morning.
October 23
Got lessons. Was in wood some.
October 24
Got lessons.
Pa to village all day. Done
chores etc, etc.
October 25
Pa, Ella Pierce and I went
to S. S.
October 26
Got lessons.
Picked up beechnuts. See Pa
draw stone. Got lessons.
October 27
(no entry)
October 28
Got lessons.
October 29
Got lessons.
Watched Pa build arch.

October 30
Ditto.
October 31
Watched Pa make arch.

Sunday, November 1, 1891
Did not go to Sunday
School. Grand ma came
down.
November 2
Got part of lessons. Aunt
Lucy Whitney came up.
I made some ink.
November 3
Got lessons for
today and what
I did not get
yesterday. Pa
gone to Election.
November 4
Got lessons. Pa went
up to Elizabethtown.
November 5
Got lessons.
Pa came home.
November 6
Got lessons. Watched Pa
build arch.
November 7
Watched Pa build arch.
November 8
Pa and I went to S. S.
afoot.
November 9
Got lessons. Watched Pa
build arch.

November 10
Did not get lessons.
Threshers was here.
November 11
Got lessons for yesterday
and today. Rained.
November 12
Got lessons. Rained.
November 13
Got lessons.
November 14
Have been down in sugar
works some.
November 15
Went to Sunday School.
November 16
Went up to Grand ma's.
Stayed all day. Did not
get lessons.
November 17
Got lessons for yesterday
and today.
November 18
Got lessons. Had cold.
November 19
Got lessons.
Went down where Pa was
once.
November 20
Got lessons. Went in
sugar works twice. Sat.
November 21
Was in sugar works a good
deal watching Pa.
November 22
Did not go to Sunday
School. Pa and Ma went.

November 23
Got lessons. Did not go
outdoors.
November 24
Got my lessons. Did not
go outdoors. Teased for
mouse trap.
November 25
Ditto.
November 26
Got my lessons. Went
outdoors.
November 27
Got my lessons. Went
outdoors.
November 28
Snowed most all day.
Wrote some.
November 29
Did not go to S. S.
November 30
Got my lessons. Awful
cold.

Tuesday, December 1, 1891
Got lessons.
December 2
Got lessons. Helped Pa
shingle sugar house.
December 3
Did not get lessons.
Ma and I went up to
Grand ma's. I came
home about 10 a.m. to
help Pa shingle sugar
house.

December 4
Got lessons. We butchered. I helped Pa cut hog up etc. etc. etc.

December 5
May Whitney came up. I played with her and helped Pa.

December 6
Did not go to S. S. Had tooth ache some.

December 7
Got lessons for last Thursday and today. Went to saw mill with Pa.

December 8
Got my lessons. Caught a mouse last night. Went to Grand ma's with Pa. Helped make sausage.

December 9
Got lessons. Ma went up to Grand ma's. I stayed at home with Pa. Helped make sausage.

December 10
56°   Pleasant
Got lessons. Pa went to Riverside after his new Evaporator. He got home about 7 p.m.

December 11
Got lessons. Looked at Evaporator and Regulator, saps spouts etc. etc.

December 12
Went from here to sugar works quite a lot. Tapped some maple trees and made some molasses.

December 13
Went to Sunday School.

December 14
Did not get lessons. Went to village with Pa and we brought home a dog.

December 15
Got lessons. Played with the dog.

December 16
Got lessons. Pa went to village. He took dog home. Pa cut apple tree down in front of house.

December 17
I had a cold and my head felt so bad that I did not get lessons. I made a Christmas candle with three legs.

December 18
Did not get lessons. Dipped little candles three or four times. Ma and I made me a cover over lounge out of bed quilt etc. etc. Grand ma came down. Sewed some on machine for Ma. Stayed in house all day.

December 19
Got lessons for last Monday. Pa went to village. Did not go outdoors.

December 20

Did not go to Sunday School. Ma did not go. But Pa went, Grand ma, Uncle Jim and Henry. Went outdoors considerable.

December 21

53°   Pleasant

Got my lessons. Pa went to Pottersville. Done chores to barn some. Slid down hill quite a lot.

December 22

40°   Cloudy, rain

Got lessons. Went up in lots with Pa after wood once and up on hill once. Went up to Grand ma's and to Grangers. Made me little sled out of old one that I made.

December 23

34° to 43°   Cloudy

Got lessons. Helped Ma sew on machine.

December 24

34°   Cloudy

Went to Grand ma's and to Granger's. Went down and see sugar house doors.

December 25

Did not get lessons. Got up in morning and I found in my stocking one mouse done up in paper, one pair slippers and a game of Fiddly Tiddley Winks. Played with them.

December 26

Played with Tiddley Winks. Went to Granger's Rained some.

December 27

Did not go to Sunday School. Uncle Jim came down.

December 28

Got lessons. Watched and helped saw wood. Helped Pa draw sugar wood.

December 29

Got lessons. Addie Allen and Edith Ferguson came up here.

December 30

Got lessons. Pa went to village. Stayed at home all day.

December 31

Got lessons. Went up to Uncle Jim's, stayed all afternoon. Sewed on machine in evening.

Good Bye Mr. Diary and old year.

Subscribers to Beacon
John Ford
Uncle Henry
Pa
Uncle Jim Whitney
Mrs. Granger

Wood chucks
Caught 1 but got away

Caught 1
Caught 1

Pa, Fred Persons, Uncle Jim
and Henry, Roll Granger and
Mr. Granger killed a deer
Sept. 23, 1891.

First snow of the year Oct. 22,
1891.

Thermometer 56 1/2 degrees
above zero Dec. 10, 1891

Bills Payable
Walter Whitney in account
with L. Bailey
1891
Oct, 16 To 1 card table   2.00
10 By 1 Bu. potatoes   .10
27 " 2 "   "   .20
1/2   ruttabague   .20

Walter Whitney in account
with Mrs. R. Carpenter
Oct. 13 By 4 qt. onions   .15
Oct. 13 Cash   .15
(log of mice caught with dates)
                           .51

What It Costs to Keep a Boy
1891   Dolls. Cts.
Jan. 14 Diary   .50
"   30 One bot. cough medicine
                           .25
Feb. 13 One lemon   .04
    13 Two bot. cough medicine
                           .50
Mar 3 Pants   .80
    17 Doctor   4.00
    29 Doctor   4.00
Apr. 6 Rubber boots   2.25
May 28 Pants   .33
       Shirts   .50
       Suspenders   .18
       1 pair shoes   1.40
       1 orange   .05
       1 lemon   .03
       1 pair shoestrings .05
       1 tablet   .05
       Fix boots, shoe   1.15
       1 arithmetic   .90
       1 pail   .08
       1 pin   .25
       1 pr suspenders   .18
       1 " shoes   1.40
       paper   .20
    1 bot cough medicine   .26
       1 mouse trap   .18
       1 pr Arctics   1.40
                         20.92

What It Costs to Keep a Boy

1 dozen pens	.10
1 pr. shoestrings	.05
Cloth for pants	.87
1 pr. No. 8 rubbers	.80
	1.82

Addresses:

Julia Lena McConley
Whitcomb
Shawano Co. Wis.

Siblie Culver
Medina . Orleans Co. N. Y
Christiana Day
14 Orleans St.
Newark, N. J.

Henry Carpenter
Division No. 14
Glens Falls

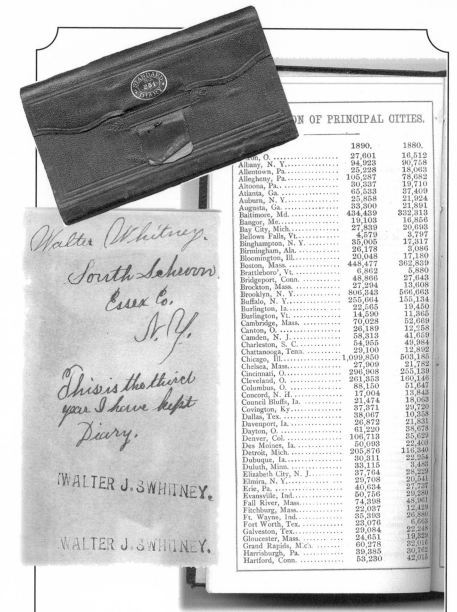

The 1892 diary *has a black composition cover with gold letters and is badly worn, but the inside pages are well-preserved.*

Stagecoach at the Wells House, Pottersville

1892 saw the election of Grover Cleveland to the Presidency of the United States. His wife was no stranger to the Schroon Lake area. In 1880 she entered her name, Mrs. Grover Cleveland and Baby, in the guest register of the Pyramid House, a grand summer resort east of Schroon Lake.

Also in this year, John Muir founded the Sierra Club for the conservation of nature. In New York State, the Adirondack Park was established and was marked off on maps with a blue line. Three years later, the Adirondack Forest Preserve was created.

But 1892 was a landmark year in United States highway travel. Plank roads and corduroy roads have their place in history and their particular purpose and need. The technology of those travel surfaces was as intricate, if not more, as the chemistry involved in today's blacktop surface that we enjoy for its even, smooth riding. The forerunner to blacktop was the concrete road, which can still be found in many small towns and particularly north and south of Schroon Lake village.

The first concrete road was poured as early as 1892 in Bellefountaine, Ohio; and the pneumatic automobile tire was patented in the same year. Teddy Roosevelt, on his ride to the presidency in

September 1901, would have welcomed the neatness of such a ride as these inventions could have offered. But he remained stalwart and resolute to the warnings of danger by his second driver, Mike Cronin; and he responded, "Push along! Hurry up! Go Faster."[1] The rain-slicked, rutted mud of the mountain roads traveled by Roosevelt from Tahawas to Aiden Lair to North Creek was a slippery, dangerous travel surface characteristic of the time.

South Schroon was no exception. Although one cannot today be sure which kind of road machine was used, a road scrapper, circa 1750, or a stamp mill for stones, circa 1870, we can be sure that the neighborhood road crews, mentioned by Walter Whitney in June 1892 and 1893, were diligent in the maintenance of their highways in keeping them open and accessible for the trade and commerce necessary to the healthy existence of their community.

TRANSPORTATION

Roads and Highways: The Great Northern Turnpike, running from Washington County to Keeseville, was started in the 18th century. Partly planked, it ran near the Whitney farm; it later became Route 9. Route 9 was paved in 1915.

In 1892 most local transportation depended on horses pulling buckboards, wagons or sleighs. Roads were maintained by landowners who either paid road taxes or donated labor. Landowners who maintained watering places by the highway for horses were given a tax break. Barrels or iron kettles were used as watering troughs. Teams were driven straight down the middle of the road, there being no right or left lanes until automobiles came along. When two teams met they worked their way around each other. Mail and merchandise were carted by wagon and stagecoach.

Railroads: The railroad in the Champlain Valley was only about 25 miles east of the Whitney farm, but mountainous terrain made it difficult to reach. When the new Adirondack Railroad, coming north from Saratoga Springs, was completed in 1872, it opened the southeastern Adirondacks to commerce and tourism. Construction of a bridge across the Hudson at the Riverside station enabled local teamsters to bring guests to the newly built summer resorts. Walter's father made frequent trips to Riverside to bring guests to Taylor's Hotel (later to become Scaroon Manor).

Steamboats: The Libbie S. Benedict (probably 1860s to late 19th Century) and Effingham (1874–1915) were used on Schroon Lake to haul rafts of logs and carry tourists. The Evelyn succeeded the Effingham. Local people also used them for the Schroon Lake-Pottersville trip. The Shew Fly was used for the same purpose on the Schroon River from Pottersville to Starbuckville.

Walter mentions trips to Mill Brook (now Adirondack). Some trips were made by road; but for others, family members went to Taylor's Hotel and took the steamboat across the lake.

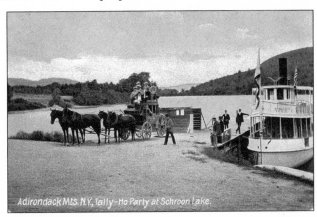

Adirondack Mts. N.Y., Tally–Ho Party at Schroon Lake.

Island House   St Andrews Church

[1] Murphy, Eloise Cronin, THEODORE ROOSEVELT'S RIDE TO THE PRESIDENCY (Blue Mountain Lake, New York: Adirondack Museum, 1977)

Walter Whitney
South Schroon
Essex County, New York
This is the third year I
have kept Diary

Friday, January 1, 1892
29°   Cloudy
I have been up to Grand
ma's all day. Pa worked
up there ceiling up their
kitchen. Ma went up and
I drove old
Nell up and
back and Pa
went afoot.
Watched Pa and
Uncle Jim work
part of the time
and part of the rest I read.
I read some in evening.
January 2
48°   Rain
Helped do chores. Pa is not
feeling very awful good.
Made a little top. Uncle
Jim came down and done
a part of the chores and I
done the other part. Played
Diddledy Winks with Pa
and Uncle Henry.
January 3
29°& 28°   Snow, cold
Did not go to Sunday
School. Pa was pretty sick

all day. Doctor Griswold
came up to see Pa. I helped
do chores in morning and
at night. Roll Granger
went after once and Uncle
Jim once to start him up.
He brought me up my
Christmas present.
January 4
11°   Cloudy
Did not get my lessons.
Pa is better today. I helped
Uncle Jim do the chores.
Went to Grangers twice.
I helped do chores at
night.

January 5
22° to 14°   Clear
Got my lessons. Helped do
chores in morning and at
night. Played Diddledy
Winks some. I heard a
crow this afternoon.
Doctor came to see Pa.
Went over to Grangers.
January 6
4° to 13°   Snow
Did not get lessons. Pa
sick. The Dr. came up and
Uncle Jim came down.
Played Diddledy Winks.
January 7
28° Cloudy, clear, snow
Did not get lessons.
Played in snow quite a lot.

Helped do chores. Chased colts around putting them in the stable.

January 8

19° & 14°   Clear

Did not get my lessons. Emory Whitney and wife came up. Found a mouse in morning in trap and caught one in afternoon.

January 9

6° to 11°   Clear

Uncle Jim, Henry and Grandma came down. I weighed my cat and she weighed 6 1/2 pounds. Helped do chores.

January 10

0° to 18°   Clear

Did not go to Sunday School. Pa sick.

January 11

22°   Cld.

Got my lessons. Went to South Schroon.

January 12

26°   Snow cold

Dr. came up in afternoon. Got part of my lessons.

January 13

31° to 29°   Snow and cloudy

Got my lessons. Uncle Jim went to village with his new sled. Pa went outdoors.

January 14

32° to 39°   Rain

Got my lessons. Helped do chores.

January 15

21° to 18°   Cld. snow

Got lessons. Pa and I did chores. Ada Persons came here to work.

January 16

5° below   Clr.

Helped Pa do chores. Drew in wood that Pa sawed. Slid down hill.

January 17

0°

Went up to Uncle Jim's with Pa. Helped do chores. Uncle Henry sick.

January 18

18° to 29°   Slpy snow

Did not get my lessons. Done every thing. Helped Pa. Went up to Uncle Jim's with Pa.

January 19

18° to 10°   Snow

Did not get lessons. Got up in morning and found 8 inches of snow on. Played in snow some.

January 20

18° below   Clear

Went up to Uncle Jim's. Pa, Ma, Ada and I stayed almost all day.

January 21

8°   Cld.

Ada Persons went over to
Granger's to work.
Went up to Grandma's.

January 22

6° to 19°   Cloudy

Got lessons. Went over
back of Granger's with Pa
after a load of wood for
Charles Stanard.

January 23

32°   Snow, cold

Went with Pa after wood
for Charles Stanard.
Helped do chores.

January 24

3°   Snow

Went up to Uncle Jim's
all day.

January 25

4°   Snow

Went to village with Pa.
Had some oysters for dinner.

January 26

10°   Wind

Got lessons. The wind
blew awful hard all day so
I did not go out much.

January 27

-10° to 2°   Wind, clear

Got my lessons. Fed the
hens in morning and at
night.

January 28

14° to 26°   Snowy

Got lessons. Went with Pa
after a load of sugar wood.

January 29

Went up to Grandma's.

January 30

21°   Clear

Got my lessons for yesterday.

January 31

21° to 16°   Clear

I have fun up to Uncle
Jim's about all day.
Helped on chores.

Monday, February 1, 1892

26° to 33°   cold

Got lessons. Pa, Ma and I
went down to see sugar
house etc. Pa and I went
down to So. Schroon and
got a bedstead for Ma.

February 2

26° to 28°   Cld. Snow

Got my lessons. Went
over to fallow with Pa after
wood. I horse sled roads
back of house.

February 3

24° to 20°   Cld.

Got my lessons. Helped
move bedsteads. Filled
straw bed. Helped do chores.

February 4

18° to 35°   Clear

Did not get lessons.
Went to Uncle Jim's with
Ma.

February 5

Got lessons. Went with Pa.

February 6

Done chores. Studied some.

February 7

6° below zero

Went up to Uncle Jim's
with Ma. Stayed till
about dark.

February 8

Cld. Snow

Got my lessons. Went
over after wood with Pa.

February 9

22° to 36°   Slippery

Did not get my lessons.
Ma and I went up to
Uncle Jim's. Done chores.

February 10

Cld. chilly

Got my lessons. Run to
barn forty eleven times
Helped do chores.

February 11

26° to 33°   Cld. clear

Got lessons.

February 12

22° to 15°   Cld. snow

Got lessons.
Went down to Richardson
Bros. farm twice after
hay.

February 13

It was so cold I did not
go out much.

February 14

Went to Grandma's.

February 15

5° to 16°   Clear

Got lessons. I helped Pa some.

February 16

5 below   Freezing weather

Got lessons. Helped saw
trees up down in woods.

February 17

1°   Clr.

Went to Grandma's.

February 18

Got lessons. Went down
in woods.

February 19

Went up to Grandma's
and stayed all night.
Pa went to the village and
got a history.

February 20

Came home. Done chores.

February 21

Went to Sunday School.
Had the headache toothache
some.

February 22

We a Went down to Uncle
Jim Whitney's. He gave
me a history of Uncle
Sam on United States.

February 23

Got my lessons. Played
snow ball some.

February 24

Got my lessons. Done
chores.

February 25

Went to village.

February 26
Went to Grandma's.
Pitched down straw from
off over barn floor.
February 27
Went up to Grandma's.
February 28
Went to Sunday School.
February 29
Got my lessons.

Tuesday, March 1, 1892
Got lessons.
March 2
Went down to Pasco's with
Pa. We got a bird.
March 3
Did not get les-
son. Had a cold.
Watched Teddy
the bird. Did not
go out doors.
March 4
Did not get lessons. Went
outdoors. Took care and
watched Teddy.
March 5
I fussed around in the
forenoon. About 1 p.m.
May Whitney and Grace
Traver came up.
March 6
Pa and Ma went to
Sunday School. I stayed.
March 7
Went up to Uncle Jim's

and stayed all day.
March 8
Got lessons. Arthur
Floyed came over. I
played with him some.
March 9
Played with Arthur
Floyed.
March 10
Went over to Mill Brook
and saw them bore for oil.
March 11
Got lessons. Quite cold.
March 12
Aunt Lib, Ed Howell, Jim
Jr. came down.
March 13
0°   Clear
I did not go to S. S.
Wrote some. Ran around
outdoors some.
March 14
Got my lessons. Pretty
cold.
March 15
Got my lessons.
March 16
Got lessons. Helped do
chores.
March 17
Did not get all lessons.
Went over to fallow
after logs.
March 18
Got my lesson.
Made 25 wires to
hang buckets with.

SUGAR
BUCKET

70

March 19
Made 25 or 26 bucket wires. Wind blew and the snow flew awful all day.

March 20
Did not any body go to S. S. from here all day.

March 21
Did not get all lessons. Uncle J. H. and H. J came down.

March 22
Did not get my lessons. Grandma went down to Uncle Jim's. Uncle Bish and Aunt Lucy came over. Ma and I went up to Grandma Cs..

March 23
Did not get lessons. I was hired girl. I brought in water, washed dishes etc.

March 24
Did not get lessons. I am 10 years old.

March 25
Went down to So. Schroon twice. Helped paint box.

March 26
Was down to sugar house most all day. Churned in the Davis Swing Churn.

March 27
Did not go to S. S.

March 28
Helped get buckets down to soak them. My printing thing came tonight.

March 29
Printed a lot. Straightened wires.

March 30
Printed a good deal today.

March 31
I was busy most all day. We boiled some sap in the new evaporator. We saw a few grass hoppers.

Friday, April 1, 1892
We boiled sap most of the afternoon.

April 2
I have been down in sugar works a good deal. Sugared off the first time.

April 3
Went to Sunday School.

April 4
I made 125 wires to put on wooden buckets. Old cat had 4 kittens.

April 5
Pa went to Schroon village. I did not do much of anything.

April 6
I have been down in

sugar works most all day.
I.C. Warren came down
to play with me.

April 7
Have been where Pa and
Abe are cutting wood.

April 8
Stayed at the house most of
the time.
Helped with sugaring off
etc.

April 9
Have been in sugar works a
good deal.

April 10
Went to Sunday School.

April 11
I have been in sugar
works most all day.

April 12
Went down in woods
where Pa and Abe are cut-
ting wood. Helped stir off
sugar.

April 13
Fussed around in the
forenoon. Harnessed old
Jill and took Ma up to
Grandma's.

April 14
I peeked sap all day while
Pa and Abe got seed.

April 15
Peeked from 10 a.m. to 6:30
p.m. Sap (water) awful
weak. Abe did not come.
Pa gathered.

April 16
Peeked all day. Abe did not
come so Pa gathered.

April 17
Went to Sunday School.
Pa and I went down in
sugar works.

April 18
Helped Abe gather sap in
the forenoon. Peeked some
in aft.

April 19
I fussed around in the
forenoon. Went down in
woods and corded up about
2 1/2 cords of slab wood.
Uncle George Whitney's
barn burnt today.

April 20
Went down to sugar house
where Pa was cutting wood.
Pa found a nest of flying
squirrels.

April 21
I lay on the lounge all
day, had some cold.

April 22
Felt awful bad in morn-
ing. Felt better in afternoon.

April 23
Have been down in woods
all aft. Helped B put up
buckets.

April 24
Pa and I went to
Sunday School afoot.

April 25
Went to school.
April 26
Went to school.
April 27
Went to school.
April 28
Did not go to school. Had a cold.
Planted some onions.
April 29
Did not go outdoors.
April 30
Did not go outdoors. Was about half sick.

Sunday, May 1, 1892
Ma and I stayed at house from Sunday School.
May 2
Layed abed all day.
Coughed pretty hard all day.
May 3
Coughed good abed.
May 4
Coughed some. Helped clean pantry.
May 5
Did not go outdoors.
Played with kitten some.
Wrote some.
May 6
Did not do much of anything.
May 7
Ditto.

May 8
Did not go to S. S.
May 9
Went outdoors. Painted some in parlor.
May 10
Planted my potatoes.
Stalked plant potatoes.
May 11
Rained all day.
May 12
Went to village.
May 13
Dropped potatoes. Helped cover some.
May 14
Pa and I finished planting taters. Pa and I went to village.
May 15
Did not go to S. S.
May 16
Did not do much in forenoon. Aft. Joseph Wilson came and bought old mares for $150.
May 17
Went to school.
May 18
Went to school. Went over and off looking after colts. Pa and I went over to Maximums etc. did not find them.
May 19
Pa and I went over to George Richerts pasture

after colts. Drew manure.
At night went off hunting
up and getting colts.

May 20
Snowed most all day.
Snowed 2 inches. Went
out some. Had slight cold.

May 21
Snowed some 3 inches or
over. Did not go outdoors.
Helped put down carpet.

May 22
Did not go to Sunday
School. Uncle Jim took Pa
down to David Hall's to
go to Elizabethtown.

May 23
Rained in morning so did
not go to school.
Set wood chuck trap.

May 24
Ditto except setting trap.
Planted balance of beets.

May 25
Ditto except plant my
beets. Planted six hills of
taters. Burpees Extra
Early.

May 26
Went to school.

May 27
Went to school.

May 28
Did not do much of any-
thing in forenoon.
Dropped corn and pump-
kin seed.

May 29
Went to Sunday School.

May 30
Did not do much worth
writing down only
watching Uncle J and H
draw manure.

May 31
Dropped corn all
forenoon and part of
afternoon. Went up to
Uncle J and H's.

Wednesday, June 1, 1892
Did not do much of any-
thing.

June 2
Went to So. Schroon.
Dropped ALA
taters.

June 3
Helped put up scare
crows on corn
ground.
Fixed a double swing.

June 4
Went to South
Schroon. Watched
Pa fix bedroom window.
Swing in my double
swing.

June 5
Did not go to Sunday
School.

June 6
Went to School.

June 7
Went to School.
June 8
Helped plant potatoes over.
About 5 o'clock Pa and I
went to Marsh Pond we
got 2 whales.
June 9
I went up to Grandma's.
Aft. Aunt Hat and chil-
dren came.
June 10
Went to Grandma's.
Went to P.O. Played with
Cyrus.
June 11
Played with Cyrus some.
June 12
Went to Sunday School.
June 13
Went over to the fallow.
Played with Cyrus.
June 14
Played with Cyrus.
Martha Richardson and
Helen Warren came up a
visiting. Grandma,
Uncle H.J., Aunt Hattie,
Cyrus, Flossie went to
Mill Brook.
June 15
Went over to the fallow.
Helped Pa fix fence.
June 16
Went to Fred Ford's.
Expected riding with Pa
but did not come. Went to

Grandma's.
June 17
Helped some.
June 18
Afternoon I went to M.
Rough. Got 49 bullfrogs.
June 19
Did not get to Sunday
School.
June 20
Uncle Jim and I went to
Riverside with Aunt Hat.
June 21
Howed in my garden.
Helped Pa hoe beans.
June 22
Went to school.
June 23
Went to school.
June 24
I went to school.
June 25
Helped hoe potatoes.
June 26
Went up to Uncle Jim
Whitney's. Came back and
went down to meeting.
June 27
Went to school. It rained
awful in evening.
Pa went down to South
Schroon and came home
in the rain.
June 28
Went to school.
June 29
Went to school. Had two or

three showers between 4
p.m. and 8 p.m.

June 30

Went over to the fallow
with Pa to get horses out of
George Huntley's. Aft
watched the road machine.

Friday, July 1, 1892

Went to school.

July 2

Pa and I went over on
Grangers a strawberrying.
Aft Pa and I went to the
village. Pa got me 2
bunches of fire crackers.

July 3

Pa and I went to
Sunday school.

July 4

Shot fire crackers. Played
with Watty Hall.
Aft Pa and I
went over
on George
Huntley's to
fix fence.
I sat
around while Pa fixed
fence.

July 5

Went to school. Shot off
some fire works.

July 6

Pa and I went to Chester
after mowing machine.

July 7

Went to school.

July 8

Went to school. Rained
hard in evening.

July 9

Rained all forenoon. Aft
Pa and I went up to
Grandma's breaking colts.

July 10

Went to Sunday School.
Awful hot day.

July 11

Went to school. Got dis-
missed. After supper Pa and
I went down to South
Schroon.

July 12

Did not go to school.
Picked 3 1/2 pounds of garden strawberrys up in
strawberry patch.

July 13

Addie Allen came up here.
Pa went to village.
After supper we tryed our
new mowing machine.

July 14

Watched mower. Mowed
some with sythe.

July 15

Watched mower. Wed out
part of beet bed. Helped
tumble up hay and rake
after.

July 16

Fed chickens. Played with

Max and Forest Allen.
Went up to Grandma's.
Wed and hoed some in
garden.

July 17
Did not go to Sunday
School.

July 18
Did not do much of any-
thing in
forenoon.
Afternoon
helped
turn hay
up and rake after.

July 19
Helped rake a good deal.

July 20
Did not do much of any-
thing in forenoon. After
fixed a bell up in shed,
helped rake after.

July 21
Spread hay. Helped rake
after.

July 22
Did not do much of any-
thing in forenoon.
Afternoon helped rake.

July 23
We a spread hay.
Afternoon Mrs. A. Day
and children came.

July 24
Played with Asher some.

July 25
Ditto

July 26
Played with Asher some.

July 27
Played with Asher.

July 28
Played with Asher. Went
to Grandma's.

July 29
Played with Asher.

July 30
Played with Asher. Went
to Grandma's.

July 31
Did not go to Sunday
School.
Played with Asher.

———

Monday, August 1, 1892
Played with Asher. Picked
berries.

August 2
Played with Asher. Caught
squirrel.

August 3
Went to So. Schroon.
Played with Asher.

August 4
Played with Asher.

August 5
Ditto

August 6
Played with Asher.

August 7
Went to Sunday School.

August 8
Played with Asher. Picked

up apples for hog.

August 9

Played with Asher. We played over in brook some.

August 10

Wed some in garden. Had toothache and sore throat.

August 11

Ditto.

August 12

Rainy
Rained most all day. Did not do much of anything.

August 13

Built a dam over to brook. Played over to brook with Arthur Granger.

August 14

Went to Sunday School with Pinky and Posy.

August 15

Did not do much of anything.

August 16

Did not do much. Stayed at home.

August 17

Did not do much. Played over to brook.

August 18

Did not do much.

August 19

Did not do much. Mrs. A. Day & Co. came up.

August 20

Went to Mash Pond. Got

skunked. Caught a squirrel.

August 21

Went to Sunday School.

August 22

Went berrying. Caught a squirrel.

August 23

Pig died. Caught a squirrel.

August 24

Went berrying and fishing.

August 25

Rained most all day. Pa went to village.

August 26

Pa and I went to Pottersville to get cold shovel.

August 27

Did not do much forenoon. Played with Asher.

August 28

Played with Asher.

August 29

Played with Asher. Old cat had kittens.

August 30

Went to Pottersville with Uncle Jim to carry Mrs. A. Day & Co. down.

Went to village.
August 31
Raked after horse. Raked oat ground. Raked after.

Thursday, September 1, 1892
Did not do much of anything.
September 2
Watched Pa fix big kettle.
September 3
Did not do much.
September 4
Went to S. S.
September 5
Hunted after Spot over to fallow.
September 6
Went to school.
September 7
Went to school.
September 8
Went to school.
September 9
Went to school.
September 10
Went to Mash Pond after hay.
September 11
Went to Sunday School.
September 12
Went to school.
September 13
Went to picnic.
September 14
Went to school.

September 15
Ditto.
September 16
Went to school.
September 17
Played with Eddy Floyd. Picked up potatoes.
September 18
Went to Sunday School down to Town Hall.
September 19
Went to school.
September 20
Did not go to school. Had cold blowed my nose over 1000 times. Caught a squirrel, skinned him and dried the skin. Chased squirrels. Set trap.
September 21
Did not do much. Only watch squirrel traps.
September 22
Caught 2 squirrels.
September 23
Did not go to school.
September 24
Did not do much but watch squirrel trap.
September 25
Went to Sunday School.
September 26
Went to school.
September 27
Went to school.

September 28
Went to school.
September 29
Pa and I went to the fair.
September 30
Went to school.

———

Saturday, October 1, 1892
Picked up taters. 17 bushels.
October 2
Went to Sunday School.
October 3
Went to school.
October 4
Went to school.
October 5
Went to school.
October 6
Went to school.
October 7
Went to school.
October 8
Went to village.
October 9
Did not go to Sunday School. Pa and Ma went.
October 10
Did not go to school. Pa about sick. Helped with chores.
October 11
Pa helped me do chores. Pa taken worse. Went up to Grandma's twice.
October 12
Helped Uncle Henry do

chores. Pa better.
October 13
Helped do chores. Pa better.
October 14
Ditto.
October 15
Helped do chores. Ciphered some.
October 16
Stayed at home.
October 17
Helped do chores. Pa went to barn.
October 18
Pa helped me do chores.
October 19
Rainy morning. Cleared off and Pa and I went to Granger's.
October 20
Went up to Grandma's with Pa. Went with Pa to set skunk trap.
October 21
Went to skunk trap with Pa.
October 22
Tinkered. Made lots of things. Pa went to village.
October 23
Did not go to S. S. Harry Ingraham was here.
October 24
Went to school.
October 25
Went to school.

October 26
Rained some. Aunt Sophia
was here.
October 27
Went to Mill Brook.
Carried over 2 kittens.
October 28
Played with Arthur and
Eddy. Came home.
October 29
Stayed at home all day.
Rainy day.
October 30
Went to Sunday School.
October 31
Went to school.

Tuesday, November 1, 1892
Went to school.
November 2
Did not go to school.
Helped Pa husk corn.

Snowed about one inch
last night.
November 3
Helped husk corn. Went up
to Grandma's to help
thrash.
November 4
Helped thrash up to
Grandma's part of
forenoon. Helped get ready
for threshers.

November 5
Pa went to village.
Threshers came in after-
noon.
November 6
Went to Sunday School.
November 7
Helped thrash and clean up etc.
November 8
Election day. School don't
keep. Stayed home.
November 9
Did not go to school.
Helped Pa put in new
water barrel to barn.
November 10
Went to school. Snowed
about five inches.
November 11
Went to school.
November 12
Went up to Grandma's.
Stayed all day.
November 13
Went to Sunday School.
November 14
Went to school.
November 15
Went to school.
November 16
Went to school.
November 17
Went to school.
November 18
Went to school.
November 19
Went to fox trap. Found

a fox and killed him and brought him to the house. Helped draw stone.

November 20

Went to Sunday School.

November 21

Went to school.

November 22

Went to school.

November 23

Went to school.

November 24

School don't keep. Helped kill 2 sheep.

November 25

Went to school. Pa went to village. He got me the following: 1 pen holder, 1 book, 1 pr. shoelaces.

November 26

Went to Grandma s. Set for trap etc.

November 27

Went to Sunday School.

November 28

Went to school.

November 29

Went to school.

November 30

Went to school.

Thursday, December 1, 1892

Went to school.

December 2

Went up to school.

December 3

Went up to my fox trap and found my trap and dog gone so Pa and I hunted after him. Pa found an awful big fox.

December 4

Did not go to Sunday School. Had a cold. Pa brought down 2 foxes this morning.

December 5

Had cold. Stayed in the house.

December 6

Stayed in the house.

December 7

Went out of doors. Pa went to village.

December 8

Did not do much. Went outdoors some.

December 9

Went to school.

December 10

Chased foxes etc. Set fox trap.

December 11

Did not go to Sunday School.

December 12

Went to school.

December 13

Went to school.

December 14

Went to school.

December 15
Went to school.
December 16
Went to school.
December 17
Was down in woods where Pa was framing Church rafters.
December 18
Did not go to Sunday School.
December 19
Had a little cold and my head felt bad. So I did not go to school.
Sold my fox skin for one dollar and twenty-five cents. ($1.25).
December 20
Went to school.
December 21
Went to school.
December 22
Did not go to school. Pa went to village. Ma went visiting down to Lou Richardson's.
I stayed at home.
December 23
Did not go to school. The wind blew awful the snow flew and it was a regular winter's day.
December 24
Cold day. Was going to have Christmas tree down to South Schroon but it was so cold they did not have it.
December 25
Went to Sunday School.
December 26
15° below zero
It was so cold in the morning that I did not go out much. It got to 1° above zero in middle of the day. Went to Christmas tree in the evening.
December 27
Went to school.
December 28
Went to school.
Examination day. I passed 100% in arithmetic in the sixth grade. And 95% in geography in sixth grade. Went up and set fox trap over.
December 29
Went to school.
December 30
Went to school. School out at noon for good.
December 31
Helped Pa cut brush out beside road. Went to South Scroon.

Noted:

First snow that amounted to
anything came Jan. 6, 1892.

We got Teddy the bird on
March 3, 1892.

Went over to Mill Brook and
saw them bore for oil
March 10, 1892.

Uncle George Whitney's barn
burnt April 19, 1892.

I saw four young flying
squirrels April 20, 1892.

May 20 and 21: snowed two
and three inches. 1892

Pa changed bedroom window
Jun 3 & 4 1892.

Aunt Hattie was here from Jun
9 to 20, 1892.
Snow came about 5 or 6 inches Nov. 10, 1892.

Caught my first fox December
3, 1892.

There is a boarding house
Not far away
Where they have pork and
beans
Three times a day.
Oh how the boarders yell
When they hear
the dinner bell.
Oh how the boarders sing
When they hear
the dinner bell.

Cash Account
Pa and I buy two dollar bill
for 10¢.

Ma and I bring water and
bring girl $10.10

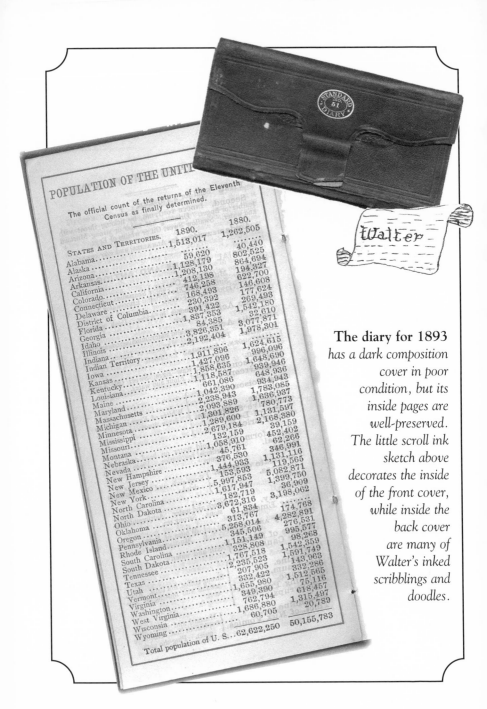

POPULATION OF THE UNIT[ED STATES]

The official count of the returns of the Eleventh Census as finally determined.

STATES AND TERRITORIES.	1890.	1880.
Alabama	1,513,017	1,262,505
Alaska		
Arizona	59,620	40,440
Arkansas	1,128,179	802,525
California	1,208,130	864,694
Colorado	412,198	194,327
Connecticut	746,258	622,700
Delaware	168,493	146,608
District of Columbia	230,392	177,624
Florida	391,422	269,493
Georgia	1,837,353	1,542,180
Idaho	84,385	32,610
Illinois	3,826,351	3,077,871
Indiana	2,192,404	1,978,301
Indian Territory		
Iowa	1,911,896	1,624,615
Kansas	1,427,096	996,096
Kentucky	1,858,635	1,648,690
Louisiana	1,118,587	939,946
Maine	661,086	648,936
Maryland	1,042,390	934,943
Massachusetts	2,238,943	1,783,085
Michigan	2,093,889	1,636,937
Minnesota	1,301,826	780,773
Mississippi	1,289,600	1,131,597
Missouri	2,679,184	2,168,380
Montana	132,159	39,159
Nebraska	1,058,910	452,402
Nevada	45,761	62,266
New Hampshire	376,530	346,991
New Jersey	1,444,933	1,131,116
New Mexico	153,593	119,565
New York	5,997,853	5,082,871
North Carolina	1,617,947	1,399,750
North Dakota	182,719	36,909
Ohio	3,672,316	3,198,062
Oklahoma	61,834	
Oregon	313,767	174,768
Pennsylvania	5,258,014	4,282,891
Rhode Island	345,506	276,531
South Carolina	1,151,149	995,577
South Dakota	328,808	98,268
Tennessee	1,767,518	1,542,359
Texas	2,235,523	1,591,749
Utah	207,905	143,963
Vermont	332,422	332,286
Virginia	1,655,980	1,512,565
Washington	349,390	75,116
West Virginia	762,794	618,457
Wisconsin	1,686,880	1,315,497
Wyoming	60,705	20,789
Total population of U. S.	62,622,250	50,155,783

Walter

The diary for 1893 *has a dark composition cover in poor condition, but its inside pages are well-preserved. The little scroll ink sketch above decorates the inside of the front cover, while inside the back cover are many of Walter's inked scribblings and doodles.*

Logging in the Adirondacks

1893 was witness to a series of "firsts." Amazingly, the first successful heart operation was performed by Daniel H. Williams on July 9th. Henry Ford completed his first useful gas motor. The first commemorative stamp, as well as the first stamp to picture a woman, was issued on January 2.

On January 3, William West Durant literally executed the first steps that led to his Adirondack Great Camp fame and recognition. On a winter holiday with friends, he walked in snow shoes to mark out the site for Camp Uncas. Camp Sagamore and Kill Kare followed, and soon the elitists' summer season would extend to the great timber palaces deep in the secluded and pristine Adirondack forest.

Durant was not alone in capitalizing on that which nature provided. Schroon Lake, in the meantime, continued to glisten in tourism; but industry had not escaped the small town and its surrounding area. Its natural resource was trees and its industry logging; and it used its lakes, rivers, and streams as vehicles to progress. This means of livelihood, however, was kept at bay during the tourist season, so as not to offend or disturb the comfort and pleasure of visitors and guests, and was allowed only during the winter and shoulder seasons of spring and fall.

South Schroon was the home of many people who participated in the logging industry. Although Walter Whitney does not refer to his father or the men of the community as loggers, and certainly not lumber jacks, many references are made in the diaries to the combined efforts of Pa and Walter drawing wood and skidding logs.

INDUSTRY

Long winters and short growing seasons led the Adirondack settlers to consider timber, itself, as a source of income. The very early market for timber was Quebec, via Lake Champlain. After the War of 1812, the market changed. The vision of William Gilliland to connect Lake Champlain to the Atlantic Ocean by way of the Hudson River, was executed in 1823 in the form of the Champlain Canal (Bernstein). This opened the timber markets to Glens Falls, Albany, and New York City. Lumbering became big business for local farmers who farmed or lumbered according to the season.

Sawmills existed on the byroads of the Schroon Lake area and kept many men working. Tanneries sprung up to accommodate the very lucrative trapping and fur-trading business. The local hemlock was needed for tanning the hides. Sanford Rawson was a tanner of leather by trade, and

Lumbering in the Adirondacks, N. Y.

he made a market for hides. He also ran a wool-carding industry and a sawmill on Hoffman Road.

Saw Mill So Schroon N.

One industry that cannot be ignored in considering Schroon Lake enterprises is the peg mill that existed in the early 1800s at Bailey Pond on Loch Muller. Alonzo and Dan Carlos Bailey made house pegs and shoe pegs, a product that preceded the use of nails in shoemaking. This product was sent to Ticonderoga by oxcart, a three-day trip, then shipped to towns in New England, where shoes were manufactured. Shoe pegs required skilled workmanship and were a good source of income for the Baileys.

Amy Godine, in a three-lecture series titled *Adirondackers Anonymous: Lost Worlds and Hidden Heroes in Northern New York*, tells of the many immigrants who found their way to the Adirondacks on the merit of their expert craftsmanship. People of all nationalities who had the skills necessary to promote and realize the full potential of New York's natural resources were hired by developers and manufacturers to exercise their skills and crafts. They were not the settlers. They were "immigrant sojourners, transient laborers, migratory craftsmen" of diverse nationalities and ethnic backgrounds. Glass, shoes, gloves, wood pulp, pottery, cigars, slate—and the list goes on—were New York products brought to fruition by the artistry of Amy Godine's "Hidden Heroes."

The tanneries of Pottersville, Adirondack, and Chestertown had largely closed by Walter's time. *Smith's History of Warren County* lists a steam mill, planing mill, gristmill in Pottersville in 1885, and a gristmill, tannery, marble works and harness making shop in Chestertown. Walter describes his own employment in a shirt factory in Chestertown.

The completion of the Adirondack Railroad in 1872 provided access to the Schroon Lake area, and the summer resort business began. Large hotels were built to accommodate New York City and Albany clientele, many of whom stayed the entire summer. This created jobs and a new way of life for local residents.

In more recent years, circa 1934, a unique business flourished in Schroon Lake. James Cheney rented an ice cream parlor on Main Street and, for pastime, made little dolls and animals out of pipe cleaners. His materials graduated to bottle caps, corks, and bobby pins in constructing small objects of interest. When plastic became available he turned to that medium and developed a line of Christmas tree ornaments, all his original ideas. His products were sent to large department stores all over the country, as well as abroad. The business employed about 20 local residents and continued until his death in 1974.

Mr. W. J. S. Whitney
South Schroon, N. Y.
(scroll drawn in ink with
lettering "Walter")
This is the fourth year I
have kept Diary

Sunday, January 1, 1893
Slid down hill just a lit-
tle. Went up to Grand
ma's with Arthur Floyd.
Went to Sunday School
Pa and I. Snowed like
"guns" towards night.
Done chores etc.

January 2
Got my lessons. Pa made
me a kind of cupboard
with curtains for doors. Pa
went to village. He got me
a Grammar.

January 3
Got lessons. Done chores.

January 4
18° below 0°
Got lessons. Went with Pa
down to the saw mill after
lumber.

January 5
Got lessons. Pa worked to
Mash Pond.

January 6
Got lessons. Done the
chores.

January 7
Jennie Brown came up
here. Sat around and "visited."

January 8
Went to Sunday School.

January 9
Got lessons. Caught a rabbit. Helped Pa.

January 10
Got lessons. Pa drawed
wood for Geo. Richardson.
Done chores.

January 11
20° below 0°
Got lessons. Pa commenced
doing off or making parti-
tions upstairs. Watched him
some awful cold in mornings.

January 12
14° below 0°   Cold
Got my lessons. Worked up
stairs. Grand ma came
down.

January 13
Got my lessons. Pa worked
up stairs. I helped him ceil
up. Uncle Henry came
down.

January 14
Helped Pa a lot up stairs.
Done chores and that was
about all I done.

January 15
Calculated to go to Sunday

School but Uncle Jim
Floyd and children came
over. I played with Eddy
some. We all went up to
Grand ma's.
January 16
Pa and I went to village.
I had tooth pulled.
January 17
Got lessons. Pa drew wood
for Geo. Richardson.
January 18
Got lessons. Pa drew wood
for Geo. Richardson. I
drew map etc.
January 19
D 24°   Hazy
Pa drew wood. Set foxtrap
over. Done chores etc.
January 20
Got lessons. Helped Pa
draw up little wood.
Went to fox trap etc.
January 21
Got lessons for last
Monday. Went up to
Grand ma's. Helped Pa
draw wood.
January 22
Went to Sunday School.
January 23
Got lessons. Helped Pa tin-
ker water. The water froze
up between house and
barn.
Made mistake and wrote
this for Sunday instead

of Monday.
January 24
Got lessons.
January 25
Got lessons. Made me a
little sled.
January 26
Pa and I went to
Pottersville.
January 27
Got lesson. Made roads
around the house for fun
etc.
January 28
Got lessons for last
Thursday. Played with
Arthur Granger.
January 29
Did not go to Sunday
School. Rained and
thawed some.
January 30
Went over to Mash Pond
to watch Pa and Clifton
skid logs. Got lessons.
January 31
Got lessons.
Pa and Ma went to vil-
lage. Got lessons.
Good bye Jan.

—————

Wednesday, February 1, 1893
Got lessons. Went down
in woods where Pa and
Clifton were cutting wood.
Helped pile brush.

February 2
Got lessons. Went down in woods.

February 3
Got lessons. Went up to Grand ma's. Helped Pa get wood down in woods.

February 4
Got lessons. Wind blew awful last night.

February 5
Went to Sunday School. Stopped at Emery Whitney's.

February 6
Got lessons. Puttered around as usual.

February 7
Went over to Mash Pond to help Pa break roads to draw logs. Did not get lessons.

February 8
Got lessons. Pa drew logs.

February 9
Got lessons. Went one load of logs with Pa.

February 10
Got lessons. Helped Pa "tinker" water.

February 11
Went to village.

February 12
Did not go to Sunday

School. Uncle Jim and Grand ma came down.

February 13
Got lessons. Went up to "Daddles".

February 14
Got lessons. Helped Pa doctor Pinkey.

February 15
Got lessons. Went a load of logs.

February 16
Got lessons.

February 17
Got lessons. Puttered with hens.

February 18
Did not do much of anything. Harry Ingraham was here.

February 19
Did not go to Sunday School.

February 20
Snowed some and blowed a great deal. Shoveled some. Got lessons.

February 21
Got lessons. Shoveled some. Pa helped shovel out roads.

February 22
Pa sick or had bad cold and the "Grip" and did not go out doors. I did most of the chores and Granger the rest.

February 23

Pa felt better so he helped me or I helped him do the chores. Got lessons.

February 24

Got lessons. Pa helped plow out roads.

February 25

Did not do much. Pa went to village.

February 26

Had cold. Did not go out doors. Felt worse toward night.

February 27

Layed abed most all day. My or Our book "400 Years of America" came tonight.

February 28

Felt better. Set up all day only when I did not lay down.

Wednesday, March 1, 1893

Did not do much of anything.

March 2

Went outdoors. Pa went to village.

March 3

Played with Claud Smith most all day. Done "my chores" tonight.

March 4

Got lessons. Helped shovel out grindstone out back of shed.

March 5

Did not go to Sunday School for I "haint" got over my cold.

March 6

Got lessons. Went up to Grand ma's.

March 7

Got lessons. Pa went to village.

March 8

Got lessons. Pa went over to Lavery's after lumber.

March 9

Went up to "Daddles" and to So. Schroon.

March 10

Got lessons. Pa went to village. Chased hens.

March 11

Pa went to village. Grand ma was down.

March 12

Went to Sunday School.

March 13

Did not do much of anything forenoon. After went with Pa breaking out sugar roads.

March 14

"Tinkered hens". Papa went to village and got me a pair of rubber boots. 5's.

March 15

Made wire loops to put on wooden buckets.

Grand ma came down.

March 16

Slid down hill. Slid down hill. Helped Pa draw up wood.

March 17

Tinkered hens. Helped Pa fix buckets down to sugar house.

March 18

Pa went over to Abe Walkers in morning. After he got back, we went down to sugar house and tried to fix and wash buckets but it was so cold we quit.

March 19

Went to Sunday School.

March 20

Clr.

Went to South Schroon with Pa in morning. After we got back, we. Roll and I, went down fixing buckets. After dinner we all went down. Arthur Geame down there.

March 21

Snow/clear

Done chores. Then went down to the sugar house, snowed awful while I was going down. I mean while Pa and I was going. Helped wash buckets some. Afternoon Pa

and I went to mill with logs.

March 22

Watched Pa build chimney down to sugar house. Henry Carpenter and Bert Ingraham came over. Fooled "with em" some.

March 23

Slid down hill. Pa drew up wood sled length from down in sugar works. I went with him some.

March 24

Arthur Floyd came down. We slid down hill some. Uncle Culver and Grand ma came down. Afternoon we went down to Post Office and rode back with Uncle Bish and wife.
Pounded out corn. Done chores. My birthday. 11 years old.

March 25

Went up to Uncle Jim's with Uncle Bish's folks and Ma. Arthur and I came home and slid and slid. Afternoon we slid and slid and slid down the road till when night came I was pretty tired.

March 26

Did not feel very well. Kindy dumped all day. Did not go to S. School Pa and Ma went. Arthur helped me do chores.

March 27

Uncle Bish came over after cedar. Arthur went home with him. I taped a few trees. Did not feel very good so I did not do all of my chores at night.

March 28

Pa and Roll tapped trees. Did not feel good nor did I go outdoors. Had little fever.

March 29

Did not go outdoors. Felt mean. Sat up when I did not lay down.

March 30

Pa went after doctor for me. When he came I was sweating awful. My pulse was 100 and my temperature 104 1/2.

March 31

Did not do anything only lay abed. Had fever etc. Grand ma came down.

Saturday, April 1, 1893

Dr. came and said I was better. April fooled women etc.

April 2

Layed abed.

April 3

Dr. came. Pa sawed wood a little.

April 4

Did not do anything but lay abed.

April 5

Layed abed.

April 6

Layed abed. Pa tinkered down to sugar house.

April 7

Pa was over to Granger's some. I am better a little.

April 8

Pa went to Pottersville after Doctor for Granger's folks and "gadded" around for G's all day.

April 9

Ma went over to Granger's. Pa stayed with me. Doctor came.

April 10

I sat up today. Henry Carpenter boiled 15 bbls. sap.

April 11

Sat up some or about 1 1/2 hours. Pa and Henry worked in sugar works.

April 12

Sat up some. Pa and

Henry saped it all day.

April 13
Rainy

Sat up etc. Rained most all day. Had thunder shower towards night.

April 14
Pa and Henry went to village. Snowed hard toward night.

April 15
Sat up some of the time and layed abed the rest. We expected Dr. but he did not come.

April 16
Grand ma, Uncle Henry and Nora Floyd came down here. Doctor came. Good sap day.

April 17
Pa and Jess Cole gathered 23 bbls of sap and snow water. The women think I'm on the gain.

April 18
Felt better. Went or Ma drawed me out in "tother room." Dr. came in Aft.

April 19
Sat up quite a lot. The Minister was here to supper. Wrote part of a letter to Aunt Lucy.

April 20
Wrote some to Aunt Lucy. Sat up some. Old cat had four kittens last night.

April 21
Sat up etc. Uncle Jim was here in afternoon.

April 22
Sat up with pants on. Nora was here a while.

April 23
Sat up with pants on out in "middle room." Layed on lounge, and then set up again etc. Dr. came.

April 24
Layed on lounge part of the time and sat up "tother" part. Ate at table and walked a little.

April 25
"Did not lay abed." Walked around considerable. Eat my dinner and supper with the rest.

April 26
Wrote a letter for "Chan." "Toddled" around the house. Took care of bird (Teddy).

April 27
Fooled with Henry. Planted watermelons in little box. Wrote quite a lot.

April 28
"Slicked up" cupboard in bedroom. Dr. came. I felt

the best today I have at
all.
April 29
Henry C. went home.
Weighed cat & kitten for
weight see memoranda.
Pa, Dolph and Roll cut
sugar wood.
April 30
53°
Did not do much. Pa
went to S. School.

Monday, May 1, 1893
Rain
Sugared off. Made 3 little
cakes. Wrote order for 23
cents worth garden seed.
Rained all day.
May 2
Planted a few beet and
onion seed.
Dr. Griswold's dog has
been here some. He would go
off and come back, he was
in the house 3 different
times. Dr. not here.
I heard frogs peep first this
year.
Ringmiddle had calf.
May 3
Did not do much.
Had headache some in after
noon.
Ma commenced me a wall
basket,

May 4
Rainy
Rained most all day.
Made little wheel barrow
gig. Ma finished my wall
basket.
May 5
Did not do much of any-
thing. Dr. came for last
time. Whittled some.
May 6
Planted a few carrots in a
little can. Pa went to
Pottersville after seed oat
and pig. Cleaned up dirt
on floor after Ma had
transplanted her tomatoes.
Fussed with kitten some.
May 7
Grand ma came down
and stayed most all day.
Pa and Uncle Henry went
to Sunday School and
Episcopal services.
May 8
Went outdoors little.
"Slicked up" around
house. Pa drew manure.
Pulled one of my teeth.
Opened barrel flour. Pulled
tooth.
May 9
Went outdoors quite a lot
for me. Wrote some to
Eddy Floyd.
May 10
Turned fanning mill out

to barn. Went out consid-
erable. Pretty hot.

May 11
Hitty Prot
Went out "bout" all I
wanted to.

May 12
Planted my taters.
Dropped sweet corn etc.
Pulled tooth.

May 13
Partly made onion bed and
it rained so I did not do
rest. Had little cold so stayed
in house. Pulled tooth.

May 14
Did not go outdoors. Had
cold. Pa went to Sunday
School alone.

May 15
Did not go outdoors.

May 16
Stayed in house. Rainy
day. Pa went off and got
12 little trout. Tooth
dropped out in my mouth
in evening.

May 17
Grand ma came down
and stayed all day. Wove
some on carpet Chan was
weaving. Rained by spells
nearly all day. Went to
bed and asleep.

May 18
Squirty
Helped Ma paste rags over
cracks upstairs. Fussed
with kitten. Helped past
paper on boards upstairs.
Printed some etc.

May 19
Windy
Helped women clean
pantry. Tinkered aft. a
thing to roll marble on.

May 20
70 ° in shade   Pls.
Went out doors again. Ma
went up "home" a "little
while." Pa tinkered water
etc. in afternoon.

May 21
Windy
Went out. Pa and Ma
went to Sunday School.
Lill Cole went with them.
Windy day.

May 22
Hot
Went out considerable.
Went up in fields and saw
Pa drag with spring tooth
harrow. Shad blowed out.
Planted my onions and
some beans.

May 23
Windy, showers
Planted two big beds beets,
one big bed onions and
carrots and turnips in
Pa's garden and a bed beets
in my own. Had an
awful shower at 6 p.m.

Planted my beets.

May 24

Helped Pa drop taters some in forenoon. Afternoon did not do much of anything.

May 25

Did not go out but once today for I coughed yesterday and got little cold etc. etc. Wrote some to Aunt Lucy. Uncle Henry got me a tablet at P.O. Ma not feeling well.

May 26

May Whitney came here and stayed until after dinner and went away. Afternoon dropped corn, cleaned guns etc. etc. etc.

May 27

Cld. Rain

Helped load a load of manure. Grand ma and I went and got some dandelions for greens and picked them over etc. etc. Kindy damp so I did not go out doors as much as usual.

May 28

Had colds all of us so we all stayed at home. I went out doors quite a lot. Grand ma came down.

May 29

Dropped corn. Pa, Roll and

Mr. Granger finished planting corn. "Holed" out 12 hills in my garden for my sweet corn. Pa helped me plant it. Planted my beans. Helped Pa plant Squashes, Sweet Corn, Potiron, Pumpkins, pole beans. Pa not feeling very good.

May 30

Pa feeling better but Dr. came. Done chores etc.

May 31

Set two crow traps and one wood chuck trap. Pa went out doors considerable. Played with Arthur Granger.

Thursday, June 1, 1893

Pa bothered to breathe so I went up to Culvers about 5 a.m. and got Uncle Jim to get Dr. Griswold. He came and stayed quite a while.
Went up to I. D. Coles after whiskey.

June 2

Papa feeling better. Dr. came. Helped do chores. "Daddle" Culver came down.

June 3

Papa feeling better. Went

up to Uncle Jim's.
Grand ma came down.
June 4
Did not do much of any-
thing. Dr. came.
June 5
86 (in wind and shade) Clear
Pa layed down little. Set
crow trap.
Uncle Bish brought colt
over to pasture. Dr. came.
June 6
Cld. rain
Pa so he layed down con-
siderable. Dr. came.
Went to crow trap and
found a wood-chuck in it.
Hoed part of my potatoes.
Wed my beet bed.
June 7
Hoed potatoes some. Wed
onion bed. Hoed beans.
Went to Post Office.
June 8
Hoed taters some and put
ashes on them.
Expected Dr. but he did
not come.
June 9
Hoed one roe peas and one
roe taters. Went up to Jess
Coles to get him to come
and work. Wed some in
garden.
June 10
82   Shd. West. Dit.
Cole worked here in

forenoon and part of after-
noon hoeing sweet corn,
potatoes, weeding beet bed,
etc. I hoed some.
June 11
Pa went out doors. Did
not go to Sunday School.
Went up to Grand ma
C's. Had awful hard show-
er. The lightning struck
not very far away.
June 12
Wed turnips and carrots.
Dr. G. came up to see Pa.
June 13
Wed carrots. Puttered
around and did not do
much.
June 14
Pa made a thing to weed
garden with. We were just
trying it when Mrs.
Sally Ann and Samantha
Green and S's boy, Arlie
Hurd, Libbie and Olive
Whitney and Grand ma
C. drove up. Did not do
much rest of day.
June 15
Wed garden etc. Puttered
around. Took care of horses.
June 16
Pa and I hoed sweet corn,
beans etc. with garden
weeder. Puttered.
June 17
Watched Pa fix up my

"Go-Cart". Hoed squashes.
Bees swarmed. Pulled
tooth.

June 18
Helped do chores. Pa and I
went and got some gum.
Went up to Daddle C's.

June 19
86°
Helped take twine of from
corn etc.
Pa and I helped Jess Cole
hoe corn little.

June 20
91°
Pa and I went to P.O.
and from there up to H. R.
King's and back. Dr. G.
came up to see Pa.

June 21
88°   Hzy. Rain
I was around where the
men of the neighborhood
were at work on the road.
Had showers toward night.
The road machine men
will stay here tonight.

June 22
57°   Rainy day
Rained most all day. Did
not do much only help Pa
ceil up bedroom upstairs.

June 23
Went up to Grand ma's
with Pa after wagon.
Afternoon Pa, Ma and I
went to village.

June 24
Rode Posy to cultivate
corn. Helped hoe some. Wed
garden etc.

June 25
Went to Sunday School
and Meeting. Wore long
pants.

June 26
Pa and I went to P.O. Pa
and I put ashes on pota-
toes.

June 27
Rode Pinkey to cultivate
potatoes. Pa and I hoed few
taters in forenoon.
Afternoon Pa and
Ma went to vil-
lage and I went
strawberrying.
I got a five
quart pail heaping full.

June 28
I was around where the
men folks were working
on the road. Went to P.O.

June 29
Pa and I hoed taters.

June 30
Hoed taters in forenoon.
Afternoon Pa and I
worked on turnip patch.

Saturday, July 1, 1893
Pa and I worked on
turnip ground below barn

most all day.

July 2

Pa, Ma, Orlie Hurd and I went to Sunday School and Episcopal meeting.

July 3

Rain

Helped get turnip ground ready. Had shower about noon and it rained part of the afternoon.
After it stopped Pa and I went down to the saw mill.

July 4

Pa and I sowed turnips.

July 5

Went down to saw mill with Pa after load of lumber.
Rained some while we were coming home.

July 6

Pa and I bugged taters. Pa mowed little with mowing machine.

July 7

Did not do much of anything. Pa went to village.

July 8

Helped patch barn in forenoon and part of afternoon. Did not do much of anything the rest of the day.

July 9

Pa, Ma, Uncle Henry, Lillie Cole and I went to Sunday School and Meeting.

July 10

Went up to Grand ma's with Pa and got some fertilizer. Wed garden.
Went up to G ma's again. Pa mowed up G ma's with mowing machine all day.

July 11

Pa mowed with machine and Jess Cole picked up after him down below road in forenoon.
I carried water to them and went up to strawberry patch and got a few strawberrys for dinner.
Pa worked up to G ma's in aft. I hoed garden some, piled up shingles etc.

July 12

Rainy

Spread hay. Preacher and his wife were here most all of afternoon.

July 13

Spread hay. Raked after some.

July 14

Went down to Blin's place with Pa to draw in hay, came back and went and got a few berries. Raking after.

July 15
Did not do much of anything.

July 16
Dolph Whitney's folks and Grand ma and Uncle J. H. and H. J. and Sally Ann Green and Arlie Hurd were here most all day.

July 17
Alice Hurd and I went up to strawberry patch and got a few berries. Wed few turnips. Jess Cole mowed in orchard. I spread hay quite a lot in aft. Had showers in afternoon and evening.

July 18
Turned grind stone. Hoed turnips. Went down to Pasco's with Pa after sack of feed.

July 19
Spread little hay in morning. Watched Pa mow. Turned grindstone. Tinkered pepper mill. Spread hay. Picked up after horse rake. Done chores.

July 20
Picked a few rasberrys. Picked up after horse rake. Tom Cole and Jess helped draw in so I did not rake after. Hoed turnips.

July 21
Hoed turnips. Carried water to Pa and Jess. Picked up after horse rake. Raked after.

July 22
Turned g-stone. Carried water to men. Hoed my turnips. Rained most all aft.

July 23
Went to Sunday School and meeting.

July 24
Hoed turnips some. Picked few rasberrys. Went down to Post Office. Picked up after horse rake. Raked after.

July 25
Cld. Rain
Hoed turnips. Raked after. Mowed away hay. Pa and Jess went to village.

July 26
Helped Pa cord up wood back of shed. Went up to Grand ma's with Ma. Raked after.

July 27
Hoed turnips. Waited on women and Pa.

July 28
Went to Grangers, brought in wood. Helped Ma paper and picked up after horse rake.

Raked after and picked up.
July 29
Did not do much of any-
thing. Pa and I hoed
turnips.
July 30
Went to Sunday School.
July 31
Pa and I went to Circus
up to village.

Tuesday, August 1, 1893
Did not do much of any-
thing. Raked after.
August 2
Followed mowing
machine around and
picked up stone out of grass
etc. Picked up after horse
rake and raked after all the
afternoon until 8 p.m.
August 3
Did not do much all day.
Pa worked down to
O'Neals.
August 4
Ditto.
August 5
85°   Fair
Did not do much of any-
thing. Pa worked down to
O'Neals.
August 6
                          Rainy
Did not go to Sunday
School. Lounged around

most all day. Went up to
Grand ma's.
August 7
                        Showers
Set out few turnips.
Arthur Granger and I
went up on hill and got
some penny royal.
Helped pick cucumbers.
Went over to Grangers.
Arthur came over and got
wheel barrow and went
back. He and Earl Brooks
came down and we played
some.
August 8
83°   Clr. all day
Went and got a few rasberrys. Made wind mill.
Wheeled up two cart loads
of saw dust from horse
barn for horse bedding. Pa
worked over to Uncle J. H.
and H. J.'s fallow. Ma
went up to Fairfield's.
August 9
88°   Fair
Went over to Uncle J. H.
and H. J.'s fallow with Pa
and stayed all day. Awful
hot.
August 10
90°   Fair
Went up to Grand ma's,
stayed a while, and came
back. Picked few berries
and peas. Pa worked over to

Uncle J. H. and H. J.'s fallow.

August 11

88°   Clear

Arthur G. and I played marbles some and that's about all I did do.

August 12

Cooler   Cld. shower

Thinned out turnips some.
Pa went to village.
Picked up potatoes. Anda Floyd came home with Pa.

August 13

59°   Fair

Pa, Ma, Uncle Henry and I went to Sunday School. Pulled tooth.

August 14

76°

Helped kill and pick eight hens. Pa went to village. Thinned out some turnips.

August 15

                                    Fair

Pa mowed oats with machine. I mowed little with scythe. Aft. Pa and I corded up wood down in woods. Caught woodchuck up in oat field.

August 16

                              Hot Fair

Raked oats forenoon and part of afternoon.
After we got oats raked up, we got in two loads.

August 17

                                   Rainy

Did not do much of anything. Rainy day.

August 18

                                    Cold

Helped catch sheep. Helped fix fence.
Picked three quarts blackberries.

August 19

Helped kill and pick eight hens. Fed hens we did not kill.
Pa went to village. Grandma and Mrs. P. M. Burbanks were here most all day.

August 20

                               Cld. rain

Went to Meeting. Rained just as we were going to Sunday School so we waited and went to Meeting.

August 21

Went up to Uncle Jim's, rode home, and went down to Post Office with Uncle Henry C.
Afternoon, Pa and I went blackberrying.

August 22

                                    Fair

Went over to Granger's.
Helped Pa tinker water. Pa and I drew stone.

August 23

77°   Fair

Arthur G. and I went to Post Office. Turned over oats. Afternoon, Pa, Jess Cole and I got up oats.

August 24

       Wind, rain

Did not do much of anything. Wind blew awful from the Northeast and rained all day.

August 25

      Clr. Cld. Sho.

Went up to Grand ma's. Played with Arthur G. Helped Ma. Pa went to village.

August 26

Did not do much of anything in forenoon. Afternoon, Pa and I went up and helped Jess Cole, Uncle Jim and Henry get in oats.

August 27

        Cld. Sho.

Did not go to Sabbath School. Had long showers in morning and evening. Toward night Pa, Aunt Lillias Richardson, Mrs. Edward Jones and I went up to Fairfield's. Stayed a few minutes.

August 28

       Cld.

Pa and I went down to David Hall's to carry Aunt Lillias and Mrs. Jones home. Afternoon did not do much of anything.

August 29

      Rainy

Fed hens. Toward night, cleared off and I went and got a few blackberries for supper. Rain! Rain!

August 30

48°   Clear

Painted roof ladder. Went blackberrying. Helped Pa make ladder. Helped milk.

August 31

Pa and I raked up oats in forenoon. Aft. Jess came down and we got em in. Pa and I went down to David Hall's and

got 16 white leghorn chickens in evening.

Friday, September 1, 1893

Pa and I hayed it over to

Mash Pond.

September 2
48°   Clr.

Went over to Granger's.
Helped mow young hay.
Boned hens. Turned
fanning mill. Helped Pa
set saw.

September 3
Fair cold.

We were going to Sabbath
School but Uncle Bish
came over so we stayed at
home. Afternoon Pa, Uncle
B. and I went up to
Grand ma's, and from
there over to our fallow
and about all over cre-
ation. Pulled tooth.

September 4
68°   Fair

Went to P.O. and up
around house by Charley
Warren's. Pulled my
beans.

September 5
Cld.

Fed hens. Pa worked up to
School House.
At noon, I carried his
dinner up to him, and
stayed a good share of afternoon.

September 6
Cld.

Went up to School House
with Arthur G. and we got

some lime for hens. Arthur
G. came home toward
noon but I stayed most
all day.

September 7
Squirty

Pa worked up to School
House. I did not do much
of anything.

September 8
Dug a few potatoes. Helped
get in oats for Jess Cole.

September 9
Picked sweet corn. Picked
up apples for hog. Aft.
went up to School House
and helped Pa paint.

September 10
Fair

Pa, Ma, Grand ma and I
went to Sunday School.

September 11
Pa and I hayed it over to
Mash Pond.

September 12
Pa and I cut our corn.

September 13
Did not do much of any-
thing in a.m. In p.m.
Pa and I went to
Pottersville.

September 14
Cld.

Helped Pa thresh oats.
Threshed my beans from
20 hills. I got 1 1/4 quarts
beans.

Helped draw corn and pumpkins.

September 15

Husked corn some. Pa went to village.

September 16

Did not do much of anything in a. m. In p. m. Pa and I went to the village.

September 17

Rainy

Pa and I went to Sunday School afoot.

September 18

Cld.

Went to school.

September 19

Went to school.

September 20

Went to school.

September 21

Went to school.

September 22

Went to school in forenoon. In aft. went to Mill Brook.

September 23

At Mill Brook, played on Henry's organ.

September 24

At Adirondack, played with Eddy Howard and Arthur.

September 25

Rainy

We was going home, but it rained so we did not go. Played with Eddy and Howard.

September 26

Fair.

Packed up and came home. Got here about 12:15 p. m. Went up to Jess Cole's, Grand ma's, etc. Went up and took up woodchuck trap and gathered few sweet apples.

September 27

Went to school. Took my grammar to school.

September 28

Went to school.

September 29

Went to school.

September 30

Helped draw in corn. Picked up potatoes.

Sunday, October 1, 1893

Pa, Ma, Grand ma and I went to Meeting. Grand ma stayed down to Emory Whitney's.

October 2

Went to school.

October 3

Went to school.

October 4

Cold Went to school.

October 5

Went to school.

October 6

Went to school.

October 7

Helped Pa bag up corn and get it to the house. About noon Uncle Bish and Aunt Lucy came over from Adirondack.

October 8

Pa and I went up to Grand ma's. Uncles Jim, Bish and Henry were here.

October 9

Went to school.

October 10

Went to school.

October 11

Went to school.

October 12

Went to school in forenoon. Aft. helped thresh our oats. Threshing machine here. Had 53 bushels.

October 13

Helped Pa lay floor in our room.

October 14

Helped Pa lay floor.

October 15

Did not go to Sabbath School.

October 16

Went to school.

October 17

Went to school. Aunt Lib and her children came over.

October 18

Went to school.

October 19

Went to school.

October 20

Went to school. Played with Eddy and Howard when I got home.

October 21

Played with Eddy and Howard.

October 22

Did not go to school for there was no school. Played with Eddy and Howard.

October 23

Eddy, Howard and I went to school in forenoon. Afternoon played some and ciphered some.

October 24

Went to school.

October 25

Went to school.

October 26

Went to school. Teacher Miss Bohrman came home with me.

October 27

Went to school.

October 28

Helped pull turnips and

get them in the cellar. Had 53 bushels.

October 29

No Sunday School.
Went up to Grand ma's and drawed. Aunt Lib's baby down home. Played with Ed and Howard. Aunt Lib went home.

October 30

Went to school.

October 31

Went to school.

Wednesday, November 1, 1893

Went to school.

November 2

Went to school.

November 3

Went to school.

November 4

Did not do much of anything in a.m. Afternoon helped Pa draw stone.

November 5

Did not go to Sunday School for there wasn't any.
Pa and Ma went to funeral.

November 6

Went to school.

November 7

No school. Election Day. Pa shot a cat. Helped skin cat and I set a fox trap.

Done chores and most everything.

November 8

Went to school.

November 9

Went to school.

November 10

Went to school.

November 11

Uncle Henry made me a pair of stilts, walked on them some. Aft. Pa and I went over to fallow.

November 12

Went to school.

November 13

Went to school. Caught a skunk last night.

November 14

Went to school.

November 15

Went to school.

November 16

Went to school.

November 17

Went to school.

November 18

Did not do much of anything in forenoon. Afternoon, Ma's Sunday School class came up here with Florence Warren, Lela Kingsley etc.

November 19

Went to Sabbath School.

November 20
Went to school.
November 21
Went to school.
November 22
Went to school.
November 23
Went to school.
November 24
Went to school.
November 25
Did not do much of any
thing. Uncle Bish came over.
November 26
Went to Sabbath School.
November 27
Went to school.
November 28
Went to school.
November 29
Went to school.
November 30
Thanksgiving. Done
everything. Snowballed.

Friday, December 1, 1893
Went to school.
December 2
Cold Fair
Did not do much of any-
thing in a.m.. In p.m.
put in window glass,
ciphered, set mouse traps
etc.
December 3
Snowy

Snow! Snowed most all
day and then it rained.
Did not go to Sabbath
School.
December 4
Did not go to school for
the road was not broken
out and there was a crust
on the snow.
Ciphered some.
December 5
14°
Did not go to school.
Went down to saw mill
after a load of saw dust
with Pa.
December 6
Caught 3 mice. Went up to
school house but there was
no school on account of
diphtheria. So I came
home. Kings Dauters were
up here.
Maud Patreau came up
with them.
December 7
1 mouse. Got lessons.
Helped Pa draw wood.
December 8
1 mouse.   Cold.
Got lessons. Helped Pa
unload wood. Pa and I
went down to meeting in
evening.
December 9
Cold
Went up to fox trap. Pa

went to village. Ma went up to Grand ma's. Fixed mouse trap. Done chores. Ciphered some.

December 10
1 mouse. Uncle Henry, Pa, Ma, Grand ma's Culver and Whitney and I went to Sabbath School and meeting.

December 11
Got lessons. Awful cold.

December 12
Got lessons.

December 13
Les Gottens. Went over to Mash Pond after load of wood with Pa.

December 14
Got lessons.

December 15
Snow
Got lessons. Snowed all day.
Pa went to the village.

December 16
44°   Thaw rain
Did not do much of anything. Pa greased harnesses. Pa made mouse trap.

December 17
Went to Sabbath School.

December 18
School commences today so I went.

December 19
Went to school.

December 20
Did not go to school. Wind blowed, snow flew etc.

December 21
Went to school. Examination day.

December 22
Went to school. Examination day.

December 23
Did not do much of anything only to make Chan a kneading board for Christmas present.

December 24
Grand ma, Uncle Henry, Pa, Ma, Lill and Jennie Cole and I went to Sabbath School and meeting.

December 25
46°   Rainy
Got up and looked into my stocking. Had a cap, a neck scarf and a diary. Slid down hill, went over to Grangers. Afternoon Pa and I went to village.

December 26
10°   Clear
Went to school. Pretty slippery going.
Had nine scholars.

December 27
Went to school. Took up
my sled and slid part of
the way home.
December 28
28°   Cold
Went to school.
December 29
Went to school. Slid part
of way home.
December 30
8°–0°   Fair
Went down in sugar
works where Pa and Clifton
Clark were skidding wood.
Slid down hill.
Uncle Henry came down.
December 31
13° 18°   Fair
Papa, Ma and I went to
Sabbath School.
Grand ma came down.

Good-by Mr. Ninety-three.

Memoranda

I had a light and short run of
typhoid fever in April 1893.

Old cat had four kittens, one
mostly black, one considerable
black with white around neck.
One yellow and one mostly
white with black spots. We kept
the latter. Cat had "em" night

before Apr. 20, 1893

History of a Cat
The first thing I can remember was an old box with some
rags in it on which me and
my two brothers lay day after
day with our mother to take
care of us until we were large
enough to run around the house
where the children fed us milk
until we were big enough to eat
potato, mice and such things as
kittens like. Soon we were big
enough to run outdoors on the
grass and eat mice our mother
brought us, but in a little while
were so we could catch them
ourselves. One day one of the
children caught me and put
me in an old dirty bag. I did
not think when I went in
that she would shut me in
which she did. I tried very
hard to get out but I could
not. Pretty soon somebody took
the bag up and put me in a
wagon in which I rode and
rode until it seemed to me that
I would be jared to peices. All
at once I stoped and somebody
took me into the house and let
me out of the "old" bag . It
seemed very good to get out but
I was in a strange
place but I soon got acquaint-
ed and liked my new home

very well. The children prom-
ised I should never go away to
another place.
If you ever are a cat and get a
good home, be a good cat and
you will never be given away.
Take my advice and good-bye.

Composed by Whitney W. J. S.
Written April 28, 1893.
Memoranda
Heard frogs sign first this year
May 2, 1893
Pa and Roll finished up sugar-
ing May 2, 1893
Pa made me a "thing" to out
my things in Jan. 2, 1893
Weighed cat and kitten. Their
weight was with:
old cat 5 Lb. 13 oz.
Little kitten 9 days old 9 oz.
Apr. 29, 1893.
Went over to Uncle J. H. and
H. J. fallow Aug. 9, 1893.
Caught woodchuck Aug. 15, '93.
Snowed and hailed some today
Oct. 29, 1893
Set fox trap Nov. 7, 1893
Caught a skunk last night
Nov. 13, 1893
School stopped on account of
diphtheria - Dec. 6 '93
School commenced - Dec. 18, '93.

My examinations - Dec 22, 1893
Arithmetic 7th Grade   84%
Geography 7th   60%
Spelling 7th   78%
History 7th   85%
Grammar 3rd   81%
Physiology Lesson
Nov. 8 & 9, '93
The skeleton is composed of
about two hundred bones. The
bones have three principal uses.
1st To protect the delicate
organs.
2nd To act as levers for the
muscles to act upon to produce
motion.
3rd To preserve the shape of the
body.
Bones differ in form according
to their uses.
Bones are composed of two
kinds of matter: animal and
mineral.
Account of Lewis W. Whitney
May 11
By plowing and dragging
garden   .28
To sowing beds   .10
,,,,,,,,,,,,,,,,,,,,,,,,,,,,,,
Account W. J. S. Whitney in
account with H. J. C
Apr. 30 By cash   .20
May 6 To seeds   .15
postage   .02
cash   .02
postal card   .01

115

RELATIVE RANK OF CITIES.

In 1870 there were but fourteen cities each containing more than 100,000 inhabitants. In 1880 this number had increased to twenty, and in 1890 to twenty-eight.

In 1880 there was but one city, New York, which had a population in excess of a million. In 1890 there were three, New York, Chicago, and Philadelphia.

The number and relative rank of cities having a population of 100,000 or more at the date of each of these censuses are set forth in the following table.

	RANK.		
	1890.	1880.	1870.
New York, N. Y.	1	1	1
Chicago, Ill.	2	4	5
Philadelphia, Pa.	3	2	2
Brooklyn, N. Y.	4	3	3
Saint Louis, Mo.	5	6	4
Boston, Mass.	6	5	7
Baltimore, Md.	7	7	6
San Francisco, Cal.	8	9	10
Cincinnati, O.	9	8	8
Cleveland, O.	10	11	..
Buffalo, N. Y.	11	13	11
New Orleans, La.	12	10	9
Pittsburgh, Pa.	13	12	..
Washington, D. C.	14	14	12
Detroit, Mich.	15	18	..
Milwaukee, Wis.	16	19	..
Newark, N. J.	17	15	13
Minneapolis, Minn.	18	..	..
Jersey City, N. J.	19	17	..
Louisville, Ky.	20	16	14
Omaha, Neb.	21	..	..
Rochester, N. Y.	22	..	..
Saint Paul, Minn.	23	..	..
Kansas City, Mo.	24	..	..
Providence, R. I.	25	20	..
Denver, Col.	26	..	..
Indianapolis, Ind.	27	..	..
Allegheny City, Pa.	28	..	..

VALUES IN UNITED STATES MONEY
OF THE
PURE GOLD OR SILVER

REPRESENTING RESPECTIVELY THE MONETARY UNITS AND STANDARD COINS OF FOREIGN COUNTRIES.

The first section of the Act of March 3, 1873, provides "that the value of Foreign Coin, as expressed in the money of account of the United States, shall be that of the pure metal of such coin of standard value," and that "the values of the standard coins in circulation of the various nations of the world shall be estimated annually by the Director of the Mint, and be proclaimed on the first day of January by the Secretary of the Treasury."

The estimates of values contained in the following table are those made by the Director of the Mint, January 1st, 1890, in compliance with the above stated provisions of law.

COUNTRY.	MONETARY UNIT.	STANDARD.	VALUE.
			D. C. M.
Argentine Repub.	Peso	Gold & silv.	0 96 5
Austria	Florin	Silver	0 34 3
Belgium	Franc	Gold & silv.	0 19 3
Bolivia	Boliviano	Silver	0 69 8
Brazil	Milreis of 1000 reis.	Gold	0 54 6
British America	Dollar	Gold	1 00 0
Cent'l Am. States	Peso	Silver	0 69 8
Chili	Peso	Gold & silv.	0 91 2
China	Tael. { Shanghai.	Silver	1 3 1
	{ Haikwan.		1 14 8
	(Customs.)		
Cuba	Peso	Gold & silv.	0 92 6
Denmark	Crown	Gold	0 26 8
Ecuador	Sucre	Silver	0 69 8
Egypt	Pound (100 piastres)	Gold	4 94 3
France	Franc	Gold & silv.	0 19 3
German Empire	Mark	Gold	0 23 8
Great Britain	Pound sterling.	Gold	4 86 6¼
Greece	Drachma	Gold & silv.	0 19 3
Hayti	Gourde	Gold & silv.	0 96 5
India	Rupee of 16 annas.	Silver	0 33 2
Italy	Lira	Gold & silv.	0 19 3
Japan	Yen	Gold	0 99 7
	Yen	Silver	0 75 2
Liberia	Dollar	Gold	1 00 0
Mexico	Dollar	Silver	0 75 8
Netherlands	Florin	Gold & silv.	0 40 2
Norway	Crown	Gold	0 26 8
Peru	Sol	Silver	0 69 8
Portugal	Milreis of 1000 reis.	Gold	1 08 0
Russia	Roubl. of 100 cop'ks	Silver	0 55 8
Spain	Peseta of 100 centim.	Gold & silv.	0 19 3
Sweden	Crown	Gold	0 26 8
Switzerland	Franc	Gold & silv.	0 19 3
Tripoli	Mahbub of 20 piast's	Silver	0 62 9
Turkey	Piastre	Gold	0 04 4
U. S. of Colombia	Peso	Silver	0 69 8
Venezuela	Bolivar	Silver	0 14 0

Walter's diary for 1894

is in excellent condition. Its beige linen cover is clean and still neatly trimmed with darker leather. The inside entries show a new attention to meticulous handwriting, even to double spacing most lines to allow a more flowing stroke.

South Schroon Union Church

1894 was the year of completion of the South Schroon Union Church, as indicated by the inscription on the bell tower. This treasure of community pride took two years to build and was erected on property donated by Emory Whitney. The church was incorporated in February and dedicated in August of 1894. It was recorded by Walter Whitney merely as "the new church," and he tells that Pa worked on it in 1894. To Walter, it was commonplace for Pa to do this. It was the instinctual, unwritten guideline of small community life—that mutual give and take, that sharing of crops, equipment, time, and labor. Walter's simple statement and the encompassing spiritual effect of the new church on the community are humble symbols of existing parallels. Since the beginning of Adirondack tourism, there were parallels of culture that ran a very close geographic proximity to each other: the grand hotel guests and the people of the community.

The funding for the building of the South Schroon Union Church, however, offers an example that breaks with that cultural habit. On July

28, 1894, Walter states in his diary that he saw Mr. H. V. Parsell and his wife at a church meeting. Walter may or may not have known that Mr. H. V. Parsell, a summer guest at Taylor's on Schroon and benefactor of many of its modern developments, had contributed generously to the funds needed to build the church. In addition, he proposed that if the citizens would contribute the labor, he would contribute the pulpit, the pews, cushions, chandeliers, bell, stove, hymnals, etc. Mr. Parsell, a New York City philanthropist, funded many good causes and in 1901 donated a free library to the citizens of South Schroon. A circulation of several hundred books was, for a time, housed in the Sunday School rooms, presumably of the South Schroon Union Church.

Lewis Whitney, Walter's father, and Lewis's brother Emory, became incorporators of the church, along with Charles F. Taylor, William J. Hall, Lorenzo Murdock, Charles Warren, George Richardson, F. W. Schneider, and H. V. Parsell. At the first meeting, officers were elected: President, C. F. Taylor; Vice-President, H. V. Parsell; Secretary, Lewis Whitney; and Treasurer, Emory Whitney.

The efforts of these men and many others provided the community a place of worship for more than fifty years. The sparkling white-clapboard building and its many gentle arches stood on a hillside overlooking Schroon Lake until 1969 when, it is speculated, it was struck by lightning and consequently burned.

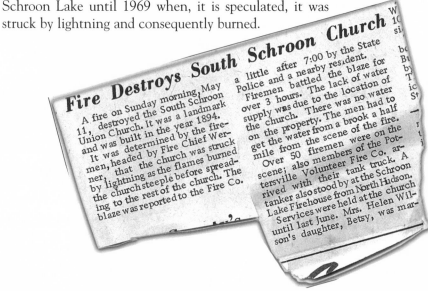

Fire Destroys South Schroon Church

A fire on Sunday morning, May 11, destroyed the South Schroon Union Church. It was a landmark and was built in the year 1894.

It was determined by the firemen, headed by Fire Chief Werner, that the church was struck by lightning as the flames spread- ing to the rest of the church. The blaze was reported to the Fire Co.

a little after 7:00 by the State Police and a nearby resident. Firemen battled the blaze for over 3 hours. The lack of water supply was due to the location of the church. There was no water on the property. The men had to get the water from a brook a half mile from the scene of the fire.

Over 50 firemen were on the scene; also members of the Pot- tersville Volunteer Fire Co. ar- rived with their tank truck. A tanker also stood by at the Schroon Lake Firehouse from North Hudson.

Services were held at the church until last June. Mrs. Helen Wil- son's daughter, Betsy, was mar-

CHURCHES

Schroon Lake Episcopal Church was set up as a separate mission from Pottersville in 1878. In 1880, 17 persons were confirmed by the Bishop from Albany. In 1888, Reverend Josepht T. Zorn became the first full-time priest in the new church, which was called St. Andrews; but he only stayed for one year. For the next three years, the church only had roving preachers. The original St. Andrews Church was located next to the Leland House and was burned along with the Leland House.

(taken from the ADIRONDACK MISSION)

The Baptist Church was the first church of Schroon Lake. It stood on a hill on what is now Route 74. According to church records, people came from North Hudson, Paradox, South Schroon, and Charley Hill to attend services at this church. It was a wooden structure with Gothic windows. The pulpit was way up in the back. The minister had to mount the stairs to get to it. He looked down on his congregation. The pews, or slips as they were called, had doors. There was no organ, but lots of singing. The church was very active for many years. However, as Methodists and others sprang up, some left to join them, and others moved away. A number of Schroon families moved west after the Civil War. The church was neglected. The roof leaked. There were no services, and the church was only used for funerals. The church was torn down in the 1880s, and the land was sold.

(taken from letters by Mrs. Louise Hargreaves, Historian)

Schroon Lake became a Catholic mission of Olmstedville under the title of "Our Lady of Lourdes" in 1867, and was a mission for fifteen years. In January of 1882, it became of mission of Port Henry. In April of 1882, Lansford Whitney deeded land to our Lady of Lourdes on Hoffman Road. In 1890, the church in North Hudson was built. In April 1909, Our Lady of Lourdes became a parish, with North Hudson as a mission.

The Congregational Church, as it now stands, was incorporated on Feb. 24, 1954. Previously, this church served as a place of worship for Methodists, Congregationalists and Episcopalians. Originally, these congregations were served by traveling preachers. In 1837, the circuit was permanently divided, with Minerva, Schroon, and West Moriah comprising the Schroon circuit. This allowed for classes to be set up in all three towns and for the preachers on the circuits to set up lay persons as their assistants.

Schroon Lake became the headquarters of Word of Life in 1947. The ground breaking for the Mountainside Bible Chapel took place in 1966. These churches may have offered a place of worship for the members of the South Schroon Union Church after it closed in the 1960s.

ARTICLE FIRST.

SECTION 1. The number of Directors of this Association shall be nine, and for the first year shall consist of the following named persons: Charles F. Taylor, Emory Whitney, Lewis W. Whitney, William J. Hall, Lorenzo D. Murdock, George Richardson, Charles Warren, Henry V. Parsell and F. W. Schneider. Said Directors shall be persons who shall each have subscribed and paid not less than the sum of ten dollars ($10) towards the support and maintenance of this Association. Said Directors shall be divided into three classes of three persons each — three holding office for the space of one year, three for two years and three for three years and until such time as their successor or successors shall have been elected, and of first year three Directors shal~~~~~ elected who shall hold o~~~ Said Directors shal~ ~~~ of the Asso~~~ ing.~~

SEC. 2. The regular annual meetings of the Association shall be held at the church building in South Schroon, Essex County, New York, on the first Saturday in the month of September in each and every year at two o'clock in the afternoon.

SEC. 3. Said Board of Directors shall, immediately upon organizing, elect a President, Vice President, Treasurer and a Secretary. These officers shall each hold office for one year and until their successor or successors shall be elected, unless sooner removed for cause by a two-thirds vote of the Board of Directors.

SEC. 4. No Director shall receive any salary for his services.

SEC. 5. All persons over twenty-one years of age, residing in Essex or Warren Counties, who shall sign these by-laws, and shall have paid or contributed for the benefit of this Association not less than the sum of $10, shall become members of this Association and shall be entitled to one vote at any regular or special meeting of the Association.

ARTICLE SECOND.

SECTION 1. A regular annual meeting of the Board of Directors shall be held at the church building in the town of Schroon, N. Y., within ten days after the regular annual meeting of the Association. At such annual meeting there shall be elected from said Board of Directors three trustees who shall hold office for the term of one year, unless sooner removed for

Articles of Association and BY-LAWS OF THE

South Schroon Union Church Association

SOUTH SCHROON, NEW YORK.

121

1894
A brief record of my diary
proceedings
Walter J. S. Whitney's
fifth diary
"Tis eh"
1894

Monday, January 1, 1894
Clear

Went up to Grand ma's and got Uncle Henry to send to J. Lynn. Slid down hill. Went to donation down to Mr. G. W. Ford's in evening. Got home about 12 o'clock.

January 2
13°   Fair

Done chores. Slid down hill. Went over to Grangers and Arthur and I sat a rabbit trap. Pa drew a load of logs to mill and brought back a load of lumber.

January 3
Cold

Got up and found my throat quite sore so I could not go to school. I felt pretty well all the forenoon but after dinner I began to feel kindy mean until night when I was sick to my stomach and vomited etc. Did not go out only to do chores in morning. Got spelling lesson in forenoon.

January 4
46°   Rainy

Felt some better today but considerable weak. My throat about over being sore I guess. Pa went over to Thilo's to funeral.

January 5
Cold

Did not do much of any thing today only lay around. My throat about the same.

January 6
Cld.

Went to the barn at noon and fed the horses, cattle etc. and found an egg. Made a puzzle. My throat little better today.

January 7

Did not go to Sunday School. Grand ma, Uncles J. H. and H. J. came down. Wrote some to Aunt Lucy.

January 8

10°

Got my lessons. Went out doors some. Uncle Henry came down a while in the evening.

January 9

10°   2

Got lessons. Went out considerable. Did few chores at night.

January 10

                        Cld.

Got my lessons. Addie and Arthur Granger came over here a while. Dr. G. came up here.

January 11

Got lessons. Went up on pasture hill where Pa was cutting wood and logs. Ellen Rounds came here and stayed all night.

January 12

-20°   Blowy

Got my lessons. Pa drew up load of lumber from the mill. I found an owl up in the hog house chamber.

January 13

5°

Puttered around and did not do much of anything. Pa went to village.

January 14

Did not go to Sunday School. Uncle Henry and Grand ma came down.

January 15

Got lessons. Helped squirt out water.

January 16

Got lessons. Ma went up to Grand ma's. I went up on pasture hill and sat a rabbit trap.

January 17

                        Clear

Got lessons. Slid down hill.
Went to rabbit trap and found trap sprung, but the rabbit had got away. Went over to Grangers and Arthur and I sat us some rabbit traps.

January 18

Arthur came over and said that I had a rabbit in my trap so I went over and killed it. Then we went up on the hill and I had one there. Skinned them and gave some of them to hens.
Got lessons. Went down in woods and helped Pa load wood.

January 19

60°   Clr.

Got my lessons. Went up to Grand ma's. Done chores. Got catalogue from W. Atlee Burpee & Co. Philadelphia, Pa. U. S. A.

January 20

Caught a rabbit. Uncle Bish and Aunt Lucy came over. Went up to Grand ma's.

January 21

28°/31°   Cld. snow

Pa, Ma and I went to Sabbath School and Meeting. Snowed considerable while we were coming home and some after.

January 22

Got lessons.

January 23

Got lessons. Chopped out my fox trap and sat a rabbit trap.

January 24

Got lessons. Wind blew and it rained all afternoon. Fixed a brake on my sled.

January 25

Did not get lessons. Emma Smith and Helen Warren were up here.

January 26

Got part of lessons. Pa, Ma, and I went to Mill Brook.

January 27

Ate breakfast up to Aunt Lucy's and then went down to Aunt Lib's and stayed to dinner and then came back to Aunt Lucy's and stayed until about 4 p.m. and then we came home.

January 28

Did not go to Sunday School. I had a little cold. Grand ma C. came down.

January 29

               Cld. snow

Got lessons. My cold little better today I think. Pa went to village.

January 30

               Snow

Got lessons. Did not go out doors. Snowed about a foot.

January 31

Got lessons. Went outdoors.

Thursday, February 1, 1894

Got lessons. Made a road to slide down hill on.

February 2

Got lessons. Slid down hill.

February 3
Slid down hill. Uncle Henry came down and got Ma.

February 4
Pa, Ma, Grand ma Whitney, Uncle Henry and I went to Sunday School and Meeting. I was baptized.

February 5
Did not get lessons. Ma went down to Mr. David Hall's with Pa and stayed all day.
I slid down hill some.

February 6
Got lessons. Slid down hill. Pa went to Schroon Village.

February 7
Went up to Grand ma's and stayed until near noon. Aft. did not do much of anything. Did not get lessons.

February 8
Thaw
Got lessons. Went up to Uncle Jim Culver's. Slid down hill.

February 9
Got part of my studies. Had headache most all day.

February 10
31°3h, 43°8h   Snow, cold
Got up and found it
snowing like everything and it kept at it until noon. Done chores etc. Gave hens some bones. Pa worked on a hand sled.

February 11
21°   West windy
Did not go to Sabbath School. The wind blew awful hard in forenoon. I had a little cold coming on. Uncle Jim came down here a little while in afternoon.

February 12
Clr. cold. snow
Went up to Uncle Henry's. Did not get lessons. Ma stayed up to "Daddles" most all day. I helped Pa draw wood.

February 13
Got lessons. Had little cold.

February 14
Got lessons.

February 15
Snow
Got lessons. Snowed every minute of the day.

February 16
4° & 7°   Blowy
Got my lessons. Wind blew quite hard all day. Done chores. One of our Silver Spangled

125

Hamburghs (speck) laid her first egg.

February 17

14° & 30°   Clear

Done chores. Brought in eggs. Pa went to village with 10 1/2 doz. eggs. Speck laid egg.

February 18

28°, 47°, 41°, 40°

West, cold, fair, blowy

Did not go to Sabbath School. Grand ma and Carrie Hall were here.

February 19

Got lessons.

February 20

Got lessons. Pa went to village.

February 21

Got lessons. Pa went to Riverside with poles. Henry Carpenter came over and went up to Grand ma's to stay all night.

February 22

Henry came down this morning and stayed until afternoon. Did not get lessons. Pa went down to Church Meeting.

February 23

Got lessons. Pa carried Grand ma Whitney down to Smith Howe's.

The wind blew quite hard all day.

February 24

21° below zero/3°   Clear

Did not do much of anything.

Pa tinkered sled.

February 25

Went to Sunday School.

February 26

Got lessons.

Pa went to village.

February 27

Got lessons.

Pa finished making sled.

February 28

Got lessons.

Thursday, March 1, 1894

Did not get lessons. Uncle Bish Carpenter came over.

March 2

Got lessons. Went up to Grand ma's.

March 3

Got lessons. Helped saw wood.

March 4

Arthur Floyd came over. Went up to Grand ma's.

March 5

Slid down hill. Arthur and I.

Went up toward Grand ma's and got some hay that was beside the road.

March 6
Pa and I went to
"Schroon Lake" Town
meeting day.

March 7
Warm Clear
Went to Post Office with
Uncle Jim Culver in
forenoon. Afternoon stayed
at home.

March 8
Went up to Uncle
Henry's. Tapped few trees.
Pa went to Schroon.

March 9
Went down to Sugar
House two three times.
Pa worked down there.
Had some new molasses for
supper.

March 10
49°   Clear
Did not do much of any-
thing in forenoon.
In p.m. Uncles Jim and
Henry, Pa and I started
hoops on sap buckets and
washed as much as half of
them.

March 11
Did not go to Sunday
School. Pa went but I did
not go.

March 12
Washed buckets. Helped tap
trees.
Roll Granger scattered
buckets.

March 13
Roll and I finished tap-
ping trees. Pa went to
Chester after "Daddle" W.

March 14
Did not do much of any-
thing in forenoon.
Afternoon I boiled sap.

March 15
Boiled sap. Helped clean up
evaporator.

March 16
Did not do much of any-
thing. Uncles J. H. and
H. J., Grand ma and Peter
Fairfield were to dinner.
The men folks cut wood.
Pa fixed buckets for Uncles
J. H. and H. J.

March 17
Helped cut wood some in
forenoon. Afternoon boiled
sap.

March 18
Went to Sunday School
and Meeting. Stopped at
Mr. Lew Richardson's and
stayed until after supper.

March 19
Boiled sap all day. Pa and
Roll gathered.
I syruped off three times.

March 20
Thawing N.E. wind   Fair
Pa and I tapped trees in
forenoon. Afternoon I

boiled sap. Done chores.
Sat around a while and
went to bed and asleep.
Syruped off once.
March 21
Went to Post Office. Boiled
sap.
March 22
Boiled sap most all day.
March 23
Helped cut wood.
March 24
Pa, Roll and I dumped
water out of buckets in
forenoon. Afternoon Pa
and I went
to village.
My birth
day 12
years old.

HAPPY BiRthdAy

March 25
Felt kindy old today so I
didn't go to S. School.
Grand ma C. came down.
March 26
Boiled sap most all day.
March 27
2°
Arthur Granger and I
went down to Mr.
Prouty's.
I ate just about 20 pounds
of sugar.
March 28
4°
Did not do much of any-
thing.

March 29
Pa and I went to village.
March 30
Corded up sugar wood.
March 31
Corded up sugar wood in
a. m p. m. I boiled sap.

———

Sunday, April 1, 1894
Fair
My throat felt kindy sore
so I did not go to
Sunday School. Arthur
and Nora Floyd came
over.
April 2
Boiled sap. Arthur and
Nora went home.
April 3
Did not go out of doors.
Had cold in my head and
throat.
April 4
Did not do much of anything.
April 5
Pa gathered sap most all
day. Ma went down and
boiled sap a while in after-
noon. Did not go outdoors.
April 6
Did not go out doors. Pa
boiled sap in forenoon and
went to village in afternoon.
April 7
Went out doors twice.
Aunt Lib, Eddy, Anda,

Howard and Jimmy came over.

April 8
Did not go to S. School. Snowed some. Aunt Lib went up to Grand ma's.

April 9
Done chores. Aunt Lib and the children went home. Pa boiled sap aft.

April 10
Boiled sap all day.

April 11
Boiled sap all day.

APRIL 12
Helped sugar off. Cleaned off hen roost. Done chores.

April 13
Went up to Grand ma and had some stick jaw. Done nothing much.

April 14
(no entry)

April 15
Went to Sunday School Pa and I afoot.

April 16
Did not do much of anything. Pa worked on church.

April 17
Done chores. Went up to "Daddle" C's and to Granger's. Pa worked down on the new church.

April 18
Worked in sugar works all day. Finished gathering and brought buckets out to the road. I wore socks today first day I ever wore socks.

April 19
Boiled sap forenoon. Afternoon Pa and I washed buckets.

April 20
Helped finish up sugaring in forenoon. Went up to Uncle Henry's. Helped put cutters etc. up in horse barn.

April 21
Pa and I went to village.

April 22
Pa, Ma, Grand ma W., Lillie Cole and I went to Edah Ford's funeral.

April 23
Went to school.

April 24
Went to school.

April 25
Went to school.

April 26
Went to school.

April 27
Went to school.

April 28
Helped cord up wood. Went fishing. Got one small trout.

April 29
Pa, Ma, Grand ma Whitney, Lillie Cole, went

to Sabbath School and
Preaching Services. Have a
new preacher: C. R. Church.
April 30
Went to school.

Tuesday, May 1, 1894
Went to school.
May 2
Went to school.
May 3
Went to school.
May 4
Went to school
(Arbor Day).
Came home at
noon.

May 5
Did not do much of any-
thing.
Uncle Bish and Aunt
Lucy came over.
May 6
Did not go to S. School.
Uncle B. and Aunt L.
went home.
May 7
Had cold. Helped Pa plant
taters. Planted my taters.
May 8
Went to school.
May 9
Pa and I hunted after
horses that were in our pas-
ture. Walked about seven
miles.

Afternoon helped plant
garden.
May 10
Went to school.
May 11
Went to school.
May 12
I went and got some dan-
delions for greens.
Helped Pa draw stone.
Planted some beans.
Took banking away from
the house. Pa went to village.
May 13
Pa, Ma, Uncle Henry,
Lillie Cole and I went to
Sunday School.
May 14
Went to school.
May 15
Helped plant potatoes.
May 16
Went to school.
May 17
Went to school.
May 18
Went to school.
May 19
Did not do much of any-
thing.
May 20
Went to Sunday School.
May 21
Went fishing. Got two
trout and twelve big
pumpkin seeds. Took
banking away from house.

May 22
Helped draw manure.
May 23
Helped plant corn.
May 24
Pa about sick. Went to Post Office.
May 25
Pa little better.
Went up to Grand ma's.
May 26
Did not do much of anything in forenoon.
Afternoon Arthur G. and I went fishing.
May 27
Did not go to Sunday School.
May 28
Howard and Eddy came down.
I wed and hoed in the garden.
May 29
Went to school.
Howard and Eddy went to school visiting.
May 30
Helped plant corn.
May 31
Did not go to school. Rained about all day. Played with Eddy and Howard.

Friday, June 1, 1894
Went to school.
June 2
Cld. rain
Played with Eddy and Howard. Rained hard part of p.m.
June 3
Went to Sunday School on Charley Hill.
June 4
Went to school.
June 5
Went to school.
June 6
Went to school.
June 7
Went to school.
June 8
Went to school.
June 9
Went to village. Got me a watch.
June 10
Went to Sunday School.
June 11
Did not feel first rate. Had a bad cold.
June 12
Did not feel like going to school.
Helped hoe potatoes.
June 13
Went to school.
June 14
Went to school.
Examination day.

June 15
Went to school.
June 16
Rode horse to cultivate potatoes. Hoed potatoes until I got sick of it.
June 17
Ma did not feel very well so I did not go to Sabbath School.
Bees swarmed.
June 18
Went to school.
June 19
Went to school. Pa went to village and got some cloth for me some pants.
June 20
Went to school.
June 21
Went to school. Hoed in garden.
June 22
Went to school. Wed onion beds.
June 23
Helped hoe corn.
June 24
Went to Sunday School.
June 25
Went to school.
June 26
Went to school.
June 27
Went to school. Herb Wood came down with me and stayed all night.

June 28
Went to school.
June 29
Went to school.
June 30
Went to Town.

Sunday, July 1, 1894
Went to "Daddle" C's.
Went over to fallow.
Uncle Bish was over.
July 2
Hoed taters, sweet corn and turnips.
July 3
Hoed and bugged potatoes.
July 4
Went down to new church where Pa was to work. Had green peas.
July 5
Helped hoe potatoes. Went to village.
July 6
Went to Picnic at the foot of the lake.
July 7
Hoed corn.
July 8
Went to Sunday School.
July 9
Helped get ready for haying.
July 10
Picked up after machine.

132

Pa went to Chester in p. m.

July 11

Helped get in hay.

July 12

Picked up after mowing machine.

July 13

Raked hay. Went to picnic up to school house.

July 14

Stired hay and helped get it in.

July 15

Did not go to Sunday School. Had small shower.

July 16

Hayed it.

July 17

Hoed turnips.

July 18

Hoed turnips. Worked up to Uncles J. & H.

July 19

Hayed it.

July 20

Hayed it.

July 21

Rain

Rainy day. Done nothing of any consequence.

July 22

Went to Sunday School.

July 23

Hayed it.

July 24

Went to So. Schroon where men were drawing dirt to grade up New Church. Uncle David came to Schroon etc.

July 25

Hayed it.

July 26

Went up to Grand ma's. Hayed it.

July 27

Piled wood over. Moved hen coop. Hoed turnips. Set wood chuck trap. Pa worked down to O'Neil's.

July 28

92°   Fair

Caught a wood chuck. Went down to Church Meeting. Saw Mr. H. V. Parsell and his wife.

July 29

Went to P.O. Uncles D. J.H. & H.J., Aunt Lib and her boys, and Grand ma C. were here.

July 30

Hoed turnips. Uncle David gave Pa money to get Ma an extention table. Pa went to village and when he came back he brought the table.

July 31

Hoed few turnips. Picked about 17 quarts of cucumbers.

Pa and I went down to saw mill and got some saw dust. Pa took Uncle

David to Riverside.

Wednesday, August 1, 1894
76°   Fair
Hoed turnips most all day.
Pa worked down to
O'Neill's.

August 2
Went up to Grand ma's.
Rained in aft.

August 3
Went down to "Taylor
House."

August 4
Picked up after mowing
machine and horse rake.
Loaded hay. Pa and
Grand ma went to Erastus
Richardson's funeral.

August 5
Pa, Ma & I went to
Sunday School.

August 6
Hayed it. Worked hard.

August 7
Went to Taylor's. Loaded
hay.

August 8
Forgot what I did do.
Can't think.

August 9
Did not do much of any-
thing. Pa worked down to
new Church in p.m.

August 10
Went down to new

Church.

August 11
Done everything. Went
black berrying. Pa
worked for C. F.
Taylor & Son.

August 12
Went to dedication
of the new Church.

August 13
Went to village.

August 14
Hayed it.

August 15
Loaded hay.

August 16
Went to Taylor's.

August 17
Helped get up oats.

August 18
Picked black berries beside road.

August 19
Went to Sunday School
in new Church.

August 20
Mowed few oats. Went
black berrying.

August 21
Went black berrying.
Got up few oats.

August 22
Helped mow, get up sheep,
and get in oats.

August 23
Got up oats.

August 24
Got up oats.

August 25
Did not do much of anything.
Pa went to Stone Bridge.

August 26
Went to Sunday School.
Went to meeting in forenoon and afternoon both.

August 27
Pa and I went to Mash Pond.
Got a load of hay home.

August 28
Went down to New Church
to see the new bell.

August 29
Pa and I went to Mash
Pond in afternoon.
Found Uncle Jim's colt
with a bad cut on his
shoulder.

August 30
Did not do much. A man
came here and took a picture of our house and family including the horses
and carriage.

August 31
Done nothing. Pa shot
hedge hog.

Saturday, September 1, 1894
Went black berrying.
Helped take care of berries.

September 2
Went to Sunday School
once and preaching services

twice.

September 3
Didn't do much. Papa
went to Chester.

September 4
Pa and I went blackberrying.

September 5
Didn't do much.

September 6
Arthur G. and I went
and got some frogs for
hedge hog bait.

September 7
Didn't do much. Pa
worked for Taylor.

September 8
Rainy
Uncle Jim and I went to
Taylor's after Aunt Lib
and her boys.

September 9
Played with Eddy and
Howard.

September 10
Commenced going to
school in So. Schroon.

September 11
Went to school.

September 12
Went to school.

September 13
Went to school.

September 14
Went to school.

September 15
Forgot what I did do.

It's too bad ain't it.

September 16

Went to Sunday School.

September 17

Went to school.

September 18

Went to school.

September 19

Went to school.

September 20

Went to school.

September 21

Went to school.

September 22

Helped Pa make out tax list. Dug potatoes.

September 23

Went to Sunday School Conference in p.m. and in evening.

September 24

Went to school.

September 25

Went to school.

September 26

Dug potatoes. Picked up apples etc. etc.

September 27

Pa and I drew in one load of corn and then we went to the fair.

September 28

Worked on threshing machine in a.m. Helped clean up in afternoon.

September 29

Husked popcorn. Uncle Bish came over. Pa worked up to Grand ma's in aft. on threshing.

September 30

Went to Sunday School afoot.

Monday, October 1, 1894

Went down to school house but the teacher did not come so I came back. Afternoon went up to Grand ma's.

October 2

Went down to school house but teacher did not come. Came home and went up to Uncle Jim's and worked on threshing machine.

October 3

Went to school.

October 4

Went to school.

October 5

Went to school. Pa gathered apples.

October 6

Aunt Emelins died this morning about 7 o'clock. I helped about the

house some.
Ma about one half sick.

October 7

Went up to Grand ma's
and back. Did not do
much else. Uncle Henry
went over to Adirondack
and got Aunt Lib and her
children.

October 8

Aunt Emeline buried
today.

October 9

Went to school.

October 10

Went to school.

October 11

Went to school.

October 12

Went to school.

October 13

Did not do much of any-
thing. Had hard cold.
Fred Cole buried today.

October 14

Felt sicker today. Aunt
Lib and her youngsters
went home.

October 15

Did not go to school. Did
not feel any better today.
Dr. Griswold happened to
come up here. Nobody told
him to come up but he was
up to Cart Squire's and he
said he thought he would
come up to see how we were

getting along as he had
not seen us in so long.

October 16

Did not set up more than
an hour. Did not feel first
rate.

October 17

Felt better.
Was around the house more
or less.

October 18

Good deal better today but
some weak yet.

October 19

Better yet.

October 20

Went out doors.

October 21

Went out doors good deal.
Uncle Henry & Grand
ma down.

October 22

Picked up potatoes.

October 23

Went to school.

October 24

Went to school.

October 25

Went to school.

October 26

School was attended by
me today. Left of ahead
tonight and seven nights
before so that makes eight
don't it eh? Uncle Bish
and Aunt Lucy came
over.

October 27

Picked up two and one half bushels of apples.
Pa and Uncle Bish went to village. Pa got me a tablet.

October 28

Went up to Grand ma's and stayed to dinner. Uncle Bish and Aunt Lucy went home. Went to Advent Church. Dedication at 2:30 p.m..

October 29

Went to school.

October 30

Went to school. Pa went to Schroon Falls.

October 31

Went to school.

Thursday, November 1, 1894

About sick. Vomited the most I ever did in my life. Was sick to my stomach about all day. Had Dr. Dunn of Schroon Lake come up in night about 11 p.m.

November 2

Some better today. All over nausea. Pa went to village. Got me 3 lemons & an orange.

November 3

Felt better. Sat up some.

November 4

Did not go to Sunday School. Pa went.

November 5

Stormy Snow

Snowed about all day. Pa fixed water works.

November 6

Hit and miss. Worked some examples in Arithmetic. Pa gone to election all day. Levi P. Morton elected Governor. Snow about 6 inches deep here. Fixed Ma's receipt book with musilage. etc. etc. etc.

November 7

20°   Fair

Worked examples. Pa went to village. Mary Whitney was up to here in afternoon. Uncle Henry down here.

November 8

Went out doors. Pa up to village all day. Done fifty examples.

November 9

26°   Cold, snowy

Done examples. Went outdoors some. Pa gone to Schroon all day. Uncle Henry down in evening. Coughed a good deal.

November 10
Cool N.E.   Snow
Coughed pretty hard all day. Snowed considerable today. Pa pulled about 10 bushels of turnips out from under snow. I pasted cards in scrap album. Did not go outdoors at all cause I or we were 'fraid I would cough worse etc.

November 11
Cold Windy little Fair
Did not one of us go to Sunday School.
Grand ma Culver down here about all day.
Uncle Henry down toward night. I did not cough quite as bad as I did yesterday but quite hard today. Didn't go outdoors at all cause same as yesterday.

November 12
25°/0°   Wintery
Coughed some but not as hard as yesterday.
Pa went to Post Office and to Mrs. J.L. Huntley's and got me some Down's Elixir.
I moved bedstead upstairs, made blue ink and done most everything. Pa pulled turnips out from under snow about a foot deep. He pulled about 24 bushels. Folks commence to go with cutters, sleds, etc. I done about sixty examples in Ratio and Proportion.

November 13
Cold
Worked examples. Wrote a letter to Uncle Ed. Wrote some on legal cap.
Pa finished pulling turnips. Had 44 bushels. Pa banked house in afternoon. Cleaned out cupboard.
Did not cough as hard as yesterday.

November 14
Thawing Snow went off some   Cold
Worked examples. Pa went to village. Got a letter from Aunt Lucy. Read books, old letters, papers etc. some. Did not cough as hard as I did yesterday. My cough on the gain.

November 15
Middling Fair
Worked examples. Wrote a letter to Aunt Lucy Carpenter and sent it over to her by Uncle Jim as he was going over there. Puttyed up windows. Pa went over on Hardhack Hill and gathered up wood. Pa fixed barnyard gate by setting posts.

November 16

Thawy Smoky
Puttyed windows. Grand ma not very well. Ma about sick she had to lay abed nearly all the p.m. I knit round tape on a spool a good deal. Knit me a silk watch cord.

November 17

30° Squally a.m. Fair p.m. Ma little better. I wiped dishes, set table 3 times, waited on Ma, brought in wood, set dog trap, knit round tape and lot of other smaller things. Pa made handle on Dr. Griswold's butcher knife. I went outdoors considerable. Snow nearly gone off ground. Bare a good deal in meadows.

November 18

Clear
Ma better today. So she sat up some of the time. Grand ma down nearly all day. I went outdoors all I wanted to. Pa went to Granger's and to Uncle Henry's. Emory Whitney up here in evening. Ma's throat quite sore.

November 19

30°, 11°, 10°, 9° 6°
Snow squalls a.m. Ma better today. I was

outdoors more or less. Pa made soft soap. I worked some examples, set table, picked up dishes etc. Awful cold toward night. (Coldest this season) and in the evening and in the night, or I suppose it will be cold in the night at least.

November 20

2°, 18°, 25°   Fair
Got up and found it the coldest morning we have had this season. Done chores. Helped Pa put up corn to take to mill to get ground.
Worked some examples in Square Root.
Quilled quills for Aunt L.A. to weave, quilled all she wove. Pa went to Schroon. Ma about same as yesterday. Picked up things around the house. Wiped dishes at night, as Grand ma W. had worked hard all day.

November 21

45°   Fair
Worked examples. Done chores. Pa went to village. He got me a pair of leggins, a pair rubbers and some sheep skin slippers. Helped Pa kill sheep.

November 22

45°   Fair

Turned grind stone. Done chores. Worked examples. Read in Youth's Companion. Carried off water that women had washed in.

November 23

Cold rain (Rainy in p. m.) Pa and myself done chores, and horses and wagon. Worked examples. Read in Youth's Companion. Went down in cedars and skidded sleepers for shed floor. Afternoon I helped move things up in shed chamber and clean out or pick up the shed and carry the duffle up chamber. Pa and I took up part of shed floor and took down shed stairs. Pa framed sleepers for new shed floor.

November 24

                                             Fair

Done chores. Helped clean out shed, i.e. drawing dirt off etc. Helped Pa lay shed sleepers etc.

November 25

                                             Fair

Pa and I went to Sunday School and Church.

Grand ma, Uncles Jim & Henry were down. Done chores, read awhile, went to bed and to sleep.

November 26

13°   Cold

Went to school again. Brought me gold pen home. The rest of the pupils had not got ahead of me as far as I expected for some had been sick and some had whooping cough etc. Missed two words and left off ahead to boot. Came home in less than half an hour. Pa worked laying shed floor.

November 27

Went to school. Rode down and back with Pa as he was working on the church.

November 28

Went to school. Left off ahead. Wore rubbers and leggins. Snow $1^1/2$ to two inches deep. Wind blew a good deal so it made it the coldest day of the season so far. Ma dumping with tooth ache or something caused by tooth.

November 29

7°   Fair

Ma dumping with tooth

trouble, her face swelled up bad. She did not set up much. Uncle J. H. & H. J. and Pa killed hogs. Pa took our hog up to Uncle J. & H. I made eraser for school blackboard. Blowed up bladder. Went up to Grand ma's. Aunt L. A. went up there. I slid down hill little snow 2 or 3 inches deep.

November 30

Went to school. Ma little better. Wiped dishes at night. When I got to school the stove pipe had got or fell down and it was awful smoky.

Saturday, December 1, 1894
Cold

Ma's tooth broke last night so she felt better.
I done house work etc. etc. Pa went to Schroon Lake. Worked examples. Got through Progression in Arithmetic. Slid down hill some. Done chores. Pa got him a fur overcoat to try. Pa went to Choir Practice in evening. Found pullet's egg to barn this morning. Grand ma and Uncle Jim came down in p. m.

December 2
29°   Stormy

Went to Sunday School. Snowed about three inches. Uncle J. H. & H. J., and Grand ma were down.

December 3

Went to school. Played "fox & geese" at noon, recess etc.

December 4

Went to school. Left off ahead.

December 5

Went to school.

December 6

Went to school. Mim Brown came home with me.

December 7

Went to school.

December 8

Brought wash water. Went up to Grand ma's. Shelled two bushels of corn in their corn shelter. Pa and I went to choir practice in evening.

December 9

Went to Church.

December 10

Went to school.

December 11

Went to school.

December 12

Went to school.

December 13

Went to school.

December 14
Went to school.
December 15
Went to school, school kept
for a day about election
time. Went to Church for a
"sing".
December 16
Went to Sunday School
afoot.
December 17
Went to school.
December 18
Went to school.
December 19
Went to school.
December 20
Went to school.
December 21
Went to school. School out
until Monday after New
Year's Day.
December 22
Went down in woods and
helped Pa saw up logs.
Went up to Grand ma's.
Went to Christmas rehears-
al in evening.
December 23
4°
Pa, Uncle Henry and I
went to Sunday School
and Church. Practiced
Xmas music after church.
December 24
Went up to Grand ma's.
Went to Christmas tree in
evening. Santa Claus
brought me a watch chain,
a metal book mark, two
bags of popcorn, a tablet, a
bag of candy, a
necktie & handker-
chief. Sent a bag
of popcorn up to
Uncle Jim.
December 25
Went down in woods
where Pa was making skid-
way. Afternoon, Pa, Uncle
Jim and I skidded logs.
Grand ma C. and Uncle
H. also down to our house.
December 26
Arthur G. and I slid
down hill. Went up to
Grand ma's.
December 27
Snow
Got up and found it
snowing and blowing like
every thing. Blew, snowed
and drifted all day long.
Helped fix hen roost. Uncle
Henry and Roll Granger
were the only persons we
saw.
December 28
7° below°   Nice day
Shoveled roads. Pa went to
village. Done chores. Done
examples.
December 29
Pa and I drew wood

143

around into the shed on hand sled. Six or seven cords. Pa went to "sing" in evening. Roll and Arthur Granger here in evening. 20° below zero this morning.

December 30

4°   Fair

Pa and I went to Sunday School. Grand ma, Uncle Henry and Carrie Hall down here little while. Elected new officers in Sunday School.

December 31

10°/15°   cold

Brought wash water and carried dirty water off again. Levi Olden came over and killed one of our cows (Jersey). Pa and Uncle Henry went up to the village with beef. I went to Grangers to look at their organ.

Done chores etc. Worked few examples.

Good-bye Mr. 1894.

The 1895 diary, *second smallest of all the diaries, only 3" x 6", has a dark, fold-over cover of composition material, which is quite worn. The inside pages, however, are surprisingly well-preserved. Note the manufacturer's mention in the foresection (above) of the several eclipses occurring in this year.*

68   Adirondack Freight Team.

CHARLIE BROWN. TEAMSTER

Early transporttion in the Adirondacks

1895 hosted many ideas that today are so much a part of daily living that their origins are no longer considered. They're just taken for granted. On May 20 of this year, while Walter Whitney occupied his time with working examples, reading old letters, and writing to Aunt Lucy, 153 Broadway, New York City, opened its doors to the first commercial moving picture. On November 27, Alfred Nobel, the Swedish inventor of dynamite, established the Nobel Prize. The next day, November 28, while Walter was making his way by horse cart to Mill Brook (now Adirondack in the town of Horicon), America's first auto race took place. The average speed of the winning car, incidentally, was 7 mph.

The Schroon Lake area was not far behind. It already had a philanthropist in H. V. Parsell, and in the 1900s it had 2 movie theaters, the Strand and the Paramount. The Schroon Lake Gas & Mining Co. was incorporated in 1895, and oil leases were purchased by community people, including H.V Parsell and Walter's father, Lewis Whitney. This enterprise ended in disappointment in the production of oil, but it supplied the fuel that kindled many conversations and some tall tales for many years.

On October 25, 1895, Walter Whitney recorded that he put his wrist out of joint at recess in the afternoon. On November 8, 1895, William Roentgen in Germany, discovered the principle of x-ray. On November 11, 1895, Dr. Dunn determined, after two weeks of consultation, that Walter's arm was, indeed broken. Roentgen's x-ray would not arrive in America for sometime; and so, in spite of the fact that Dr. Palmer, of Schroon Lake and Dr. Dunn, and Dr. Griswold all examined Walter's arm, Walter, unfortunately, experienced the trial and error method of diagnosis characteristic of the era. The diary entries regarding this and other medical incidents are good examples of the tenacity and resolute quality inherent in the character of the Adirondack people.

ILLNESS AND MEDICINE

Some of the doctors in Pottersville around Walter Whitney's time were Dr. E. J. Dunn, who practiced from the late 1870s to the end of the century, and Dr. Frank A Griswold, who was licensed to practice pharmacy and dentistry during the same period. Early in the 20th century Dr. George Bibby, who came from a Pottersville family, graduated from Albany Medical College and began a practice in Pottersville that lasted until his death in the 1960s. Walter makes several references to Dr. Dunn's visits to treat his father. He also speaks of a Dr. G. calling him Dr.

Jim G. once; this may have been Dr. Griswold.

Walter's frequent illnesses may have been colds and bronchial infections, which were treated with homemade concoctions like boiled thoroughwort and slippery elm with licorice and flax seed to which molasses and sugar were added. Salt and baking soda were mixed with hot water to gargle. Drops of a slippery elm-based remedy were put in the ear.

Common problems for country people were frostbite, most often affecting the fingers and toes, and farm accidents. Head lice sometimes infected whole families and whole school groups. It was treated with kerosene or turpentine. Serious medical problems included heart disease and strokes (called shocks) and liver and kidney disease (treated with elixirs and patent medicines). Tuberculosis affected both city and country people. During the period of Walter's diary, a revolution in its treatment was in progress in Saranac Lake, only about 70 miles northwest of South Schroon, where Dr. E. L. Trudeau was prescribing Adirondack air and rest for TB patients.

J. S. Whitney
South Schroon
Essex Co., N.Y.
1895

Tuesday, January 1, 1895
30°   Clr. Cld.
Went up in meadow with
Pa after load of wood.
Helped Pa unload wood.
Slid down hill some.
Done few examples. Did
chores. Helped Pa unload
lumber.

January 2
                          Fair
Went to school. Mr.
Church of Mill Brook had
horse drowned in lake.
They saved one horse. I
saw him on the lake and
saw him all the time when
the horse was in the water.

January 3
19°/20°   Cld. Fair
Went to school. Uncle
Henry down a while in
evening. Pa drew wood
and broke road over on
hardhack hill.

January 4
0°   Blowy
Went to school. Pa drew
wood. Wind blew hard
especially in the evening.

Left off ahead in
spelling.

January 5
10°/16°/4°   Fair clear
Slid down hill on skip-
jack. Went to Post Office.
Done chores. Pa drew wood
in a.m.
Worked examples. Pa went
to choir practice.

January 6
5°/29°   Stormy
Went to Sunday School
and Church. My class had
new teacher who was
Thurman C. Warren who
was a good one.

January 7
33°/36°   Warm Cld.
Went to school. Sliding
down hill was the play
today. I had no sled at
school so did not slide
only when I slid with
someone else. Rode home
with Deb Hall.
Pa laid part of bedroom
floor.

January 8
Went to school. Took my
sled down, broke sled and
Mr. Richardson fixed it.
Pa and I went to singing
school in evening. Pa
singing master.

January 9
Went to school. Hurt my
ankle in morning sliding
so that I could not walk
home. Rode down to
F. Fords in stage and up
home with John Wood.

January 10
                    Stormy
My foot pretty sore and
stiff. Uncle Jim and
Henry cams down. I
never stepped on my foot
at all. Pa made storm door
for bedroom.

January 11
                        Cld.
My foot little better. I
played on mouth organ
some. Pa hung bed-room
door. Worked few examples.
Pa went to singing school.

January 12
                        Fair
Pa took Aunt L. A. to
Chestertown. I played on
mouth organ etc. some.
My foot so I can bear
my weight on it.

January 13
39°   Fair
My foot so that I could
walk on it a little.
Pa, Ma, and Uncle Henry
went to Church.
Grandmas W. and C.
stayed at home with me.

C. Tyrrell came here and
took supper.

January 14
                        Cld.
My foot better today. Did
nothing of much account.
Popped little popcorn.
Sugared off. Pa cut wood.
Uncle Jim came down lit-
tle while. Uncle H. down
in evening.

January 15
                        Cld.
Played on harp. Read
some. Worked few exam-
ples. Luna Fairfield came
here visiting. Uncle Jim C.
not feeling very good
today.
Frank G. worked here.

January 16
                        Cld.
My foot better. Did not do
much of anything.
Luna Fairfield here. Pa
and Frank Granger cut
and skidded wood. A pack
peddler came here this
forenoon. Went outdoors
first since hurting my
foot.

January 17
18°   Sql. Fair
Played on mouth organ
little. Cut pictures
out of a book
and framed four

or put in frames. Pa cut
and drew logs.

January 18

Played on mouth organ.
Luna here. Went out some.
Went to singing school in
evening. Luna. went
down too.

January 19

Did few chores. Shelled
corn. Pa went to a kind of
singing school at which
only children came. I
had headache.

January 20

6°   Fair
Pa, Ma, both Grandmas,
Uncle Henry and I went
to Church and Sunday
School. Brought in wood.

January 21

Went to school. Pa went to
village. I rode down and
back with him. Done
chores. Luna here yet.

January 22

Went to school. Stayed
with Thurm Warren
until singing school.
Went to Singing School.
Had quite a school tonight.
Got through my arith-
metic.

January 23

Went to school. Rode from
schoolhouse down to Geo.
Richarson's with E. Page

and then with Pa, then
with Geo. Bailey, then
with Uncle Jim.

January 24

Went to school. Miss
Brown had row with
Harry Richardson because
she put him in lower
class.

January 25

Went to school. Grandma
and Uncle Henry and
Arthur and Nora Floyd
came from Mill Brook.
I rode up from school with
them. Went to singing
school.

January 26

                              Snow
Played and visited with
Arthur and Nora.
Snowed ten or eleven
inches. Commenced to
blow at night from west.

January 27

                              Blowy
The wind blew and the
snow flew about all day to
beat the cars. Pa went to
Sunday School.
There were 7 to S. School.

January 28

Went to school. Pa carried
me to school and came
after me at night. Miss
Brown did not come this
morning until 9:30 a. m.

January 29

Went to school. Pa carried me down to Fred Ford's. I stayed down to Thurm Warren until singing school. Came home with Pa.

January 30

Went to school. Walked down and part of way back. Rode with a man by the name of Lynn from Minerva.

January 31

Went to school. Went afoot down and back. When I got home I had most of the chores to do. Got tired.

Friday, February 1, 1895

Went to school. Stayed down to Emory Whitney's until singing school. Rode home with Pa.

February 2

Helped Pa unload wood that he was drawing up to house. Wrote some to Chan. Done chores etc.

February 3

We all went to Sunday School and Church. Uncle Henry went down afoot and road back with us.

February 4

Went to school. When I came home the wind blew and the snow flew considerably. Wrote some in the evening about the Indians.

February 5

16 below

Went to school. Pa came after me. It is awful cold. Way down to 16 below zero and the wind a flying and the snow a blowing to beat the cars.

February 6

23 below   Cold. Blow

Too cold to go to school. Helped melt maple sugar over. Uncle Henry was down in forenoon. Wind blew awful. Quite a winter day.

February 7

Cold. Blow.

Went to school. Examination day. I was examined in Arithmetic and Geography today. Wind blew hard. Pa came after me at night. Pretty cold today and blowy also.

February 8

Cold. Blow.

Went to school. Examination day. I took History, Spelling, Physiology, and

Grammar today. I passed the ninth year in Arithmetic and Geography. Pa came after me at night. School is out for this storm.

February 9

8° Wind west Blowy hard. Brought in wood and water. Ma not feeling first rate.

Pa sawed green wood. I brought some of around from wood pile. Wind has awfully blown.

February 10

12° Shoveled snow Clr. Did not go to Sunday School. Lots of big drifts. Done chores. Give hens some meat.

Wrote and read some. Pa went up to Grand ma C.

February 11

15° Fair. Slid down hill on skip-jack. Shoveled snow. Went up to Grand ma's with team that were plowing out road. Arthur Granger came over and we played.

February 12

25° Fair Sawed wood. Helped Pa draw logs down from up on hill. Went up to Grand ma's. Uncle J., C.

Whitney up here to dinner. Done chores.

Got ready and went to singing school.

February 13

Pa got up and started for Riverside about 5 a.m. I had all chores to do both night and morning. Sawed wood. Pa got home in evening with load fertilizer.

February 14

Slid down hill. Sawed wood. Did chores.

Pa drew wood for Abe Walker. Puttered with hens giving them meat bones and such things as hens like etc. etc.

February 15

Made hand-sled to slide on. Uncle Bish and Aunt Lucy cams over. Grand ma and Carrie came down. Went to singing school. Got examination papers back.

February 16

32° Extra Fair. Slid down hill. Done chores. Cleaned out hen roost. Sawed and split wood. Brought and carried off water. Brought in wood. Read some. Pa went to village. He got me a Civil Govt.

February 17

Fair

Pa, Ma, Grand mas C. & W., Uncle Henry and I went to Sunday School and church services. Done chores. Went to bed and asleep.

February 18

21°/35°   Pleasant

Slid down hill. Done chores. Helped women folks. Studied some. Pa drew wood for Abe Walker from his house to Fred Ford's through swamp.

February 19

Slid. Filled straw bed. Went up to Grand ma's. Aunt Lucy Ann came home from Chestertown. Abe Walker and U. S. Ingraham worked here. Went to singing school.

February 20

Middling

Went to South Schroon. Went over with Pa to Abe Walkers after wood. Came home. Sawed little wood. Studied some in evening on C. G.

February 21

25°   Sql.

Slid down hill. Chored it etc. Went down in the woods where Pa and the men were cutting wood. Got ready and went to donation down to Wesley Bailey's. Got back 1:10.

February 22

Cut wood. Done chores. Pa, Abe Walker, and Sam Ingraham cut wood. Got ready and went to singing school. Were but few there tonight.

February 23

Slid down hill. Sawed wood for today and tomorrow. Uncle Henry came down. Pa and Abe Walker cut wood down in sugar works.

February 24

Pa, Ma and I went to Sunday School. Maude Patreau and Lettie Stowell were taken out of my class. Heard that Henry Carpenter had got a baby.

February 25

Went to Grand ma's. Pa drew wood to village. Went down in sugar works and helped Pa load wood. Done chores. Studied some. Wrote some. Ate some too.

February 26

6°   Plst.

Made wind mill. Slid down hill. Sawed wood. Done chores. Pa drew load

wood to village in a. m.,
Grand ma and Carrie
down a little while.

February 27

Slid down hill. Got
throwed off the sled head
over heals. Sawed wood.
Studied some.
Went to singing school.

February 28

46°   Thawing
Sawed wood. Studied some.
Pa went two load of wood
to village. Done chores.
Went up to Uncle Jim's.

Friday, March 1, 1895

43°   Thaw
Sawed wood some. Got
Grammar and Civil
Govt lesson. Pa and
Uncle Jim drew wood to
Schroon in forenoon.
Went to school but had no
school.

March 2

Snow Cold
Sawed wood. Slid. Pa drew
load of logs up to Ed
Richardson. Got ready
and went to Post Office
and then to singing
school.

March 3

Pa, Eddy Floyd and I
went to Sunday School
and Church. Aunt Lib
and the children went
home. We boys slid down
hill some on snow crust.

March 4

12°   Old Snow
Slid down hill on snow
crust. Hurt my finger
helping Uncle Jim load
logs. Sawed wood.
Studied some. Pa drew
logs. Uncle Henry down.

March 5

6°   Fair
Scraped roads. Grand ma
and Carrie down.
Pa went to Town Meeting.
Sawed wood.
Got ready and went to
P.O. and to singing
school.

March 6

Mid. Fair
Studied some. Went with
Pa over on hard-hack hill
plowing out road.
Sawed wood. Uncle Henry
down. Pa drew two loads
wood.

March 7

Cld.
Went over on hard-hack
hill with Pa after wood.
Helped unload wood.
Sawed wood. Gave hens
bones etc. Went to singing
school. Got back 10 p.m.

March 8

42°/50°/48°/55°   Fair

Went over on hard-hack hill with Pa after wood. Sawed wood. Helped unload wood. We went up to Grand ma's today as Grand ma was not feeling very well.

March 9

Blowy

Helped unload wood. Helped skin a fox for Uncle Henry. Got ready and went to singing school. Had a pretty good school.

March 10

Pa, Ma and I went to Sunday School. We went up to Emory Whitney's and stayed until nearly 6 o'clock. Saw eclipse of moon in evening.

March 11

Slid down hill. Shoveled snow. Helped unload wood. Aft. Pa and Ma went to village. First time Ma has been to village in 1 1/2 year's.

March 12

Sawed wood. Split wood. Slid down hill. Grand ma and Carrie down today. Pa finished drawing wood.

March 13

32°   Cld.

Sawed wood. Went up to Torn Coles aid got Lill's Grammar. Ma went to K.D. Meeting. Pa went to P'ville with load wood.

March 14

Sawed wood. Pa went up to Schroon Lake village with a load of wood for Abe Walker. Went to S. School.

March 15

Slid down hill. Sawed wood. Studied some. Went over to Grangers to see Arthur about sliding but he did not come over.

March 16

Slid down hill on snow crust some. Sawed quite a lot of wood. Pa went to village and Ma went to Uncle James C. Whitney's.

March 17

Fair

Pa, Ma and I went to Sunday School and Church.

I was the only scholar in my class. Maud P. hurt her arm so May W. played the organ.

March 18
Sawed wood under wood shed. Pa went to Chestertown. Quite windy today. Done chores etc. Pa brought me candy etc.

March 19
Helped draw off snow from behind the shed.
May Whitney came up here. We slid down hill some. Sawed little wood. Went to S. School.
May rode down with us.

March 20
Pa, Ma and I got ready and went to Mill Brook. Got there 9:15 a.m. Went up to Aunt Lucy's.
Came back to Aunt Lib's and stayed all night.

March 21
Went up to Aunt Lucy's and back to Aunt Lib's. We boys slid down hill. Uncle Henry came over and we rode back with him. Went to singing school.

March 22
Brought in and carried off water. Went up to Grand ma's in forenoon. Gave hens bones.
Pa drew load wood to village for A. Walker.

March 23
Emory and Mary Whitney came up. Emory and I went up to G Ma's where men were shoveling.
Helped saw wood. Went to S. School.

March 24
Pa, Ma and I went to Sunday School. Got cold yesterday which made my head ache.
G Ma down.

March 25
Got up and did not feel very first class.
Did not sit up any. Had head ache good deal and nausea.

March 26
Felt about so. Jesse Cole and Papa fixed buckets. Jesse sawed wood in afternoon some.
Uncle H.J. came down.

March 27
Felt about so. Pa went after Dr. Dunn who came about some time after noon. Howard Foster dropped dead today.

March 28
Felt better today. Grand ma and Carrie came down.

Pa went to village to see Dr. Dunn who was over to E. Page's so Pa had to wait.

J. M. Lealand died today.

March 29

Did not feel any better today. Think that I got a little cold yesterday so did not feel quite like talking. Uncle H. J. came down.

March 30

Felt the best I have at all since I have been dumping. Pa not feeling very good so we had Dr. G. come up. Grand ma came down.

March 31

Sat around and read. Uncle Jim went over to Mill Brook after Aunt Lib & Co. I played with the children. I felt better today.

Monday, April 1, 1895
Cld, Snow

April fooled the folks. Uncle Bish came over. Made a checker board and played some. Eddy came down. Played dominoes.

April 2
Fair

Mended rubber boots etc.

Played checkers etc. Went outdoors. Uncle Henry and Eddy came down. Eddy stayed most all day.

April 3

Went out doors considerable. Watched chicks under tree in orchard etc. Pa and Jess worked sugaring.

April 4

Went out doors. Played checkers. Pa and Jesse worked in sugar works nearly all day tapping.

April 5

Went out doors good deal in am. Pa and Jess finished tapping and got things ready to boil. I boiled some in afternoon toward night.

April 6

Did not do much of anything in forenoon. Aft boiled sap made four buckets of syrup. Pa and Jess gathered. Pa boiled little toward night.

April 7

Did not go to Sunday School. Pa and Ma went with carriage. I had hiccough quite bad but cured it by taking lemon juice.

April 8
47°   Rainy

Eat maple sugar. Went up

to Jesse Cole's to see if he was coming to work. Stirred sugar etc. Played with E. & H.

April 9
Sprouted taters. Aft Pa and I went all over sugar works emptying water out of buckets.
Aunt Lib & Co. came down.

April 10
Done chores. Pa went to the village. He took up some sugar. Played with E. & H.

April 11
Eddy, Howard and I went down and thawed out the evaporator. Aft Pa and I sawed wood some.

April 12
Boiled sap. Pa gathered 8 1/2 barrels. Eddy and Howard were down to sugar house good deal. Jese Cole came down.

April 13
Eddy and I gathered four barrels of sap and I went to boiling. Rained in p.m. so Pa went down and boiled. Ate sugar.

April 14
Rain

Rained all day. Done chores. Played with E. & H. Pa cut my hair and cropped off his whiskers.

April 15
Rain Cold

Helped gather two barrels of sap and rain water. Then went to boiling and boiled the rest of the day. Went and got sheep.

April 16
40°   Cld.

Went down to sugar house helping take out evaporator. Sawed wood. Emptied water. Done chores.

April 17
Helped cut wood. Ate stickjaw. Eddy and Howard down. Went down to sugar works. Sap run good.

April 18
Helped gather two barrels of sap and then went to boiling and boiled all day. Got about 5 buckets of syrup. Men cut wood in p.m.

April 19
71°   Boss

Helped cut wood. Ate stickjaw. Eddy and Howard down until three p.m. or such a matter.

April 20
Pa, Jesse and myself gathered two bbls. sap and I went to boiling. They

gathered 6 1/2 barrels.

April 21
Went up to Grand ma's twice in forenoon.
Got ready and went down to Sunday School.
I drove the mule. Stayed to C. Whitney's to tea.

April 22
Cut wood Pa, Abe and I. Women sugared off so we men folks went in and ate about 10 pound apiece.

April 23
Packed my duds and went to school. May Whitney came up home with me to see Jess.

April 24
May and I went down to sugar house. Went to school.

April 25
Went to school.

April 26
School was attended by me.

April 27
Helped draw stone. Talked of going fishing but did not go. Aunt Lib & Co. went home.

April 28
Went up to Uncle Henry's. Went to Sunday School afoot. Uncle Henry went down and Jess came back with us.

April 29
Went to Post Office and then up to school.

April 30
Went to Post Office and sent to Burpee after garden seeds.
Went to school. After school was out helped Deb Hall unload wood and rode home with her.

Wednesday, May 1, 1895
Went to school.

May 2
Went to school.

May 3
Went to school. Arbor Day.

May 4
Took banking away from house. Helped plant potatoes. Went to Choir Practice in evening.
Set hen upon hay.

May 5
Went up to Grand ma's. Went to Sunday School afoot. Hottest day we have had this year.

May 6
Went to school. Sowed garden.

May 7
Went to school. Sowed garden.

May 8
Went to school. Hot today,

had showers.

May 9
Went to school. Awful hot.

May 10
Went to school. School was out little after 3 p.m. Came home. Pa and I went to lake fishing. Got 7.

May 11
Clr. Cold Rain

Pa, Uncle Henry and I planted potatoes. Got them all done but one row. Had small showers toward night.

May 12
Pa, Uncle Henry and I went to Sunday School and Church. We went up to Emory Whitney's and stayed to dinner.

May 13
Went to school. Played dog and deer at noon.

May 14
Had frost last night. Went to school. Played dog and deer at noon. Saw a wood-chuck. Wrote our Geography this afternoon. Helped pick up stone. Set hen in bee hive under hen roost.

May 15
Went to school. Coughed good deal at school.

May 16
Cold felt worse so I did not go to school. Did not feel very good. Felt worse along toward night. Pa set hen in basket in cow stable.

May 17
Felt worse if anything. Dr. G came in afternoon. Pa shot wood chuck. Dr. took it home.

May 18
Felt better. Ate at the table. Wrote some to Aunt Lucy.

May 19
Felt better. Wrote some to Aunt Lucy. Grand ma Culver came down and stayed nearly all day. F. Granger's baby very sick today.

May 20
Fair. Plst.

Worked examples. Read old letters. Went outdoors. Wrote some to Aunt Lucy. Printed some.

May 21
Went out considerable. Had eye ache in right eye. Grand ma came down, Chan coming or came down with "Grip".

May 22
Aunt L. a little better. Ma little worse. Went to barn and helped Pa get hens shut up.

My eye commenced to ache and ached awfully-most of p. m.

May 23

Clear

Wind blew hard. Did not do much of anything in forenoon. I expected my eye to ache again but it did not. Shelled corn and went up and dumped fertilizer while Pa done the rest. Ma sick. Aunt L.A. nearly sick.

May 24

Pa and I planted corn.

May 25

Finished planting corn, and then went to Thurman pond fishing.

May 26

Went to Sunday School and Church.

May 27

Went to school.

May 28

Went to school.

May 29

Went to school. Hoed in garden and dropped beans.

May 30

Pa and I worked getting mangle beet ground ready and then sowed half of them.

May 31

Cld.

Went to Mrs. Huntley's and then up to school. Case Stone left school to get ready to go to Hague.

Saturday, June 1, 1895

Pa and I went over to fallow. We finished sowing mangles and turnips. Went to choir practice.

June 2

90°

Pa and Grand ma went up to Thurm Barnes' boy's funeral. Grandma C. down. Jess Cole and I went down to So. S. in evening.

June 3

Went to school.

June 4

Went to school. Played ball.

June 5

Went to school. Took down my "Higher Lessons in English." Rained or hard shower after school was out.

June 6

Cld.

Went to school. Played ball. Wed some in garden.

June 7

Fair

Went to school. Came home up around by Schneider's. Wed some in garden. Pa and Frank G. fixed fence.

June 8

Helped draw rails. Wed some in garden. Went to choir practice.

June 9

Pa, Ma, Uncle H. and I went to Sunday School.

June 10

Went to school.

June 11

Went to school.

June 12

Went to school.

June 13

Went to school. Examination day.

June 14

Went to school. Examination day. Rode horse to cultivate.

June 15

Pa and I hoed taters, sweet corn and beans. Went to Choir Practice in evening.

June 16

Went to Sunday School. Pa, Ma, Patreau and I went to Children's Day up to village.

June 17

Went to school.

June 18

Went to school.

June 19

Went to school.

June 20

Went to school.

June 21

Went to school. Last day. Had entertainment that lasted $1^1/2$ hours. Pa and Ma down. Got my sheep skin diploma.

June 22

Pa and I hoed two rows of corn. I went down to Schneider's to tell them that the horses that were in their pasture were out.

June 23

Felt better today. Uncle Bish, Aunt Lucy, Uncles H. & H. J. and Grand ma C. here.
Uncle B. and Aunt L. went home. Pa and Grand ma Whitney went to Church.

June 24

Fair

Wrote some or a good deal. Picked over greens. Papa hoed beets below barn. Got smart and smoked part of cigar and got sick.

June 25

Fair

Pulled weeds in garden. Hoed beans.
Felt good deal better today but some weak. Pa cleaned out cellar etc. and done

164

numerous jobs.

June 26

Fair

Felt about same. Helped Pa hoe mangle beets. Nose ached quite bad all day. Pa made me a thing to run salt water through my nose.

June 27

Did not feel so well. Layed on lounge all day. Ate too many greens for a few days back. Had lameness in side caused by hoeing or throwing stones which I did yesterday.

June 28

Felt better. Was up all over the house. Samuel Ingraham here to supper. Pa killed a rooster for me to eat.

June 29

Thinned out carrots. Wed few onions. May Whitney and her mother up here. Mabel and I had lots of laughable fun.

June 30

Pa and Ma went to Sunday School. Uncle Henry and Grand ma came down. Went up and saw corn and potatoes.

Monday, July 1, 1895

63°

Fair

Went up to Grand ma's. They were raising their corn house. Came home and wed onions and beets. Aft. Pa and I wed beets, hoed sweet corn, beans and potatoes.

July 2

Pa and I hoed all of our field potatoes. Ma down to Emory Whitney's dressmaking it. Uncle Henry down in evening.

July 3

Went up to Grand ma's. Saw a deer. Hoed mangle beets. Pa and I bugged taters till I or we got awful sick of it.

July 4

Went to picnic.

July 5

Pa, Uncle J. H. & H. J. and myself cuffed our corn over. Pa and I went to village in afternoon.

July 6

Worked on road. Went up to school house and to Fred Ford's. Pa and Jess went to Choir Practice.

July 7

Went to Sunday School and Church. Rode down

and back with Jess. Aunt
Lib and the boys came
over and stopped to church.
July 8
Pa and I painted on
Church sheds and fence.
July 9
Went to village. Helped
hang grind stone.
July 10
Went to lecture in
evening. Pa, Uncles J. H.
& H. J., Elmer Warington
and I mowed. Pa and I
painted tater bugs.
July 11
Hoed garden. Helped get in
hay. Went up to Grand
ma's.
July 12
Mowed and picked up after
mowing machine.
July 13
Helped Pa put in new sec-
tions. Helped squirt water.
July 14
Pa, Ma, both grandma's.
Uncle Henry and I went
to Church. Rev. Blanchard,
a blind man, preached.
July 15
Picked up after mowing
machine. Helped get in two
loads of hay.
July 16
Painted on bedroom
floor. Helped Pa make

screen door.
July 17
Helped make screen door.
Picked up after mowing
machine and horse rake.
Loaded one load hay.
July 18
Picked up after machine.
Loaded hay.
July 19
Picked after mowing
machine. Mowed swath
next to fence. Pa and Ma
went to village.
July 20

Cld. clr.
Helped hang screen door.
Picked up after horse rake.
Uncle Henry came down
and helped us get in two
loads. Went to Choir
Practice.
July 21

Clr. Rain
Pa, Ma, Uncle Henry and
I went to Sunday School
and Church. I rode down
with Jess Cole and back
with Pa and Ma.
July 22
Picked up after mowing
machine and horse rake.
We got in two pretty good
sized loads of hay.
July 23
Hayed it. Got in one big
load.

July 24

Pa and I mowed the lot west of corn. Uncle Jim Whitney and wife came up. He helped us get in two loads. We got in one load alone.

July 25

Pa and I mowed the piece above the muck bed. Also muck bed. Stove peddler came here in afternoon.

July 26

Helped mow in orchard. Pa and I got in two pretty good loads up beyond muck bed.

July 27

Helped unload hay. Pa and I went up and got some that we did not get last night. Uncle H. J. came down and helped us get in hay in orchard.

July 28

Pa, Ma, both Grandmas, Uncle Henry "Chan", and I went to Sunday School and Church. Rev. J. H. Blanchard preached. Quite a lot of city people up among whom were Mr. and Mrs. Parcell.

July 29

Catched potato bugs in pan. Canned string beans.

Pa mowed down to O'Neal's. Helped get sheep and lambs.

July 30

Pa and I went to Schroon.

July 31

Picked berries. Hoed garden. Pa worked down to O'Neal's.

Thursday, August 1, 1895

Picked peas. Helped patch barn. Thinned out beets.

August 2

Pa and I went over to Uncles J. H. and H. J.'s fallow.

August 3

Uncle Jim and I went over to their fallow after hay. Helped Pa patch barn. Uncle Henry and I went over to our fallow berrying.

August 4

Pa, Ma, Uncle Henry and I went to Church. Uncle Henry and I went afoot.

August 5

Pa and I worked haying on Uncles J. & H. fallow.

August 6

Ditto.

August 7

Did not do much of anything. Pa went to South

Schroon. Went to lecture meeting.

August 8
Picked blackberries. Went over to Uncles J. & H. fallow.

August 9
Thinned out beets. Pa got home in afternoon. We picked and shelled 8 quarts of peas.

August 10
Thinned out beets. Picked blackberries. Went up and helped Uncle J. H. and H. J. get in one load of hay.

August 11
Pa, Ma, Uncle Henry, Grand Ma W. and I went to Church.

August 12
Gathered some pennyroyal and picked blackberries. Pa went to Riverside for C. F. Taylor.

August 13
Picked peas. Went blackberrying. Mowed oats.

August 14
Waited on women. Helped rake in and draw in two load of oats. Pa and I went down to Taylors in evening.

August 15
Went blackberrying. Got fourteen quarts.

Pulled weeds in garden.

August 16
Went up to Grand ma's after sour milk. Pa went to village.

August 17
Dug and picked up potatoes. Run all over pasture after sheep.

August 18
Pa, Ma, Uncle Henry, Grand mas C. & W. Chan and I went to Sunday School and Church. Rev W. H. Graut preached.

August 19
Picked berries and cucumbers. Cleaned out stable.

August 20
Picked 8 quarts berries. Pa not feeling very awful well so he did not do much of anything only go to Taylors with milk twice. Sold fifteen chickens to E. Clark.

August 21
Picked berries. Went up to Grand ma's. Pa and Grand ma Whitney went to Alex Landing's funeral.

August 22
Mowed oats alone. Helped mow away hay.

August 23
Helped rake and

draw in oats. Pa, Uncle Henry and I mowed oats in afternoon.

August 24

Helped turn over, load and mow away oats.
Uncles H. J. and J. H. helped me. Grand ma and Luna down here.

August 25

Pa, Ma, Grand mas C. & W., Uncle Henry, Lunc and I went to Church.

August 26

Did not do much of anything. Uncle Jim and I went to Taylors with milk. Pa off after leases for oil etc.

August 27

Worked up to Uncle J. H. and H. J. helping them get in oats. Got home and found Mrs. Day, Jim Seaman, wife and three children.

August 28

Fooled around with Henry Seaman and the rest. They went off in afternoon. Mrs. Day stayed here.

August 29

Played over to brooks. Christina went down to David Hall's. Pa went to Riverside.

August 30

Boiled corn and got ready to dry.
Played over to brook.
Picked up apples. Pa went to Riverside.

August 31

Helped take up carpet.
Filled straw bed.
Dug potatoes.

Sunday, September 1, 1895

Went to Sunday School and Church. Rode back with "Stub" Floyd. We went up to Charley Hill to meeting.

September 2

Went blackberrying with Mrs. Day. Pa went to Riverside.

September 3

Uncle Jim and I went to Carding Machine.

September 4

Did not do much of anything. Papa and Grand Ma W. went to Uncle Henry Kellenbach's funeral.

September 5

Pa and I went to village.

September 6

Corded up wood little.

September 7

Helped Pa copy off by-laws

of Church Association.
Went to Church Meeting.

September 8
Pa, Ma, Grand Ma and I
went to Church.

September 9
Went up to Grand Ma's
to get straw to bind corn.
Rained in aft. Corded up
wood.

September 10
Cut corn.

September 11
Helped cut corn. Got it
done.
Helped pull beans. Went to
show lecture down to
Church.

September 12
School was attended by
me today for the first time
this term.

September 13
Went to school.

September 14
Helped put cover on wood.
Picked seed peas.
Went over to Grangers.
Helped gather apples and
squashes.

September 15
Anda F. brought Chan
home.
We went up to Grand
ma's and she and Uncle
Jim came down.
Anda went home about 4.

September 16
Went to school.

September 17
Went to school.

September 18
Went to school.

September 19
Went to school.

September 20
Went to school.

September 21
Helped draw in corn.
Aft. helped kill and dress
hens and chickens.
Went to Taylors and to
Choir Practice.

September 22
Had headache and did not
feel very good.
Pa and Uncle Henry went
to Sunday School.

September 23
Did not feel very well on
account of taking pill last
night.
Husked little corn.

September 24
Went to school.

September 25
Shucked corn.

September 26
Uncle Jim & Henry and
I went to fair.

September 27
Pa and I went to fair.

September 28
Husked corn and dug pota-

toes. Lizzie Day came here from Pottersville.

September 29
Went to Sunday School and Church.

September 30
Went to school.

Tuesday, October 1, 1895
Went to school.

October 2
Went to school.

October 3
Went to school.

October 4
Went to school.

October 5
Dug corn and husked taters.

October 6
Went to Sunday School.

October 7
Went to school.

October 8
Went to school.

October 9
Went to school. Lizzie went to Pottersville.

October 10
Went to school.

October 11
Went to school.

October 12
Helped gather onions and spade up weeds. Husked corn.

October 13
Went to Sunday School.

October 14
Went to school.

October 15
Went to school.

October 16
Went to school.

October 17
Went to school.

October 18
School was attended by me today.

October 19
Helped put corn stalks up over head out to barn. Helped thresh beans. Threshing machine here in afternoon. Had little cold.

October 20
Had cold so did not go to Church. Pa and Ma went.

October 21
Head felt bad did not feel very good.

October 22
Felt little better. Did not do much. Pa pulled mangles. Went out where he was.

October 23
Went out doors all I wanted to. Winnowed out and picked over beans. Helped pull mangles and turnips.

October 24
Went to school.

October 25
Went to school. Put my wrist out of joint at recess in the afternoon. Emory Whitney took me to Schroon and Dr. Palmer put it back.

October 26
My wrist ached awfully all last night so I couldn't sleep. Ached pretty good all day but not as hard as it did last night.

October 27
Wrist better or did not ache so hard. Pa, Ma, and Grand ma went to Jane Hall's funeral.

October 28
Slept good last night. Sat up and walked around.

October 29
Snow
Wrist good deal better. Wrote some.

October 30
Wrist about the same. Aunt Lillias came up here visiting. Pa went to village. He got a single bedstead.

October .31
Aunt Lillias came up here. Worked examples.

Friday, November 1, 1895
Wrist about the same. Worked examples. Fooled with women. Pa plowed. Emory Whitney came up.

November 2
Wrist better. Worked examples. Aunt Lillias went home.

November 3
Read some. Grand ma C. and Mrs. Burbank came down here. Dr. G. came along and his woman got out and stopped here. Dr. stopped when he came back and looked at my wrist. He said that one bone of arm was cracked.

November 4
Worked examples.

November 5
Worked examples. Pa went to Election.

November 6
Went outdoors good deal. Deb Hall cleaned out our well.

November 7
My wrist getting better

slowly. Read and worked examples some. Eleanor Rice came here. Ma went down to Uncle Jim's.

November 8

Fooled around home in forenoon. Helped Pa draw stone in afternoon.

November 9

Rained about all day. Thought my wrist was getting crooked.

November 10

Squly

Read good deal. Pa went to Pottersville to see Dr. G. about my wrist. Grand ma and Uncle H. down.

November 11

Pa and I went to Schroon to see Dr. Dunn about my wrist. He said the bone was broken.

November 12

Arm about same. Worked examples. Wrote some Watched Pa draw out rocks.

November 13

Ditto.

November 14

Ditto.

November 15

Ditto.

November 16

Ditto.

November 17

Arm little better. Pa and Ma went to Sunday School.

November 18

Worked examples. Pa and Uncle Henry drew rocks. Aunt Sophia and Lillias came here.

November 19

Worked examples. Aunt S, and L. went home. Went up to Grand ma's.

November 20

Pa went to village to get corn and oats ground.

November 21

Worked examples. Pa went down to Taylor's.

November 22

Uncle H.J. and J.H. and us killed hogs. Swatched them. Grand ma and Carrie down here.

November 23

Worked examples. Pa went to village. He got a little meat chopper.

November 24

We took bandage off my arm and washed it off. Pa and Ma went to Church.

November 25

Went to school.

November 26

Went to school.

November 27

Went to school.

November 28
Went to Mill Brook.
November 29
Went to school after I got back from Mill Brook which was a little after 9 a.m. Stub Taylor took picture of school. Ma stayed at Mill Brook.
November 30
Cld. & Clr.
Had a cold so stayed in house most all day. Hulled some corn. Pa cut wood on Hardback Hill. Wrote some.

Sunday, December 1, 1895
Cold Fine
Pa went to Sunday School. My cold a little better but don't feel first class yet. Ma at Mill Brook.
December 2
My lungs ached some and felt tight today. Pa tinkered around in forenoon. Aft. he went to Pottersville after Ma. She came home and doctored me up.
December 3
Felt good deal better today. Grand ma and Carrie W. down here. Uncle Henry

and Deb Hall worked for Pa. Hulled some corn and run it through meat cutter.
December 4
Wrote composition. Pa, Uncle Henry and Deb cut wood on hardhack hill. Ma went to "King's Daughter" meeting.
December 5
Wrote some. Pa cut wood in a.m. Uncle Henry down in forenoon.
December 6
Didn't do much of anything.
December 7
Wrote some. Pa cut brush down in sugar camp.
December 8
Did not go to Sunday School. Pa and Ma went. Uncle Jim came down here.
December 9
Went to school.
December 10
Went to school.
December 11
Went to school.
December 12
Went to school.
December 13
Went to school.
December 14
Pa cut wood upon hill so I went up and piled some. Went to Grand ma's and

to Choir or Christmas practice.

December 15
Pa and Ma went to Sunday School. I did not go.

December 16
Went to school.

December 17
Went to school.

December 18
Went to school.

December 19
Went to school. Examination day. I took teachers' examination just to try.

December 20
Went to school. Finished my examination.

December 21
Went up to Grandma's. Chased sheep. Helped Pa put kindling wood into hog shop.

December 22
Went to Sunday School and Church.
First time I have been since Oct. 13.

December 23
Went up to Grand ma's. Got ready and went to Christmas rehearsal in evening.

December 24
Popped some popcorn for Xmas. Went down to Xmas rehearsal in afternoon. Went to Charley Hill to Xmas tree.

December 25
Popped corn. Went up to Grand ma's. Played on Carrie's accordion some. Arthur Floyd came over. We all went to Xmas tree in evening.

December 26
Went up to Grand ma's. "Stub" and I. We played games and carried on generally.

December 27
"Stub" and I played games in the house and ran and capered outdoors. Pa went to village afoot. Grand ma and Uncle Henry down.

December 28
Pa and Ma went down to Uncle Jim Whitneys a visiting. Went up to Grand ma's twice.

December 29
Went to Sunday School.

December 30
Rain
Went to school. Rained most all the afternoon and

in the evening.

December 31

It rained most all night last night or until 3 o'clock. Wind blew awfully in last part of night and all the forenoon and more or less all day. Went to school. Left off ahead. Uncle Henry and Deb Hall worked for Pa.

Memoranda

Hurt my ankle and foot sliding down hill on Jan. 9, 1895. Aunt L. I. went to Chestertown Jan. 12 came back Feb. 19, 1895.

Went to Mill Brook Mar 20, 1895.

Came back Mar, 21 with Uncle H. J. Howard Foster dropped dead Mar. 27, 1895.

J. M. Lealand died Mar. 28, 1895.
Had "Grip" May 16 to 24, 1895. Had Dr. twice.
Got my diploma June 21,

1895.
Down to last day of school. Saw a deer when I was going up to Grand ma's July 3, 1895.
Put my wrist out of joint down to school at recess in the afternoon. Emory Whitney took me to Schroon and Dr. Palmer and Emory pulled it back. Oct. 25, 1895.

Jane Hall died. Oct. 25, 1895.

Pa, Ma and I went to Mill Brook Nov. 28 and Pa and I came back Nov. 29. Ma stayed until Dec. 1895.
Stub" Taylor took picture of school Nov. 29, 1895.

I got a pair of slippers, an ink stand, a set of colored pencils, a diary, a globe and a looking glass for Xmas.

....

Dec. 4, 1895.
This morning is the coldest one that we have had this season. The thermometer registered just zero, I have got cold so I cannot go out of doors but I can get some idea of the cold by going to the door and by the amount of wood it takes to keep warm. Uncle Jim has just come with a load of wood for

"Chan". Pa, Uncle Henry and Deb Hall are cutting wood over on Hardhack Hill. Ma is going down to "Quaker Meeting" this afternoon.

Why is a hedge hog like some proud folks?
Because he is too much stuck up.
Quite a puzzle ain't it? Yes. KB

Roll Granger and his new wife came home over to Frank Granger's Saturday night. June 22, 1895.

Account with Lewis W. Whitney
Jan. Balance from 1894
$12.50
Examinations: Ninth Year
February 1895

Arithmetic	80%
Geography	78 3/4%
Spelling	82%
Physiology	98%
History	Not passed
Grammar 7th year	100%
Drawing 5th and 6th year	100%

Got 7th year certificate

Examinations June 1895:
Civil Govt. Ninth Year
Drawing
Grammar
History

Spelling
24 Grams = 1 pint
20 Pint =10 2I.
12 oz. = 1 Lb.
12 inches

A cat is an animal that is kept in houses to catch mice and to play with.

W. J. Whitney Mar. 6 1895
Sunday Have been having kind of eye ache today.
Arthur Floyd went home today.
Four Dutch Governors:
Peter Minute
Wouter Van Twiller
Win. Krift
Peter Stuyvesant

Cost to keep a boy:

Jan. 1 Diary	.40
One pr. shoe strings	.03
Flannel shirt cloth	.83
Rub. boots No. 7	3.00
Tablet	.05
Civ. Govt.	.80
Dr. G.	
Cloth for pants	1.08
Grammar	.75
Straw hat	.15
Legal cap	
Cough drops	.10
Bot. elixir	.25
Collar	.30
Suit clothes	6.50

Pair shoes	1.75
Shirt cloth	
Buttons	
Slate pencil	.01
Lead pencil	.01
Tablet	.05
	$16.56
Composition book	.05
2 pr. drawers	1.00
Neck tie	.25
x Ink stand	.15
x Looking glass	.10
x Colored pencils	.10
x Pr. slippers	.75
x for Xmas	3.00
	16.56
Total	$19.56

Account of accident: I saw
horses coming up lake. By
and by, I looked down on
lake and saw horses in lake.
We ran to tell Miss Brown.
Soon the whole school were on
stools looking at the team.
Within half hour eleven men
were on the lake helping. One
horse drowned. The man was
Mr. A. Church of Adirondack.
He had a fore head sled on and
a barrel of apples and two good
sized horses.
The above happening Jan,
1895.

Mr. N. Floyd had a team of
horses drown in lake Jan. 4,

Cake of ice slipped or tipped up
and let them in sleds and all.

Lizzie B. Day, Sheffield St.,
Newark, N. J.

J. E. Brown, Chestertown,
Warren Co., N. Y.

I. C. Warren, 14 80th St.,
Boisie City, Mo.

P. F. Smith, 21 Brick St.,
New Strong, Conn.

Mabel Whitney

Arthur D. Perkins,
11 & 13 St.
New Haven, Conn

Peter Pewter, 16 First St.,
Boston, Mass.

Diary for June 22, 1895
Uncle Bish and Aunt Lucy
came over. Afternoon I was
about half sick with sore throat,
nausea and head ache. Pa and
Uncle Bish went to
village.

Farewell Address to 1895
Farewell dear year. You have
behaved very well for a tricky
fellow as you. We have enjoyed
your visit greatly and it has

been a prosperous year for us.
Me anyway for I have got
my diploma. With thanks for
your kindness and goodness we
remain, the inhabitants of the
earth. Dec. 31, 1895.

Compliments of
W. J. S. Whitney May 23
8:34 p. m.
After a few hours work in the
p. m..

"Why is the letter A like 12
o'clock a. m.?"
Because it is in the middle of
day.

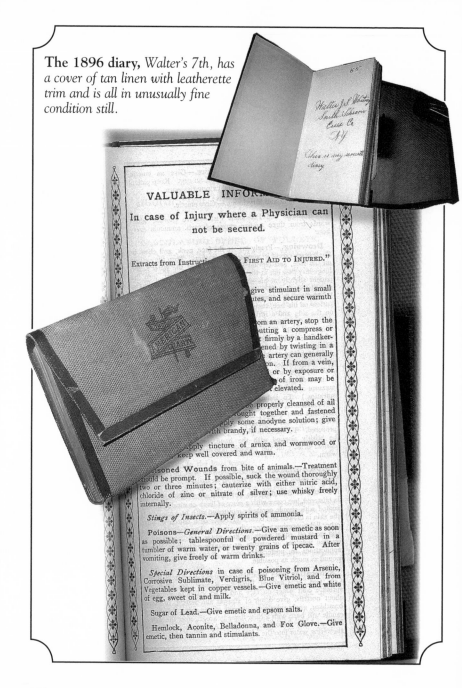

The 1896 diary, *Walter's 7th, has a cover of tan linen with leatherette trim and is all in unusually fine condition still.*

South Schroon Schoolhouse

1896 yielded to further expansion of the United States borders, admitting Utah as the 45th state. Expansion continued in other venues, as well. Automobiles were seen on the streets of big cities. The medical profession was making progress using radiation for the treatment of cancer; and the first modern Olympic games took place in Athens, Greece, where American, James Connolly, brought home the first gold medal.

Unfortunately, Mother Nature also left her mark on modern history in 1896. A tornado hit Texas, killing 78 people, and a tsunami struck a beach celebration in Japan killing tens of thousands, leaving 9,000 injured and 13,000 homes destroyed.

There were alarming statistics during this year, as well as futuristic promises by the visionaries at this time; but there is little evidence in Walter' s diaries that he was aware of such current events. His subscription to *Youth Companion* magazine, his mention of Levi Morton's election to the governorship in 1894, and McKinley's assassination in 1901, were hints of peripheral world knowledge that were scattered throughout his life. By today's standards and technology, it would seem strange for a fourteen-year-old boy to be so sheltered from the rest of the world. But we learn through Walter's story that the focus of life in 1896 in the Adirondacks was on the world of the community; and for Walter, especially, there was a focus on school. He was a scholar. He valued his books, his teachers; and his story conveys that he had a penchant for learning.

The old school bell, that may have summoned the scholars to the small clapboard building in South Schroon in 1896 and brought them back to their desks at the end of recess, has a story of its own, and one that lends credence to the strength in, and the allegiance to, the sense of community. This story cannot be told better by anyone than by Lucille Murdock Roblee, a resident of South Schroon, whose father was instrumental in the preservation of the bell. Lucille gives this account:

The South Schroon School Bell

When the new school in South Schroon was built, around 1920, the bell from the old school was placed in the downstairs hall.

During World War II, the bell was taken to the pasture in back of the Harold Swan home where a platform was built to hold it. The bell was used for an air raid warning, if needed, as well as the church bell at the other end of the road.

In later years a man who had purchased Coles Motel, nearer Schroon Lake village, wanted to purchase the bell, so he could have it near his office. The reason being he could be down by the lake, and if someone needed him they would ring the bell. He approached the people in South Schroon and was told it wasn't for  *sale. He then went to the Schroon Lake Town Board and said he wanted to buy it. They said they weren't aware of the bell but would sell it* *to him for $25.00. Later that night, the Town Clerk called Mrs. Swan and told her a man would be there to pick up the bell in the morning. She immediately called Hobart Murdock to tell him. Hobart called a member of the Town Board and asked why they thought they could sell it. The reply was "We didn't know anything about it, but thought if he wanted to pay $25.00, we would sell it to him." Hobart was very annoyed, and said to him, "The next thing you would be selling is our church, cemetery, and town hall." The next morning Hobart went over and put a sign on the bell saying it belonged to the people of South Schroon.*

The bell remained there until the people of South Schroon gave it to the Historical Society in Schroon Lake.

HISTORY OF THE SCHROON LAKE SCHOOLS

Soon after Simeon Rawson settled in the area in 1800, a school was started about a mile north of the present village of Schroon Lake. The first teacher was Clark Rawson, son of Simeon. By 1813, Schroon Lake had seven school districts.

There was a schoolhouse south of the village at Baker Street in 1834, because the first Methodist Episcopal Church of Schroon met there that year.

A school building was built in 1866 on South Street in Schroon Lake village. It consisted of "three apartments, two school rooms and a large hall above for school uses. There are (were) two departments in the School."

(History of Essex County, Edited by H. P. Smith, 1885)

Many small schools can still be located in the Schroon and South Schroon area. One is a stucco private home located on the west side of South Schroon Road. There is an old stone wall near the road, which was the location of the old schoolhouse. This was probably the school attended by Walter Whitney. Another early school is located on the west side of Route 9 near Airport Road. This was the Lockwood School. Walter Whitney taught in the schoolhouse on Route 74 to the east of Knox Road. It is painted red and is now a private residence.

There were two Academies in Port Henry; one was run by the Sisters of St. Joseph. It started in 1891 and was called the Champlain Academy. In 1892 "the old Sherman Academy was torn down and replaced by a new one"

(History of Essex County, Edited by H. P. Smith, 1885)

Walter Whitney mentions taking exams in Port Henry, Crown Point, and Chestertown. These seem to be schools accredited to give regents' and teachers' exams.

Many Schroon Lake residents remember going to the Union Free School, which was located on the top of the hill behind Maincare. It was closed when the new school on Main Street was opened. Centralization of schools took place in the late 1920s and early 1930s. The present Schroon Lake School was built in 1938 and was one of the first WPA Projects.

1896
Walter J. S. Whitney
South Schroon
Essex Co.
N. Y.
This is my seventh diary
1896

Addresses and Memoranda
W. J. S. Whitney
South Schroon
Essex Co.
N. Y.
Timothy Hoehandle
South Schroon
N. Y.
Lizzie Day
71 Sheffield St.
Newark, N. J.

The World 53 to 63 Park
Row New York City

There is from four to six
inches of snow on the
ground now, but not
enough for sleighing. People
still continue to travel
with carriages.
It seems nearly time to
commence to use cutters
but we cannot until more
snow comes which we hope
will be very soon.
Jan. 12, 1896 5:53 p.m.

What is the sum of ten
cents and five mills?
Why a cent and a half of
course. Any fool like me
could see that.

Wednesday, January 1, 1896
21 to 23   Cld. Snow.
Went up to Grand
ma's with my
rubbers and a lot
of old shoes and
Uncle Jim
nailed my shoes
and tapped my
rubbers. Emory
Whitney and fam-
ily came up here visiting.
May and I had more fun
than a little. Deb Hall
and Uncle Henry helped
Pa cut wood down in
sugar works.
Commenced to snow about
five o'clock.
January 2
Went to school. Will and
Aunt Sophia Kettenbach
and Uncle Jim Whitney
came up here in evening.
Will and Aunt Sophia
stayed all night.
January 3
Went to school. Aunt Lib
and Co. came over.

January 4

2° to 4°   Fair

Aunt Lib, Uncle Jim,
Floyd, and the boys,
Uncle Jim, Henry and
Grand ma came down
here to dinner. Eddy,
Howard, Jimmy and I
played.
Aunt Lib and Co. went
home.

January 5

5° to 7°   Fine

Nice day but pretty cold.
Went to Sunday School
and Church. I was Sect.
and Treasurer.

January 6

Went to school.

January 7

Went to school.

January 8

Went to school.

January 9

Went to school.

January 10

Went to school.

January 11

Went up to Grand ma's.
Brought wash water.
Pa worked for Uncle Jim
and Henry. Pa and I
went to "Choir Practice."

January 12

Went to Sunday School.
Snowed some while I was
gone. Pa and Ma went

with carriage. Came back
with Uncle Henry.

January 13

Went to school. Took trial
Regents Examinations or
part of them.

January 14

Went to school. Finished
Regents Examinations.
Passed 90% in Arithmetic,
Grammar and Geography
and 94% in spelling.

January 15

Went to school.

January 16

Went to school.

January 17

Went to school.

January 18

Went up to Grand ma's.
Pa and I went down and
put sugar wood under wood
shed.
Went to Choir Practice.

January 19

Went to Sunday School.
Rode down with Uncle
Henry.

January 20

Went to school.

January 21

Went to school.

January 22

Went to school.

January 23

Went to school.
Pa took Grand ma

Whitney to Chestertown.
January 24
Went to school.
January 25
Greased harness. Went up
to Grand ma's.
Done chores. Snow balled
hen that was up in the
apple tree. Pa and I went
up to Grand ma's in
evening.
January 26
Had cold. Pa and Ma went
to Sunday School. "Chan"
and I stayed at home
alone.
January 27
Had cold so I did not go
to school. Puttered around.
Did few examples. Pa
went to village.
Uncle Henry down in
evening.
January 28
My cold about the same.
Worked examples.
January 29
My cold better. Worked
examples.
January 30
Worked examples. Pa
worked for George
Richardson. "Rich" Cole
came down here.
January 31
Worked examples. Pa went
to Chester after Grand ma.

Ma went to Mill Brook.
Grand ma and Carrie
down here.

———

Saturday, February 1, 1896
Snow
Worked examples. Deb
Hall and Uncle Henry
down here in forenoon.
February 2
Did not go to Sunday
School. Pa and Uncle
Henry went. Wrote a letter
to Ma.
February 3
Worked examples. Pa drew
wood for George
Richardson. Pa chored and
gave hens bones.
February 4
Worked examples. Read
more or less. Uncle Henry
down at noon.
February 5
Went to school.
February 6
Went to school.
February 7
Went to school. Last day.
Wind blew and snow flew
to beat the cars. Pa went to
Mill Brook after Ma.
February 8
Did chores. Uncle Henry
stayed down here last
night. Pa and Ma came

home from Mill Brook I went up to Grand ma. Pa and I drew two loads of wood from Hardhack Hill.

February 9

20°   Snow.

It has snowed every minute of the day.
Pa. and I went up to Grand ma's.

February 10

Helped plow out wood road and draw one load of wood.

February 11

Wind

Shoveled out wood road down in lot east of lane. Aft. Pa and I worked on squirrel cage Uncle Henry down in p.m.

February 12

Pa and I worked on squirrel cage in forenoon. Helped plow out wood road. Went up to Grand ma's in afternoon.

February 13

Pa and I finished squirrel cage. Helped unload wood.

February 14

Helped unload wood. Went up to Grand ma's.
Pa went to village in p.m.

February 15

Helped Pa plow out wood road as far as the sugar house. Helped unload wood.

Went over to Granger's and had Frank string up our violin.

February 16

50°

Pa, Uncle Henry and myself went to Sunday School and Church.

February 17

60°

Guess I ate too many chestnuts yesterday and got some cold too, for I have been sick to my stomach most all day and have "heaved up Jonah" three or four times. Head ached and I didn't feel very first class so laid abed all day. Pa went to Post Office and then drew wood from Hardhack Hill. Uncle Henry down.

February 18

20°

Feel some better but feel pretty weak from the result of taking four pills yesterday. Read a good deal.

February 19

Cold

Fixed our "fiddle" and "fiddled" more or less all day. Read some. Cold it's little better.

February 20

Puttered around at most

everything. My cold feeling little better.

February 21

10°   Wind

Worked examples. Played on violin. Uncle Henry came down in afternoon. He and Pa plowed out road down to So. Schroon and back.

February 22

Worked examples. Puttered around at most every thing.

February 23

Grand ma, Uncle J. H., and H. J. and Carrie came down here. Arthur F. "Babe" and George Nichols came over here. Pa not very well.

February 24

Pa feeling pretty weak or some weak any way. Puttered around at most every thing.

February 25

Pa to village all day on auditing business. Sawed wood and puttered around.

February 26

Pa went to village on town auditing business and didn't get back until seven o'clock. I sawed wood and went up to Grand ma's. Pa, Ma and I went to donation down to Emory W's in evening. Got home 1:25 a.m.

February 27

Pa started for Riverside early so I had nearly all the chores to do. Sawed wood. Went up to Grand ma's.

February 28

Helped Pa fix wood rack and skin calf. Also to load a load of straw. Aft. we went to village with load of straw and did not get back till 6:30 p.m.

February 29

                         Rain

It has rained all day. Helped move my bed up stairs. Pa fixed or I mean built a buck saw frame.

Sunday, March 1, 1896

Puddled around in the water. So much water in the road we couldn't go to Church.

March 2

Colder now so guess the thaw is over. Sawed wood. Pa went to village and got the horses shod.

March 3

                         Windy

Slid down hill. Grand

ma and Carrie down.
Pa went to town meeting.

March 4
10° to 15°   Wind
Went down in woods and
helped Pa load a load of
wood. Did chores. Fed hens
meat and bones etc. Sawed
wood. Pa and Ma went to
Taylor's to see Dr.
McAllister.

March 5
Sawed wood. Pa and I
went up and got Uncle
Henry's straw cutter. Slid
down hill.

March 6
                    Fine
Helped load wood. Sawed
wood. Uncle Henry down.

March 7
                    Snow
Sam Ingraham and
Thurm Warren came up
here and stayed to dinner.
We played dominoes.

March 8
24°   Wind
Uncle Henry and I went
to Sunday School and
Church. Pa and Ma went
with cutter.

March 9
10°
Pa, Sam Ingraham and
I cut wood down in sugar
works.

March 10
22°
Uncle Jim, Henry, Grand
ma C., Ma, Carrie and I
went to Mill Brook. Mrs.
George Huntley rode over
with us. Played with the
boys and girls and had
lots of fun. Got back about
7 p.m..

March 11
16°   Snow in p.m.
Went down and helped Pa
load wood. Puttered with
hen. Aft. "King's" daugh-
ters were up.

March 12
12°   Snowy
It snowed about 17 inches
so of course we had to dig
out.
Sawed wood in afternoon.

March 13
Pa and I plowed road in
forenoon. Ma's
glasses came
today. Aft.
Pa and I
sawed wood under shed.

March 14
Went to Grand ma's. Pa
went to Schroon with
wood for D. C. Bailey.
Sawed wood.

March 15
Pa, Ma, Grand ma W.,
Uncle Henry, Carrie and

myself went to Sunday School and Church.

March 16

Squally

Pa and I drew dry wood from back shed around under front one on hand sled. We fixed pole between horses etc. Had concert in evening here. Pa played zither and I the violin.

March 17

21°   Windy

Took two pills last night so don't feel very muscular today. Pa and I cut 3/4 cord wood in forenoon. Aft. he shoveled out skidway down in woods. Went to show down in hall in evening. Got back at 10:30 p.m.

March 18

Pa, Sam I. and myself cut wood. They cut wood in p.m. but I rested or I mean slept up for the show. Went to show in evening.

March 19

26°/31°   Snow, rain

It has snowed a foot today and turned to rain and is thawing a good deal. Puttered around at everything.

March 20

35°

Pa and I plowed roads. We went down and shoveled out skidway and cut up two logs.

March 21

35°/25°   Hzy

Pa not very well or I mean had a cold and was hoarse and did not work any. I did chores etc. Went down in wood after aro. Played dominoes.

March 22

Went to Sunday School.

March 23

Went down to P.O. and ordered lesson leaves. Pa not very well so I had to do all the chores. He felt worse toward night and evening and had Roll go and telephone for Dr. G. who came about 11 o'clock.

March 24

Pa feeling better. Dr. stayed here until most noon. Did all chores at night.

March 25

Pa better. Did all chores. "Fiddled".

March 26

Tinkered on squirrel machine. Pa put new rivet in my knife and fixed clothes bars. Did chores.

191

March 27
Did chores. Dr. came again today. Pa better.

March 28
30°/39°   Fair
Sawed little wood. Did all chores. Pa went out twice. Played on violin.

March 29
26°/30°   Rain Snow
It snowed all the forenoon and stopped about 1 p.m. so I got ready and went to Church.
George Brooks preached.

March 30
Pa and I broke road down to wood and brought up one load.

March 31
Pa and I broke out sugar roads and drew up wood from down in woods.

Wednesday, April 1, 1896
We went down to sugar house and puttered around. Aft. we tapped 90 trees.

April 2
                    Snow
Pa and I sent down to sugar house and took down wooden buckets. Aft. corded up wood and gathered 1 1/2 bbls. of sap.

April 3
24°   Wind
Helped Pa get ready to go to village. May Whitney came up here. Aft. went down and thawed out evaporator. Leslie Nichols came over.

April 4
25°   Wind
Pa and I corded up wood. We went over on George Rickert's to look at maples and went from there up on Schneider's hill. Made handles for squirrel cage.

April 5
Went to Sunday School. Went down in sugar works. Pa and Ma went to village to church evening.

April 6
Pa and I scattered buckets in a.m. and tapped trees in p.m.

April 7
We tapped trees in a.m.. and p.m. Pa gathered 8 bbls. sap while I boiled.

April 8
Boiled sap in forenoon while Pa went to Amos Ingraham's funeral. Aft. we scattered buckets.

April 9
Pa, Uncle Henry and I tapped trees in forenoon.

Got 'em all tapped. Aft.
Pa and Uncle Henry gath-
ered while I boiled.

April 10
Helped gather two bbls of
sap and boiled all the rest
of the day while Pa gath-
ered. Henry Carpenter and
Grace came over just dark.

April 11
Pa and I gathered 2 bbls
of sap while H. B. C. boiled.
I boiled while he came up
and got Grace. I boiled
all afternoon. Made 7
buckets syrup = 150 Lbs..

April 12
Fine
Went up to Grand ma's.
Henry C. and Grace went
home about 10:30. Anda
F., Grand ma and Uncle
Henry down. A lamb got
into the water tub and got
nearly drowned. Went to
Church.

April 13
76°   Warm
Pa and I gathered two
barrels sap and I went to
boiling. Boiled nearly all
day.

April 14
Went down to Stanards.
Went up to Grand ma's.
Helped put sleds up in horse
barn. Pa and I went
down to So. Schroon.

April 15
78°
Pa went to village. I
went down in sugar works
twice.

April 16
Pa gathered 12 bbls of sap
and I boiled.

April 17
67°
Pa and I went down and
finished boiling up sap
and finished up with
water. Aft. Pa and I cut
little wood down in woods
but the saw went so hard
we quit. Pa and I made
squirrel trap.

April 18
Pa and I cut wood down
in sugar works.

April 19
Went to Sunday School.
Pa, Uncle Henry, Anda
F. and I went to C. E.
meeting in evening.

April 20
Pa and I went to village.
We cut 1 1/2 cords of wood
in aft.

April 21
Pa and I worked gather-
ing buckets.

April 22
Pa and I finished up sug-
aring. We went to party

up to Jesse Cole's in evening.

April 23
Pa and I cut wood.

April 24
Pa and I cut wood.

April 25
Pa and I cut wood.

April 26
Went to Church and C.E. in evening.

April 27
Cut wood.

April 28
Cut wood.

April 29
Cut wood.

April 30
Pa, Uncle Henry and I cut wood.

Friday, May 1, 1896
Pa and I fixed fence in forenoon. Aft. he went to village.

May 2
Pa and I went over and put up the line fence between us and John Wood. Aft. we drew

manure on the garden and plowed it.

May 3
Pa, Ma, Grand ma W., Mrs. E. Tripp, Uncle Henry and I went to Church. Elder Torins Slit preached.

May 4
We drew stones some. Helped plant few potatoes.

May 5
Pa and I drew manure. I worked in garden some in p.m. Pa and I drew few stone.

May 6
Pa and I drew stone off last year's potato piece. Pa went down to Emory Whitney's. Pa went to village in p.m.

May 7
Pa and I went up to Emory Richardson's with cow but failed up there and went to Fred Ford's and left her until noon. We tinkered farrow and after dinner we took Ma down to K.D. meeting and got cow. Dragged in oats.

May 8
Pa and I drew manure a.m. Aft. I dragged while Pa sowed oats, fertilizer and grass seed.

May 9
Dragged in oats. Drew stone.

May 10
Went to S. S. and Church.

May 11
Sowed garden. Called down sheep. Fixed sweet peas. Tied up wool. Pa and I went up and got Gerta Cornell's organ.

May 12
Helped women and did lots of things.

May 13
Puttered in garden. Aft. we planted 10 rows taters.

May 14
Planted taters. Drew manure.

May 15
Planted taters.

May 16
Cut pea brush. Helped plant sweet corn.
May came up and gave me a music lesson.

May 17
Went to Church.

May 18
Cleaned off hen roost. Planted few taters.

May 19
Dug stones out of barnyard. Drew manure.

May 20
Drew manure.

May 21
Followed around after plow. Aft. went down and took music lesson.

May 22
Dragged corn ground and helped plant corn.

May 23
Planted corn.

May 24
Went to Church. Pa went to Schroon with Mrs. Tripp.

May 25
Went to school.

May 26
Went to school.

May 27
Helped plant corn. Went to school. Went to speech in evening.

May 28
Went to school.

May 29
Went to school.

May 30
Pa and I went to Fred Ford's with cow. We planted fodder corn.

May 31
Went to Sunday School and "Swamp Angel Church."

Monday, June 1, 1896
Went to school.

June 2
Went to school.

June 3
Went to school.
June 4
Went to school.
June 5
Was about half sick. Layed on lounge good deal. Pa and Ma went to village. Bees swarmed.
June 6
Cold better today. Did not do much only play on organ.
June 7
My cold little better. Went up to Grand ma. We did not go to Church. Pa doctored Spot.
June 8
Hung around home. Cold little better. Painted wagon.
June 9
Ditto.
June 10
Painted wagon. Got ready and went to Chester to Will K's wedding.
June 11
Hung around Chester until 3 p.m. and came home.
June 12
Went to school.
June 13
Pa and I worked in garden.
June 14
Went to church.

June 15
Went to school.
June 16
Went to Schroon and took examination in Arithmetic and Geography today. Ma went down to Uncle Jim W's. I stayed all night there.
June 17
Went up and took exam in grammar and spelling. Came back to headquarters at 2 or 3 p.m.
June 18
Took ex. in History in forenoon, and nothing in afternoon. Came down to Watson's and stayed to supper.
June 19
Took ex. in Physiology. Looked at Drawing but did not take it.
June 20
We started to hoe corn but got sick of old cultivator and made a new one. Cultivated garden taters, sweet corn and few rows of field corn.
June 21
Went to Sunday School and Church.
June 22
Went to school.
June 23
Went to school.

June 24

Went to school. Hoed two rows of corn this morning.

June 25

Went to school. Came home around the road.
Mrs. E. Whitney up here this afternoon.

June 26

Went to school.

June 27

Went up to Grand ma's after garden rake. Hoed garden etc., churned etc. Aft. went strawberrying.

June 28

Went to Church.

June 29

Went to school.

June 30

Went to school.

Wednesday, July 1, 1896

To school I went.

July 2

Went to school. Brought my books home.

July 3

Hoed corn. Picked up after mower. Helped put up hay.

July 4

Pa, Chas. Stanard and I fixed fence. Pa and I went to Schroon aft.

July 5

Went to church.

July 6

Hoed garden.

July 7

Puttered around home a. m. p. m. went down to talk by Miss Church. Picked up after mower.

July 8

Mowed little. Aunt Lucy and Howard came over.

July 9

We mowed below lower barn and got up small road.

July 10

Pa and I mowed forenoon. Aft. got up hay. Howard and Aunt Lucy went home.

July 11

Went and picked few berries. Aft. got up hay.

July 12

Went to Church.

July 13

Uncle Henry and I bugged tatoes.

July 14

Painted tater bugs. May W. up here.

July 15

Played on organ. Picked raspberries. Pa worked for O'Neal.

July 16

Puttered around in

forenoon. Aft. helped get in hay up to Grand ma's. Pa mowed for C. F. Taylor & Son.

July 17
Picked a few peas and just a few berries.
Hoed garden. Went up to Grand ma's to see if they wanted me to help them.
Pa worked for O'Neal.
Went to Taylor's with Pa in evening.
Will Traver killed chipmunk.

July 18
Went down with Pa and took music lesson.
Paris greened taters by hog pen. Aft. went up and helped Uncle J. H. and H. J. get in hay.
Pa worked for O'Neal.

July 19
Went to Church.

July 20
Rained all day. Fooled around home.

July 21
Pa worked for Taylor. Mowed behind house.

July 22
Pa worked at Taylor's.

July 23
Hayed it.

July 24
Cloudy

Did not do much of anything only hoed garden little.

July 25
Picked up after mowing machine. Pa helped get in hay.

July 26
Fussed with chickens.

July 27
Went fishing.

July 28
Pa worked for Uncle J. & H. I stayed around him.

July 29
Hayed it.

July 30
Hayed it.

July 31
Hayed it.

Saturday, August 1, 1896
Bugged taters and got in hay.

August 2
Went to Church.

August 3
Puttered around at everything.

August 4
Hayed it west of taters and oats.

August 5
Mowed orchard.

August 6
Worked at hay in orchard

but it rained and stopped us.

August 7
Got in hay.

August 8
Pa and I cut little orchard.

August 9
Went to Sunday School and Baptist preach.

August 10
Fair

Pa and I mowed oats. Got nearly tired out.

August 11
Cold rain

Got in oats.

August 12
Mowed and got in oats.

August 13
Went with milk and got in oats.

August 14
Went with milk. Raked oat ground over with horse rake. Picked berries.

August 15
Got in oats.

August 16
Went to S. School.

August 17
Puttered around. Went and picked few berries.

August 18
Did chores. Pa went to Pyramid Lake with city folks. Picked berrys.

August 19
Went blackberrying twice.

August 20
Ma went down to Stanard's with Pa and he went to I's and up to Pasco's. I went berrying over to fallow in forenoon, aft. pulled weeds in garden.

August 21
Took Ma down to Fred Ford's and came back with milk horse wagon while Pa and Ma went to village. Puttered around and stayed with Grand ma.

August 22
Pa went to Riverside for Taylor & Son. I milked and went to Taylor's. Went up to Grand ma's. Picked few blackberrys. Dug potatoes for minister. Milked again.

August 23
Went to Sunday School and Baptist meeting. Aunt Lib and her boys came over.

August 24
Pa went to Riverside for Taylor. I puttered around home and played with boys.

August 25

Played with Aunt Lib's boys. Aunt Sophia here.

August 26

Played with the boys. Aunt Lib and Co. went home.

August 27

Pa went to Chester with Aunt Sophia. I stayed around "hum."

August 28

Got up early and milked and got team ready to go to Riverside. Pa sick and sent after Dr.

August 29

Did all of chores as Pa was sick but better than he was yesterday.

August 30

Went to Church. Telephoned for the Dr. not to come and afternoon told him to come.

August 31

Got up at 4 a.m. and got team and milk ready and took them down to Chas. Warren who drove them to Riverside.

———

Tuesday, September 1, 1896

Got team and milk ready and took 'em.

September 2

Went with milk and up to Pasco's and got sack of middlings.

September 3

Went to Taylor's and then to Pottersville and got medicine for Pa.

September 4

Pa feeling better. I helped do chores, got milk ready etc. etc. etc. etc.

September 5

Picked up apples. Went down to Church meeting in afternoon.

September 6

Pa did not go to Church or do much of anything. Ma and I went to Mrs. Sherman's funeral.

September 7

Pa and I cut corn.

September 8

Went to school.

September 9

Went to school.

September 10

Went to school.

September 11

Went to school.

September 12

Hot rain.

Picked up apples and chored it around generally. Pa went to Riverside.

September 13

Went to Church.

September 14
Went to school.
September 15
Went to school..
September 16
Went to school.
September 17
Went to school.
September 18
Went to school.
September 19
Rained all day. I made
out tax. Pa and I made a
scrap book.
September 20
Went to Sunday School
and Baptist meeting.
September 21
Stayed at home and helped
draw in corn.
Pulled beans and bound
up sweet corn.
September 22
Went to school.
September 23
Went to school.
September 24
Pa and I went to fair.
September 25
Pa and I drew in corn.
Dolph Whitney and wife
came home from fair and
stayed here all night.
September 26
Visited with Dolph's folks
some. Husked corn.
Went up and helped Uncle

J. H. and H. J. get in nig-
ger wheat. Went down to
political meeting.
September 27
Uncle Henry and I went
to Church afoot.
September 28
Went to school.
September 29
Went to school.
September 30
Went to school. Miss
Brown came up and will
stay all night.

Thursday, October 1, 1896
Went to school.
October 2
Went to school.
October 3
Pa got cold so I did all the
chores. Uncle Henry and
I went down to Taylor's
after pigs.
Went up to Fred Squire's.
May Whitney came up in
p.m. Went to speech down
at hall.
October 4
Had cold so I did not go
to Church. Pa's cold better.
Grand ma down. Uncle
Henry went to Church.
October 5
My cold a little better.
Didn't do much of any-

thing. Pa started to dig taters but had asthma and couldn't.

October 6
Cold about the same. Did not do much.

October 7
Rained all night. Pa went to village. I stayed at home.

October 8
Snow
Pa helped do chores this morning but his chest was lame. Stayed at home.

October 9
Stayed at home. Pa's side awful lame.

October 10
Went over to Granger's to see about fence.
Pa and I went to speech in evening.

October 11
Stayed at home. Pa and Ma went up to Charley Hill to meeting. Mrs. Church stopped here.

October 12
Husked corn.

October 13
Gathered apples.

October 14
Gathered apples.

October 15
Finished husking corn. Gathered apples.

October 16
We finished gathering apples and then dug taters.

October 17
I dug taters in forenoon while Pa fixed fence. Then we both dug.

October 18
Rain
Stayed at home. Rained so we did not go to Sunday School.

October 19
Dug taters awhile then went to Mrs. Burbank's funeral.

October 20
Went to school.

October 21
Went to school.

October 22
Went to school.

October 23
Went to school.

October 24
Ma and I went to Mill Brook.

October 25
Went to Church at Mill Brook. Came home in afternoon. "Stub" came over as far as Taylor's with me.

October 26
Went to school.

October 27
Went to school.

October 28

I attended the great acadamy at South Schroon today I did.

October 29

Went to school.

October 30

Attended school.

October 31

Attended to pick up stone all day. Pa and myself.

Sunday, November 1, 1896

Went to Sunday School and Baptist meeting.

November 2

Went to school.

November 3

Went to elections.

November 4

Went to school.

November 5

Attended school.

November 6

Attended school.

November 7

Banked up the house. Mabel Whitney and her mother were up here. Pa and I went to Schroon to Rep. parade and Prof. Wiseman's show.

November 8

Rainy day. Pa and Ma went to Church but I stayed at home.

November 9

Went to school.

November 10

Went to school.

November 11

Went to school.

November 12

Went to school.

November 13

Went to school.

November 14

Pa and I put apples in cellar and went down and got load of saw dust.

November 15

Went to Church.

November 16

Went to school.

November 17

To school I went.

November 18

Went to school.

November 19

Went to school.

November 20

Went to school. Uncle Henry came home from Mill Brook and Nora came home with him.

November 21

Pa and I went down to saw mill and got a load of saw dust. Snowed $4^{1}/2$ inches.

November 22

Went to Sunday School and Church.

November 23
Went to school.
November 24
Went to school and to
donation down to Jacob
Hall's in evening. Got to
bed about 3 a.m.
November 25
Went to school when I got
up.
November 26
Helped shell corn. Grand
ma C. Louis R. and Oscar
R. were here to dinner. We
visited and sang and had
a lot of fun.
November 27
Put up corn to take to
mill. Aft. Pa, Ma, Nora
and I went to the village.
Got me a new suit of
clothes, a pair of rubbers, a
pair of leggins, a cap and
a collar.
November 28
Pa and I cut wood over
on hardhack hill when we
didn't go hunting and
trapping.
November 29
Pa, Ma, Grand ma, Nora
and I went to Sunday
School.
I wore my new suit of
clothes. Will Taylor came
up in the evening to see
Nora.

November 30
Took Nora down to Emory
W's and hitched horse and
went to school. Came home
with horse at night. Nora
went home with Harry
Floyd.

———

Tuesday, December 1, 1896
31°
Went to school.
December 2
Went to school.
December 3
Went to school. Mabel
Whitney came home with
me.
December 4
Went to school.
December 5
Pa cut wood over on hard-
hack hill in forenoon.
Aft. we ground my "new
made over from an old
one" ax.
December 6
Went to Church.
We voted to change lesson
leaves i.e. from Pelonbet's
to Cooke.
December 7
Went to school.
December 8
Went to school.
December 9
Attended school.

December 10
Attended school.
December 11
Went to school.
December 12
Pa went to Pottersville. I
stayed around home. After
Pa got back, he made me a
drawing board while I
fixed meat.
December 13
Went to Sunday School
and Baptists preach.
December 14
Went to school.
December 15
Went to school.
December 16
Went to school.
December 17
Went to school.
December 18
Went to school.
December 19
Cold
Puttered around in the
forenoon. Aft. went over
and "Dick" and we went
to the fallow and got what
sheep we found.
December 20
Went to Sunday School.
Mrs. Susan Squires and
Mr. Flavor Barney were
buried today.
December 21
Went to school.

December 22
Went to school.
December 23
Went to school. School
closed until after New
Year's. Brought home some
of my books.
December 24
Went up to Grand ma's.
Went up to Uncle Jim
Whitney's and went up to
Christmas tree in evening.
Got back 10:30 p.m.
December 25
Pa went to village so I
rode up with him.
He stopped to the
church and I
came home. I
fixed apples to
put on the tree. Went to
Xmas tree in evening. Got
a diary and a "Columbian
Atlas of the World."
December 26
I got a cold yesterday so
I didn't feel very good.
Read some. Doctored up all
over and went to bed.
December 27
My cold a little better
today. Dolph U. and wife
stopped here a little while.
Thurm Warr stopped here
few minutes. Pa and Ma
went to Church. Stayed in
house.

December 28

My cold better. Walter "Fud" came here this forenoon. Also Emory Whitney. Toward night, Aunt Sophia, Will Kettenback and his wife came here. Stayed in house.

December 29

Visitors went away toward noon. Pa ceiled up little, and I painted little, played a good deal, studied some and ate some. Went outdoors.

December 30

Studied quite a lot. Played on organ some. Wrote composition some. Read a little. Pa went to Pottersville. Ma went down to L. Richardson's. I went outdoors some.

December 31

Studied quite a lot. Played on organ. Went to Grand Ma's. Did quite a few chores, but my throat feels mean to be out in the cold air. Pa and Ma went down to the "social" at Len Murdock's. Uncle Henry down here in evening. This is the page called "finis."

Memorandum
Will K. let me take his violin to try Jan. 31 but we did not get it strung up until Feb. 11. Sent it home Dec. 13, 1896.

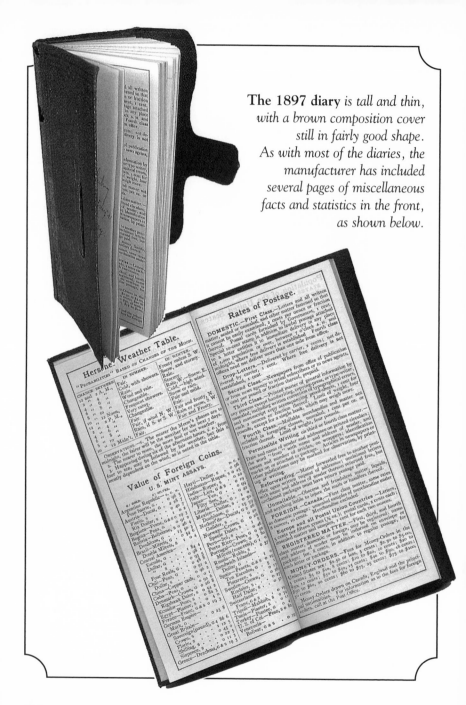

The 1897 diary *is tall and thin, with a brown composition cover still in fairly good shape. As with most of the diaries, the manufacturer has included several pages of miscellaneous facts and statistics in the front, as shown below.*

Taylor's Hotel at Schroon Lake

1897 was the Diamond Jubilee year of England's Queen Victoria. She had been queen for sixty years and would remain so until her death January 22, 1901. Her name was attributed to everything from architecture to interior décor to Christmas decorations. She ruled for so long that most of the 19th century is considered the Victorian Era, and the world still feels the effects of her reign. A great reception was held in her honor on July 5, 1897, given by the Corporation of the City of London and held in the Guildhall, the place for civic gatherings.

This may seem a stretch from the world of Walter Whitney and his family in South Schroon, but it is another parallel; and there is a correlation. The Guildhall in London was the counterpart to South Schroon's Town Hall, the place for civic gatherings. We can only imagine the pomp and circumstance associated with Queen Victoria's Jubilee, but we have a first-hand description of South Schroon's festivities. Virginia Fish, a lifetime resident of South Schroon, gives this account:

South Schroon Town Hall

The hall was on what is now Dykeman Road. It was a large, white building: one big room, a clothes room and a big kitchen. There

was a basement with a wood furnace.

In the summer the women of the South Schroon church put on suppers there. During the winter, the women met at the different homes one day every week or two. They made "fancy goods," embroidered pillow cases, dollies, etc. At the suppers, booths were set up in two corners. One to sell the "fancy goods." In the other corner was a booth with baked goods.

At these suppers, homemade ice cream was served.

In the winter, the neighbors would have card parties and dances at the hall.

Cecil Butler played the fiddle and called the sets. Edith Kipp played the piano, and her husband Vernon played the drums.

The land was owned by Charlie Traver, and after the hall was torn down in the late 1940s or 1950s the land went back to the Traver family.

TAYLOR'S HOTEL

Taylor's was a popular summer resort located near the Whitney farm on a point in Schroon Lake (on the site later to be known as Scaroon Manor.) It was founded in 1879, seven years after completion of the

Adirondack Railroad allowed tourists to visit the Schroon region. The land on what was to be called Taylor's Point had been cleared, and a prosperous farm existed there. C. F. Taylor and Sarah Noble Taylor ran both the farm and the hotel and provided fresh meats and vegetables for their guests.

The hotel had a dock at which the steamers Effingham and Evelyn made regular stops. Guests from New York City and other urban centers

kept the hotel full, often booking rooms for the entire summer. The guests played croquet and tennis and went hiking, fishing, and boating.

One guest, Henry Parsell, was an inventor who had worked with Thomas Edison. He set up an electrical generating plant at Taylor's in 1891 and produced enough electricity to light the grounds and some of the buildings. Parsell also helped the people of South Schroon build their church in 1894 and funded its plate-glass windows and large cast-brass bell.

Many South Schroon people, including Walter and his father, performed various tasks at Taylor's. The "Stub" Walter mentions at various points may have been Stub Taylor (C. F. Taylor, Jr.), the eldest son, who ran the hotel in later years. The hotel continued until the early 1920s and reopened with many of the same buildings in 1924 as the soon-to-be famous Scaroon Manor.

1897

Walter J. S. Whitney's
Eighth Diary
1897
Addresses and Memoranda
W. E. Whitney,
M. D. B.S.S
Marshaltown, Iowa

Asher Day
68 Warren St.
Newark, N.J.

Friday, January 1, 1897
Fair
Studied quite a lot. My
throat doesn't feel very
good when I am out in
the cold air.
Grandma and Uncle
Henry down today. Pa
went to village. Lute
Fairfield was here in
evening.

January 2
36°   Fine
Studied some. Mabel
Whitney came up here. We
fooled and had lots of fun.
I ruled Sunday School
book.
Pa and Uncle Henry cut
wood out on hard hack
hill.

January 3.
32°   Fair S. S. registered
                              98°.
Went to Sunday School
and Church. Had new
superintendent Mr. Oren
Murdock. Mr. and Mrs.
John Youngs were both
buried today. Aunt Lib
and the boys came over.
Grandma C. came down.

January 4
40°   Cld.
Went up and took up fox
trap. Played with the boys.
My throat quite sore and
am beginning to cough
some. Uncle Jim killed
their dog.
Aunt Lib and Co. went up
to Grandma's. Pa skidded
wood.

January 5
33°   Rainy
Did chores. Studied.
Played on organ. Eddy
and Howard came down
in afternoon. We played
dominoes etc. Awful
muddy around out of
doors.

January 6
Studied some. Eddy and
Howard came down from
Grandma's. By and by

Aunt Lib and Grandma did. Played on organ and with the boys. Pa skidded wood in a.m..

January 7
Aunt Lib and Co. started home about 1 p.m.. I helped them get ready. Studied some in afternoon. Pa and Uncle Henry cut cedar down by J.J. Wood's.

January 8
Fine.

Studied quite a lot. Fussed with the squirrel. Played on organ. Pa and Uncle Henry cut cedar down by John Wood's. They have got 96 pieces cut.

January 9
25°   XXtra

Studied quite a lot. Did chores. Pa and Uncle Henry and Frank Granger skidded cedar.

January 10
Went to Sunday School and Church. Sunday School thermometer registered about 95°.

January 11
Cold.

Went to school. Thurm Warren came today and we were together in Physics. Pa went to Schroon. He got me a new slate pencil and begged a ruler.

January 12
4°   Clr.

Went to school. Got a little cold yesterday or this morning and the wind blew awfully and and it was awful cold coming home and I got more cold and I got more sick.

January 13
Didn't feel very first class all day for I laid about all day. Pa telephoned for Dr. Jim G. and he came about 4 p.m.. Was sick, sick, sick to my stummick and sore and tight on me lungs.

January 14
Felt better today. Coughed hard all forenoon. So that Pa went and got me some cof med. Emory Whitney came up here in afternoon and stayed a while.

January 15
20°   Cold.

I feel quite a lot better today. So I walked around quite a lot. Pa and Uncle Henry skidded logs down by John Wood's. Uncle Jim and Grandma came down.

January 16

15°   Cld

Studied some. Felt quite a
lot better today.
Pa cut logs and kindling
wood. Mary Whitney
came up here in afternoon.

January 17

32°   Snow little

Did not do much of any-
thing. Pa went down to
church. Uncle Henry and
Grandma C, down. Uncle
Jim came down after her.
Played on organ etc.

January 18

15°   Fair

Studied and finished writing composition. Went out
to barn twice. Uncle
Henry came down little-
while in afternoon. Pa cut
cedar over in swamp.
Played on organ.

January 19

14°   Cold Fair

Studied some. Drew pic-
tures. Uncle Henry down
nearly all day. Did not
go out at all for it was so
cold. Played on organ. Pa
puttered around home all
day.

January 20

20°   Cold, Snow

Played on organ. Studied
some. Pa and Uncle Henry
cut cedar. Went out to
barn and did a few chores.
Commenced to snow lit-
tle in evening.

January 21

                                    Snow

Studied. Shoveled roads.
Did chores. Pa went to
village.

January 22

Studied. Did chores.
Shoveled path. Pa and
Uncle Henry skidded logs.

January 23

                                    Cold

Did chores. Studied. Made
Ma a thing to make pies
with. Shoveled roads
around. Pa and Uncle
Henry skidded logs.

January 24

0°   Fair

Went to Sunday School
and Church. Wore Pa's fur
coat. Pretty cold day.

January 25

6°to 18°   Windy

Went to school. Pa carried
me down in morning.
Came afoot to Geo.
Richardson's and rode
from there home with Jen
Cole.

January 26

18° to 20°   Blizzard

It was so cold and the
wind blew so bad that I

did not go to school.
Studied Arithmetic.
Played on organ. Wind
blew to beat the curs all
day.

January 27
Went to school. Rode down
to the church with Pa.
Rode home from the corner
with Uncle Jim and
Henry.
Got a letter, some badges
and some papers from
Asher Day.

January 28
Snow
Went to school. Snowed
all day. Pa came after me
at night.

January 29
Blowy
It was so blowy that I
did not go to school.
Worked examples.

January 30
Experimented with tele-
phone.

January 31
Went to Church.

Monday, February 1, 1897
Went to school.

February 2
Went to school.

February 3
Went to school.

February 4
Went to school.

February 5
Went to school.

February 6
Fixed a telephone from
house to shop.
Went down with Pa when
he was drawing logs.
Grandma, Uncle J. H.,
H. J., and Louis R. were
down here.

February 7
Rainy
We all stayed at home all
day. It rained all day.

February 8
Went to school.

February 9
Went to school.

February 10
Went to school.

February 11
Went to school.

February 12
Holiday
Puttered with telephone.

February 13
Went with Pa after logs
so to help him load them.

February 14
Pa, Ma and I went to
Mill Brook.

February 15
Went to school.

February 16
Went to school.

215

February 17
Attended school.
February 18
Went to school.
February 19
Went to school. School out.
February 20
Pa and I went down in farther swamp and cut some timber for sled beams etc. Lew Richardson and wife were up here in afternoon. They had choir practice here.
February 21
Went to Sunday School and Church. Pa and Ma went to church again in evening.
February 22
Pa and I cut a big pine that stood way up above the meadow and took it to the saw mill.
February 23
Puttered with telephone from house to barn. Pa went to Schroon on Town Auditor business.

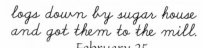

February 24
Pa and I cut a few logs down by sugar house and got them to the mill.
February 25
Pa and I drew wood from hard hack hill.
February 26
Pa went up by Tom Cole's and shoveled snow a little while and then we drew wood.
February 27
Drew wood Pa and I.
February 28
Ma and I went to church with Posy. Pa and Uncle Henry went afoot.

Monday, March 1, 1897
We drew wood from Hardhack Hill.
March 2
Went to Town meeting. We brought home a load of lumber.
March 3
                              Rain
Turned grind-stone for Uncle Henry to grind Pa's ax. Rainy day. Ma about sick.
March 4
Helped draw wood. We cut little wood in afternoon.
March 5
Pa and I drew two loads of wood. Finished it up.

Aft. we went over and cut down sled crook but it was'nt any good.

March 6

Fair

Puttered with hens and fooled around. Pa went to Schroon.

March 7

Aunt Lib and her boys came over. We boys slid down hill if it was Sunday. Pa went to church. Ma not very well.

March 8

Pa and I cut wood some. Emory Whitney up here little while.

March 9

We cut wood all the forenoon and part of the afternoon or until it commenced to rain.

March 10

Split wood. Cut wood. Made cow pen. Thurm Warren came up here.

March 11

Pa and I cut wood all day. Emory W. and Mabel came up. He helped us cut wood.

March 12

Pa and I cut wood in afternoon. He made an ax helve in forenoon.

March 13

Pa, Emory and I cut wood all day.

March 14

Snow

It has snowed all day. We stayed at home.

March 15

Shoveled snow. Pa and I skinned calf. Cut wood in p.m.

March 16

Sawed wood. Went up street and helped shovel out road. Pa worked for E. Whitney.

March 17

Pa, Emory and I cut wood. I went up and helped shovel out road.

March 18

Split wood. Pa and Grandma went to Elijah Hall's funeral.

March 19

Pa, Emory and I cut wood when we was not off around the neighbors. Aft we went down and helped put tablets in the church.

March 20

Pa and I went down and looked at buckets. Aft he went down to So. Schroon.

March 21

Pa, Ma and I went up to

Uncle Henry's. Went to church.

March 22
Pa and I went down and steamed our buckets and drew sugar wood. Aft we scattered buckets.

March 23
Pa, Frank and Arthur G. and I worked at scattering buckets and tabbing trees. Got nearly done. Made a mistake and wrote this again over on April 19.
ED.

March 24
Pa and I sawed wood until it commenced to snow. I went up to Uncle Henry's in afternoon.

March 25
Went over to fallow and emptied snow out of buckets. Came up and sawed wood little while. Went down in sugar works after dinner and found lots of sap. Gathered 8 bbls.

March 26
We got things ready to boil sap. Boiled an hour before dinner and all afternoon. Pa gathered 8 bbls.

March 27
Sugared all day. Frank G, Helped us in afternoon. I boiled all day. Pa taken sick.

March 28
Pa felt better in forenoon. I went down to Frank Hall's and had him telephone for Dr.

March 29
Frank and I sugared hard all day. Pa felt better.

March 30
F. and I sugared all day. Pa boiled some.

March 31
Frank and I sugared all day. Henry Carpenter came over and boiled some in p.m.

Thursday, April 1, 1897
We all worked at sugaring nearly all day.

April 2
H. B. C., Frank and myself worked at wood all day.

April 3
Henry, Frank and I cut wood in forenoon. Aft Frank and I gathered sap while Henry boiled.

April 4
Went to Sunday School and B. Church.

April 5

Frank and I worked in sugar works all day. Had shower just night.

April 6

Worked at sugaring nearly all day. Cut little sugar wood.

April 7

Cut little wood. Helped stir sugar and ate some while I was stirring it. Went up to Grandma's and got large steel yards. Weighed our sugar. Had about 1200 Lbs..

April 8

Cld.

Pa and I got ready and went to village. We carried up some sugar.

April 9

30°   Snow

Did chores. Brought water to wash. It has snowed hard all day.

April 10

Went up to Grandma's. Fixed can into a bucket. Aft Frank and I went and emptied snow and water out of buckets. Cut wood after we got back.

April 11

Stayed around home all day. Pa and Ma went to church.

April 12

Pa and I went to Schroon. Aft we drew some sugar wood.

April 13

Pa, Frank and I worked sugaring all day. Frank and I gathered 18 bbls. of sap.

April 14

Pa, Frank and I worked at sugaring part of a.m. Frank and I cut wood and Pa finished boiling sap.

April 15

Rain

Frank and I cut wood little while in morning but it rained so we stopped. Ma sick. Dr. G. came up to see her.

April 16

Pa, Frank and I cut wood. I went up to Uncle Jim's a little while after dinner to see them saw wood with wood mill. Have got a little cold.

April 17

My cold feels worse today. Played on organ. Read a good deal. Wrote some and blew my nose a good deal. Went outdoors once.

April 18

52°   Fine

I felt some better today but not well enough to attend church. Grandma and Uncle Henry came down. Pa went to church. I went outdoors some.

April 19
Pa and I boiled down what sap there was in evaporator. It rained in afternoon.

April 20
10° to 18°
Did chores. Pa sick. I felt worse toward night.

April 21
I felt better today. Stayed around the house.

April 22
22°   Fair
Played on organ. Read some. Played dominoes. Did not go out of the house. Henry Carpenter came over.

April 23
Fair
Andy and Howard Floyd came over.

April 24
Went down to sugar house. Boiled some. Pa and Frank gathered sap.

April 25
Stayed at home. Uncle Jim Whitney came up here in p. m.

April 26
Pa, Frank and I finished sugaring.

April 27
It has been so cold today that Pa and I have not dared to work in the wind.

April 28
Split wood. Helped load the organ which Pa took home. Pa went to Schroon and got new stove.

April 29
Pa and I went to the village. After we worked on garden.

April 30
We sowed oats on piece by hog pen. Went to Grangers and got fanning mill. Mrs. Maxim burned today so she died.

Saturday, May 1, 1897
Worked on garden. Drew manure.

May 2
It look like rain so we got scared out of going to church. Pa went over to Maxims.

May 3
Pa and I went to village and to Mrs. Maxim's funeral. Set up stove.

May 4
Drew manure. Sowed oats.

May 5
Drew stones and manure.
May 6
Drew manure and dragged in oats.
May 7
Planted taters some.
May 8
Pa and I sawed kindling wood. Went to the lake fishing.
May 9
Went to S. S. and Church, Rev. J. S. Hunt preached.
May 10
Planted taters.
May 11
Planted potatoes, sweet corn and beans.
May 12

Rain

Did not do much only go down in brook and get 3 little trout.

May 13

Rain

Did not do much of anything.
May 14
Pa and I went to Schroon.
May 15
Pa and I drew stone and

dug stone off corn ground.
May 16
Went to S. S. and Church.
May 17
We drew stone and manure.
May 18
We drew manure.
May 19
Drew manure. Pa went to Pottersville in forenoon.
May 20
Drew manure. Picked up grubs.
May 21
Worked in garden. Pa went to Schroon.
May 22
Dragged corn ground.
May 23
Went to Church.
May 24
Pa and I planted corn for E. Whitney.
May 25

Rain

Pa and I went to Thurman pond fishing.
May 26
Planted corn.
May 27
Planted corn.
May 28
Pa and I finished planting corn.
May 29

Rain a. m.

Pa and I fixed fence in p. m.

May 30
Went to Church.
May 31

Fair

Dragged sweet corn piece and garden. Aft Pa and I went to Memorial services.

Tuesday, June 1, 1897
Planted corn for Uncles J. H. and H. J.
June 2
Pa and I hoed garden. We watched them throw out rocks with dynamite.
June 3
Worked some in garden. Helped clean out hog shop.
June 4
Worked on road. Worked in garden.
June 5
Puttered in garden. Dragged fodder corn piece. Uncle Bish and Aunt Lucy came over.
June 6
Went to Sunday School once and meeting twice.
June 7
Pa and I got the fodder ground ready and planted part of it. An organ agent was here.
Miss Eugenia Smith was buried today.

June 8
Hoed potatoes some.
June 9

Rain

Did not do much of anything. It has rained all day.
June 10
It has rained all the forenoon. Did nothing much.

June 11
Pa put moulding on doors etc. I helped him some.
June 12
Puttered around. Pa went to saw mill and got some lumber planed. Played with Eddy and Howard.
June 13
Played and fooled around with E. and H. Pa went to S. S.
June 14
Did not feel very good. Eddy and Howard were here.
Pa began tearing up old stoop floor.
June 15
Helped Pa fix stoop. He went to saw mill and got some lumber.
June 16
Eddy and I chased horses quite a while in morning. Worked in garden. Aunt Lib and Co. went home.

June 17

Helped fix new floor in piazza.

June 18

Set some crow traps. Aft we went to fallow and hunted for sheep. Caught a crow in afternoon. Went to school entertainment.

June 19

Cultivated and hoed taters some.

June 20

Went to Sunday School & Church. Rev. Noble of Ti preached.

June 21

We hoed taters some in afternoon. Pa went down to Taylors.

June 22

Pa and I hoed potatoes in forenoon. Aft. Pa and Ma went to Schroon.

June 23

Uncle Jim and I went to Mill Brook. Pa went to Pottersville.

June 24

Uncle Bish, Uncle Jim C., Eddy, Floyd and I went up to Gregoryville. Aft. we came home.

June 25

Pa and I painted woodwork. Hoed some below barn and cultivated part of corn and hoed two rows.

June 26

Pa and I hoed corn. May Whitney was up here.

June 27

Went to Sunday School and Baptist Church. Pa came home after Sunday School to watch the bees.

June 28

We finished hoeing corn and hoed some in garden. Pa went down to Taylors.

June 29

We cultivated taters in afternoon until Emory Whitney came up here to have Pa make a bee hive. I plastered some in house.

June 30

I dug phone pole holes. Aft. Pa and I cut brush and dug few holes.

Thursday, July 1, 1897

Pa and I went down to Taylors and commenced to cut hay.

July 2

We worked at Taylors. Charley Stanard helped us.

July 3

Pa and I worked down at Taylors.

July 4

Went to Sunday School and Church.

July 5

Went to Schroon. There was a big crowd there but not much to see. Arthur Floyd was over here and went home on the boat.

July 6

Pa and I went to John Fey's. Hoed taters.

July 7

We dug phone pole holes and cut brush and cultivated taters and went to strawberry festival.

July 8

Hoed bugs and painted potatoes.

July 9

We cut telephone poles and scattered them beside the road.

July 10

Pa, Jesse Cole and I set telephone poles. Hoed in garden some.

July 11

Went to Sunday School and Baptists meeting.

July 12

Pa, Jesse and I hoed corn in a.m. In p.m., Jesse and I went to Mash Pond and got 3 pickerel and some bullheads.

July 13

Went to Grangers and got old shingles. Aft. Jesse and I patched barn roof.

July 14

Rain.

Whitewashed hen stable. Pa made a screen door.

July 15

We mowed in a.m., hoed corn in the p.m. and mowed again after sup.

July 16

Pa, Jess and I hayed it all day.

July 17

Mowed lot south of muck bed. We got in three loads of hay in the afternoon.

July 18

Pa, Ma, Grandma and I went to S. S. and Church.

July 19

Pa trimmed brush away from phone wire in forenoon, Jess and I cut meadow above muck bed. Aft. Pa and Jess went to Chester.

July 20

Helped fix mower in forenoon. Aft. we got in a load and jag of hay. Had hard shower. Lightning struck a phone pole down below brook.

July 21

Worked in garden. Stirred out hay. Aft. we got in 2 loads.

July 22

We moved our haying apparatus down to Taylors in the rain. Came back home.

July 23

Hayed it at Taylor's.

July 24

Rainy

Pa and I fixed telephone to barn.
Went up to Culvers in afternoon.

July 25

Fair

Went to Sunday School and Baptist meeting. Rev. Pettibone preached.
I had a time vomiting after I got home.

July 26

Puttered around home. Pa went down to the church.

July 27

Hoed it for Taylor's or at Taylor's for Whitney.

July 28

Rain

Stayed at home. Rain Rain!

July 29

We tore up old floor in hog shop and put down a new one.

July 30

Pa and I worked at Taylor's.

July 31

Worked at Taylor's.

Sunday, August 1, 1897

Went to Sunday School and Church.

August 2

Worked at Taylor's.

August 3

Pa, Jess and I hayed it at Taylor's.
Our telephone was put in today.

August 4

Jess and I worked at Taylor's. Pa went to Schroon and it rained up there and he thought it did down here, so he did not come down.
It didn't rain here and we looked our eyes for him.

August 5

Worked at Taylor's. Pa went to Pottersville and got tilting bar mended.

August 6

Hayed it at Taylor's. Mort Stanard helped us.

August 7

Worked at Taylor's at haying. We got in six big loads.

August 8
Went to Sunday School and Baptist Church.

August 9
Hayed it at Taylor's.

August 10
Hayed it at Taylor's.

August 11
Had a big rain and washout.
We fixed road home in afternoon.

August 12
Worked at Taylor's.

August 13
We finished the tame hay at T.'s. Moved home. Got here about 9.

August 14
We hayed it here at home. Aunt Lillias and Aunt Sophia were here visiting.

August 15
Had a big shower. Went to church.

August 16
Pa and Ma went to Schroon. Pa phoned down for me to dig taters. Aft. we dug potatoes.

August 17
We started to mow but it looked so much like rain we gave it up. Pa broke mower wheel coming to the house and went to Chester. I puttered with mower.

August 18
Pa came home from Chester. We mowed in forenoon but in afternoon did not do much on account of rain.

August 19
We mowed and spread out hay. In afternoon it rained.

August 20
Hayed it. Got in five loads.

August 21
Worked at hay. Got in four loads.

August 22
Went to Sunday School and Baptist meeting.

August 23
We went down and put in new bridge over the first brook. Then hayed it in orchard and lot east.

August 24
Rain
Did not do much of anything.
Sam Ingraham was up here a while.

August 25
Pa and I went to Taylor's. Went to village in afternoon.

August 26
Pa and I hayed it in orchard and below horse-

barn. We went to Chester after 3 p.m.

August 27
We worked haying below barn. Mr. Bishop came up here and is going to stay over night.

August 28
We unloaded little jag of hay and fooled around the rest of the day.

August 29
Went to Sunday School. Went up to Culver's and got road cart for tomorrow.

August 30
Commenced going to school in Schroon.

August 31
Went to school.

Wednesday, September 1, 1897
Went to school.

September 2
Went to school.

September 3
Went to school.

September 4
Went over on Granger's fallow and got their horse rake and raked over our oat ground. Aft. helped Jess Cole get in oats. Worked hard too.

September 5
Went to Sunday School.

September 6
Pa, Jess and I hayed it on Taylor's swamp.

September 7
Went to school.

September 8
Went to school.

September 9
Went to school.

September 10
Went to school.

September 11
Rainy a.m.
Uncle Sam and Aunt Jennie were here. We visited etc. In evening we all went down to David Hall's and saw Uncle Will and his wife after they came.

September 12
Went up on Charley Hill to meeting.

September 13
Went to school.

September 14
Went to school.

September 15
Went to school.

September 16
Went to school.

September 17
Went to school.

September 18
Went up to Uncle Jim Whitney's to dinner. Uncle Will and Sam and

their wives were there.

We went to Schroon. I went in and saw the man who was mur-
dered.

September 19
Went up to Grandma's. Aunt Lib and the boys were there.

September 20
Went to school.

September 21
Went to school.

September 22
Went to school.

September 23
Had cold. Did not go to school. Uncle Will and Sam and Aunt Alice and Jennie started home today.

September 24
My cold little better and boil is worse. Pa stayed at Chester last night and came home today. I tele-phoned up to Watson Hall to bring my books home.

September 25
Worked at my bookkeeping and school tax list.
Aft. Pa and I made out tax list.

September 26
Went to S. S. and Church.

September 27
Dug potatoes. Bound up fodder corn. Picked up taters.

September 28
Bound up corn.

September 29
Pa and I fixed up things in lower barn. We went down and cut fodder corn poles and set corn up around them.

September 30
Pa and I went to the Pottersville fair.

Friday, October 1, 1897
Pa and I dug potatoes in a. m. Afternoon we went to fair. Pa got lap robe for $2.25.

October 2
Pa and I dug potatoes. H. P. Jones was here little while in afternoon. We have 22 bushels of potatoes in cellar now.

October 3
Went to Sunday School.

October 4
Attended school. Quite a lot more scholars came today.

October 5
To school I went.

October 6
Attended school at Schroon. Like Union School.

October 7
Went to school.
October 8
Went to school.
October 9
Pa and I drew in some pumpkins and some fodder corn. Gathered few apples. Thurman C. Warren came up here a little while in afternoon.
October 10
Went to Sunday School.
October 11
Went to school. Took up an old stove pipe hat to drawn.
October 12
Went to school.
October 13
Went to school.
October 14
Went to school
October 15
Went to school.
Went to a conundrum supper at Fred Ford's in evening.
October 16
Showery
Went down in sugar dump and helped fix fence. Aft. we went down to saw mill and drew logs on to the roll way.
It has thundered Lisa today.

October 17
37°   Colder
Went to Sunday School.
October 18
Attended school.
October 19
Went to school. "Bird" R. rode up with me.
Had wagon fixed and had to wait for it so did not get home until 6:45.
October 20
Went to school. "Chan" went down to David Hall's with me.
October 21
Went to school. Bird went home this morning. Pa went to Chester and Grandma went with him.
October 22
Went to school. They had exercises in the afternoon. School was out at quarter past three.
October 23
Pa and I husked corn in forenoon. Aft. we threshed beans, drew in fodder corn, and went down to saw mill and got 5000 shingles.
October 24
Went to Sunday School and Church. Mr. Bishop was down here to church.
October 25
Went to school.

October 26
Went to school.
October 27
Went to school.
October 28
Went to school.
October 29
Went to school.
Took up corn and had it ground. We have just got through division in algebra and in pendulums in Physics.
October 30
Pa and I shingled all day on back side of house. Mabel Whitney was up here to supper.
Pa went to choir practice.
October 31
Went to Sunday School and did not stay to Baptist meeting. Ma rode down to church with Uncle Henry.

Monday, November 1, 1897
Attended school. It has rained all day so I had a nice time going and coming home from school.
November 2
Election Day   Rain
Pa and I husked corn. It has rained nearly all of the time today.

November 3
Blowy
Van Wyck was elected Mayor of New York.
We husked corn. I have a cold today so did not go to school.
In the morning it rained and was so damp that I was afraid that if I went perhaps I might take more cold. There was a Quaker meeting here today.
November 4
Fine
My cold was a little farther advanced but I did not feel like going to school.
Pa went to Schroon on auditor business. Grandma C. was down here.
I wrote a letter to Eddy Floyd and his folks.
Pa got home about eight p.m.
November 5
Worked problems in Algebra. Aft. went outdoors a good deal. Emory Whitney came up to help Pa shingle. Finished shingling house.
November 6
We finished husking corn and put up the stalks. Pa went to "sing."

November 7

29°   Cold

Went to Sunday School
and Church. Mr. Hunt
preached.
Saw first snow.

November 8

                    Cold, Snow

Attended school. Mr.
Bishop went off to
Saratoga last week and
Miss Jones was boss. The
kids carried on pretty well
while he was away I guess.
He gave it to them to beat
the cars this morning in
chapel.

November 9

Went to school.

November 10

Went to school.

November 11

Went to school. It has
rained in Schroon and
down as far as Stanard's
but up here it is snowing
very hard.
Pa is down in Chester and
going to stay all night.

November 12

                         Hairy

It snowed about six inches
last night, and as Pa was
off in Chester and I did
not have a good horse and
the roads were so bad I did
not go to school.

November 13

Went up to Culver's. Made
a box to carry books in.

November 14

Went to Sunday School
and Baptist Church.

November 15

Went to school.

November 16

Went to school.

November 17

Went to school.

November 18

Went to school. Went up
to Uncle J. H. and H. J.'s to
a party in the evening.
Got home half past twelve.

November 19

                         Snow

Have a cold so have not
been to school today.
Studied some.

November 20

                         Snow

Went outdoors some. Worked
in Algebra. Pa worked on
preacher study table.

November 21

                         Fair

Went to Sunday School
& Church. Ma stayed down
and went to church again
in evening. My cold some
better but throat and cough
feels worse.

November 22

Did not go to school.

Throat did not feel first class.

November 23
Studied some. Throat don't feel first rate and got tooth ache some.

November 24
Cold, Snow
Studied some. Telephoned some.

November 25
Uncle Henry and Grand ma came down here and we had a chicken dinner. Pa and Ma went down to Emory Whitney's to dinner.

November 26
Rained so I did not go to school.
Pa went down and got a load of sawdust.

November 27
Helped Pa get ready to go to the village. He carried up some apples.

November 28
Went to Sunday School and Baptist "Union" prayer meeting.

November 29
Went to school. The "thermometer" was pretty well up tonight or to about 100°.

November 30
Went to school. The "thermometer" dropped down to

97° today.

Wednesday, December 1, 1897
When I got up my stomach felt kind of sick but I went to school but came home at half past three. Had to vomit up my breakfast and dinner after I got home.

December 2
10°   Extra fine.
Feel kindy weak from the effects of vomiting up so much and taking a pill last night.
Pa went to Chester. He got home about nearly six o'clock. He got me a fur coat.

December 3
Took two more pills last night so I was awful busy for a while from four to eight o'clock. Felt better all over after the first effects of the pills worked off.

December 4
Felt better. Studied some. May Whitney came up here and stayed a while. Went over and got sheep.

December 5

Went to Sunday School and Church.

December 6

Went to school.

December 7

Went to school.

December 8

Went to school.

December 9

Went to school.

December 10

Went to school.

December 11

Pa went down to the saw mill in forenoon.
We went down to the church in evening to see about Christmas.

December 12

Snow

It snowed quite hard in the a.m. but a good deal of it melted. Pa and I went down to Sunday School and to C.E. meeting in evening.

December 13

Went to school.

December 14

Went to school.

December 15

Attended school at Schroon. Am kindy sick of going on account of the road and other causes.

December 16

Went to school. The road is very, very muddy.

December 17

Went to school.

December 18

Have a cold. Went out of doors some. Studied etc.

December 19

Did not go out. Read, slept etc. Pa and Ma went to church.

December 20

Don't feel very good. Have a cold in my throat and head.

December 21

Felt some better. Uncle Henry went to the village and got my books.

December 22

Felt pretty kindy bad all day. Gave me more medicine than a little.

December 23

Don't feel first class. Eye ached pretty hard all last night. Pa did not lay down all night. Pa went to Christmas practice.

December 24

Felt little better but nothing to brag of.
Pretty weak. Pa has sore thing on lip.

December 25

Don't feel very good. Dr.

233

G. up to see Pa and I.

December 26

Pa's lip pained him badly all day.

Mr. Hunt stopped here a while in afternoon and Emory & Mary came up in evening.

December 27

Feel better. Aunt Libs boys were here some. Emory W., Mr. and Mrs. C. Warren and Edna were here in p.m. Pa feeling better.

December 28

Fine

Feel about the same. Aunt Lib and Co. went home. Nate Sherman was here a little while.

December 29

XXtra

Feel better. Did some chores. Pa feels better too. Uncle Henry helped do chores.
Studied some.

December 30

Did chores. Studied some. Read some.
Puttered with telephone. O.K. some.
Pa on the gain. Uncle Henry went over and drove sheep home. Chas. Stanard and we here played dominoes.

December 31

21°

Snow

Did chores. Went down to Frank Hall's after medicine. Emma Fey came by and phoned to North Creek. Pa feeling better. Began snowing in afternoon.

Williams Jackson, a negro, was killed by three Lagoy fellows Frank, George and Will, on the night of Sept. 17 about 8 or 9 p.m. Will Lagoy was caught Monday. George and Will on Tuesday.

Memorandum

Thunder on Oct. 16, 1897.

Heavy thunder on Oct. 28, '97.

Finished shingling the house Nov. 5, 1897.

Pa got me a fur coat down to Chester for $8.50
Dec. 2, 1897

Charles Stanard caught a bear Oct. 27, 1897.

Big rain and washout all over town Aug. 11, 1897.
Telephone put in Aug. 3, 1897.

Cash Account
1897

Eggs sold   Received
Jan 11 $2/3$ doz. @   .18
"   21 $3^1/3$ doz. @   .60

Cash account Received
Grammer   .85
Algebra 1   .15

I am studying
the following studies from
Aug. 25 to January:
Algebra
Bookkeeping
Physics
Drawing

Lillie Cole came home
from Saranac Nov. 21,
1897

The Modern School System

Ram it in, cram it in,
Children's heads are hollow.
Slam it in, jam it in,
Still there's more to follow.
Hygiene and history
Astronomy mystery
Algebra, histology,
Latin, etymology,
Botany, geometry,
Greek and trigonometry,
Ram it in, cram it in,
Children's heads are hollow.
Scold it in, mould it in,

All that they can swallow,
Fold it in, hold it in,
Still there's more to follow.
Faces pinched, sad and pale,
Tell the same unvarying tale,
Tell of moments robbed from
sleep,
Meals untasted, studies deep,
Those who've passed the furnace
through,
With aching brow will tell to
you.
How the teacher crammed it in,
Rammed it in, jammed it in,
Crunched it in, punched it in.
Rubbed it in, clubbed it in,
Pressed it and caressed it in,
Rapped it in and slapped it in,
When their heads were hollow.

Dec. 29, 1897
2:45 p.m.

Whitney's Station
Oct. 11, 1897
10:20 a.m.
Cold morning. Wind blows.
The potatoes are dug.
Had 46 bushels. Not much of
the corn husked. Apples
are gathered All gardens except
onions are gathered.
The fodder corn is not all in
yet. Pa is going to draw logs
on to the roll way down to the
saw mill this week.

We drew corn on yesterday afternoon. I got a cat down at Stanard's last night. His name is "bump". I have got nearly through multiplication in my algebra and over into forces in Physics. Last Friday we drew a cylinder on the blackboard. There are four boys in our drawing class.

Yours truly,
Walter W.

Cash Account
W. J. S. Whitney

1 diary	.30
Slate pencil	.01
Dr. Jim G.	4.00
Lemons	.15
Pr. shoes	2.88
(erased)	1.40
shirts	.80
Suit clothes	9.00
Algebra1	.10
Bookkeeping bk	.70
Tablet	.05
Pencil pen	.05
Ink	.05
Grammar	.85
Pr. shirts	.50
Pr. pants	1.65
Hat	1.50
Bag oats	1.00
Halter	.25
Tie	.25
Scythe etc.	.70
Snath	.70
Lead pencil	.01
Pen	.03
Fur coat	8.50
Tuition	3.50
	3.50
	$18.57

Schroon, N.Y. Jan. 6 1754

One minute after sight,
pay to the order of Joe
Potter Eighteen Dollars
and Fifty-seven Cents,
value received and charge
the same to the account of
Jo G. W. Bishop J. W.
Wisemann Portageville,
N.Y.

Order of Units

1. Units
2. Thousands
3. Millions
4. Billions
5. Trillions
6. Quadrillions
7. Quintillions
8. Sextillions
9. Septillions
10. Octillions
11. Nontillions
12. Decillions
13. Undecillions
14. Duodecillions
15. Tredecillions
16. Quatuordecillions
17. Quindecillions
18. Sexdecillions
19. Septendecillions
20. Octodecillions
21. Novendecillions
22. Vigintillions

The Missing Diary
for
1898

The rustic, handmade, wooden box that contained the Walter Whitney diaries had space for one more little leather-bound book. But, somehow, the diary of 1898 escaped its confines.

The possibilities of what may have happened to it are too vast to allow speculation here. The 106 years between then and now give reason enough for the loss. This loss, however, confirms our belief in the importance of preserving our past for the children of the future.

The diary for 1899 *has a dark-brown, composition cover with a flap tab. The condition of the book is good, and the entries are clear and complete. Walter used the lengthy memorandum section in the back for miscellaneous notes and personal records.*

The Whitney Cottage, where Mrs. Jessie Cole offered rooms for tourists and summer boarders

1899 marked Walter Whitney's 17th birthday on March 24. There appears to be a subtle change in our subject since last we heard from him, one year ago.

The boy who frequently weighed the household cat, and "teased" for a mousetrap for the sake of a little boyhood sport, has placed those playful, youthful days gently towards the back shelf of his mind to be reflected on in memory now as one might reflect on a trinket on the mantle or family portraits hanging in the hall.

While Walter was growing into what Shakespeare considered the fourth age of man, the United States expanded its territory. President McKinley signed the peace treaty ending the Spanish American War, acquiring the possessions of Puerto Rico and Guam. At the same time, the Boer War began in South Africa in an attempt to maintain its independence and keep Britain from acquiring possession of its territory and gold mines.

During this year, Walter Whitney quietly and subtly demonstrated an expansion of his horizons that suggest a sense of independence and a vision for his future. He began school in Schroon. He took more responsibility for chores, frequently taking on Pa's share, as well as his own. A social life began to emerge, and attention was paid to personal appearance. He received his bookkeeping card. He studied for examinations that he took in Chester, and he looked over the shirt factory there as a possible means of employment.

On January 7, 1899, Walter recorded that he read Longfellow's poems. Henry Wadsworth Longfellow died in 1882, the year Walter was born; and his boyhood days go back to the early 1800s. But, the memories of childhood and youth have a universal flavor that defies generation and time. As Walter marked the gossamer transition from youth to young manhood, it would not be surprising if one of his Longfellow selections might have been, "My Lost Youth." It begins:

> Often I think of the beautiful town
> That is seated by the sea,
> Often in thought go up and down
> The pleasant streets of that dear old town,
> And my youth comes back to me.
> And a verse of a Lapland song
> Is haunting my memory still:
> A boy's will is the wind's will,
> And the thoughts of youth are long, long, thoughts."

HOUSEHOLD

Farm houses of the day were simple wood frame structures, usually with two stories. Insulation in the walls could be from any handy material, including newspapers. The houses were heated with wood-burning stoves. Because chimneys were warm and contributed to the heat, the more exposed chimney the better. Some wood stoves contained wells to heat the water for cooking and laundry.

For those near the lake, blocks of ice in ice houses kept food cool. Root cellars kept vegetables cool. Farm families raised most of their own food. Milled molasses, vinegar, and salt pork came in barrels, although some people made their own salt pork.

Laundry was done in large pots, with the clothes being scrubbed against washboards. Flatirons were heated on the stoves. Laundry dried on outdoor lines bore the sweet smell of Adirondack air.

Lighting came from oil lamps. Although Henry Parsell built an electrical generating plant to service parts of Taylor's Hotel (only a few miles from the Whitneys) in 1891, electricity did not come to the farm homes of lower Essex and northern Warren Counties until some years later.

Note that the Whitneys got telephone service in 1897.

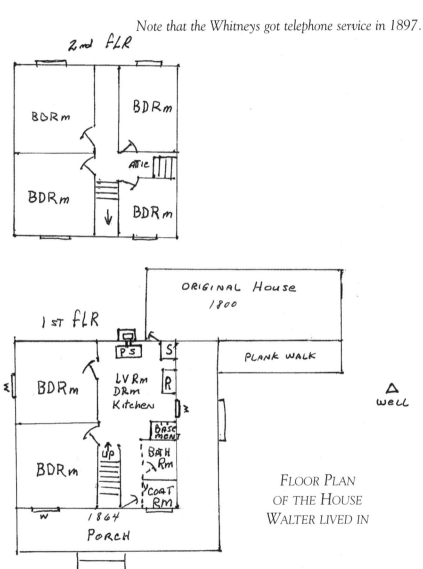

FLOOR PLAN
OF THE HOUSE
WALTER LIVED IN

1899
Walter J. Whitney
Tenth Diary
1899

Sunday, January 1. 1899
Went to Sunday School and Church. Pa went down early to see about singing. Grandma C. and Mary De Lorme were down here today.

January 2
-10°   Fair. Aft. Cold
Pa and I cut brush down beside the road.

January 3
14   Fair
I went to school. Pa went to the village.

January 4
40   Cold rain
Went to school. It has rained some today. Snow has gone off fast. Sarah W. came here just dark.

January 5
Went to school.
The snow has nearly gone off in the lots.
The road is awful icy. Pa went to Schroon with the wagon.

January 6
Snow came about 9 or 10 inches deep in these two days. Went to school. It has snowed all day. Probably it is about 5 inches deep. Road is all glare ice under the snow.

January 7
20   Squally
Wind has blown hard all day. Pa has a sore on his ear. I went up to Culver's in the afternoon. Read Longfellow's poems. Pa and I went to So. Schroon in the morning. We got a box of things from Gertie and Lizzie.

January 8
Went to Sunday School. I played the organ in Sunday School. The Baptist preacher did not come. Mary D. went to S. S. too. Uncle Henry carried her down.

January 9
Went up to school house and got my books, school being out for the present. Drew off wash water and brought in water. Pa went to Schroon.

January 10
-14° to 11°   Clear cold.

We went down in swamp and made roads. Oren Murdock helped us with his oxen. Chauncey Bruce went with us. He was here to dinner.

It was so cold we did not work in p. m.

January 11

-25° to -11°   Clear

We did not do much in forenoon only keep warm if we could. 42° below zero at Schroon Lake.

Aft. Pa and I went down and cut roads around to our wood.

January 12

-15°

Pa and I got our sleds out and drew wood from swamp. Drew three loads. Road poor at farther end.

January 13

Cold. Snowy

Went into Culver's. Drew wood from swamp.

I went three trips and Pa went early in morning. He stayed down and fixed roads while I came up with a load. Went to Culver's in evening down-river.

January 14

Rainy

It has rained hard nearly all day so we have not done much.

January 15

Went to Sunday School and Church. I played the organ in both Sunday School and Church.

January 16

I cut brush down beside of road. Pa has a boil on his wrist so he could not work. Uncle Jim and Mary D. went to North Hudson. Grandma and Uncle Henry staid down here.

January 17

Cut brush in forenoon. Aft. Pa and I went to Schroon.

January 18

Cut brush in p. m. Pa and I took sawdust out of hen house and put in some clean straw.

January 19

We drew wood from swamp. Three loads.

January 20

I went two loads of wood from swamp. Pa drew one load.

Mr. and Mrs. Hunt were up here visiting.

I went up to Culver's in evening.

January 21

Unloaded wood. Split

wood. Pa finished drawing our wood from swamp. I puttered with hens. Pa made an ax helve and I hung it and cut my thumb etc.

January 22
Went up to Culver's and got my hair cut. Went to Sunday School and Baptist meeting. Uncle Henry and Mary went too. A new kid arrived at Walter Ford's today.

January 23
30°   Fair
Pa, Sam Ingraham and I cut wood down in swamp.
Emory Whitney came up here in evening.

January 24
Snow, Rain
Pa drew one load of wood. It snowed, rained, hailed, squalled all day. I went up to Culver's in afternoon. Hurt my thumb.

January 25
Pa and I cut wood down in swamp. It snowed about seven inches last night.

January 26
We drew one load wood afore dinner. I went to Culver's to borrow neck

yoke. Pa and Uncle Henry went to Schroon in afternoon. I drew two loads of wood.

January 27
Windy
Did not do much of anything in a.m. Wind blew very hard. Fixed neck yoke. Aft. I went up to Culver's. Uncle Jim is ailing with the grip.

January 28
-14°   Fair, Cold
Drew one load of wood in forenoon. Have all drawn that we cut. Pa has boils on his wrist so he can't work. Aft. we (Pa and I) went to Schroon. Uncle Henry went to Mill Brook on lake.

January 29
Sunday School and I went to Church. Pa has two boils on his wrist so he and Ma did not go. Uncle Henry and Mary stopped here a while en route.

January 30
Split wood. Unloaded four

foot of wood.
Made an O.K. pill. Went
to Grangers and got a cat.
The boils on Pa's hand are
very bad.

January 31

Went to Culvers after their
"bobs". Went to Aunt
Olive Whitney's funeral.
Grandma W., Ma,
Uncle Henry and I went.

Wednesday, February 1, 1899

Did chores. Pa did not do
much work because of boils.
I cut up sugar wood down
under sugar house shed,
and drew five loads of
sugar wood.

February 2

Drew sugar wood. Drew
two loads from Hardhack
Hill. Grandma and
Molly were here today.

February 3

Snowy

Pa sick so I did not do
much of anything besides
chores. Dr. Dunn came
up to see Pa.
Snowed two or three inches
today.

February 4

Have cold so have not
worked any. Went down
to Uncle Jim Whitney's
after Chan. Pa is feeling
better. I fixed two O.K.
pills.

February 5

Fair

We all stayed at home.
Mary D. and Grandma
C. were down here. Aunt
Lib & Co. came over in
afternoon. They went up
to Culver's at night. My
cold is quite bad but I do
all the chores.

February 6

Went to Grangers after
mouse trap. Eddy K. was
down here in forenoon.
Split wood.
My cold is better but outdoor air makes it feel worse.
Aunt Lib & Co. went home
in p.m.

February 7

Puttered around but did
not work much. Cold does
not get well very fast.
Wrote part of story.

February 8

Snow

It snowed hard all day
about 10 or 11 inches in
all. I went up to Culver's
in afternoon.
Wrote some on story.

February 9

The wind blew and the
snow flew hard all day.

247

We did not do any work. Pa made a mouse trap. I finished my story.

February 10

-8°   Cold, Windy

We sat around the house all day. Pa has not got over his cold and me ditto. Cold winter day, the worst day we have had this winter except yesterday.

February 11

-12° to -7°   Clr

Split wood. Shoveled roads. Went down after mail in p.m.

February 12

-3°   Cold

We all stayed at home all day. Grand Ma and Molly Todd were here in afternoon.

February 13

Did not do much of anything. It snowed all day but not very hard till just night.

February 14

Split wood. Shoveled snow. Went down toward Stanards with Charley to see about shoveling out roads. Uncle Henry took our horses and went after mail.

February 15

Drew three loads sugar

wood from Hardhack Hill. Snowed in forenoon some.

February 16

Drew sugar wood from Hardback Hill. Got it all done.

February 17

We drew sugar wood from down beside road. Afternoon we made new barnyard gate and put up grist. Went up to Culver's in evening. 9:30.

February 18

Pa and I went to Schroon. Republican caucus in afternoon. We took up some corn to have ground.

February 19

Went up to Culver's to see about going to Mill Brook. Pa, Ma, Mary and I went over there and came home just dark. Made three trips to Culver's.

February 20

Went to Culver's after cross cut saw. Pa and I cut down the old sweet apple tree and partly cut it up. We went to Democratic caucus in afternoon.

February 21

Cut up apple trees. Pa and Ma went to Eleanor Jones Cole's funeral in a.m.

Ade G. and her kids were over here visiting today.

February 22

It rained hard in morning. I fixed my rubbers and split wood in a.m. In p.m. we cut wood down in orchard.

February 23

Pa went to Riverside after fertilizer for Uncle Jim Whitney. I split wood. Went up to Culver's after milk. Ade & Co. were up there on a grand visiting tour.

February 24

We split wood. I went down after mail toward night. Went up to Culver's in evening.

February 25

Pa and I cut wood. We killed calf and skinned it. I went down after mail.

February 26

Went up to Culver's and got my hair cut. Cut Uncle Jim's hair. Went to Sunday School and Church. Played organ in Sunday School. Oscar R. stopped here after meeting. We had a sing.
Mary rode home with him.

February 27

Pa and I went to Schroon. I got my pass-card in Book-keeping that I passed last June. Pa and C. F. Taylor Jr. fixed up the milk contract.

February 28

Pa went to Schroon. I cut four foot wood. Uncle Jim and Molly Todd were down here in evening.

Wednesday, March 1, 1899

We cut wood. Pa and Ma went to Quaker meeting at Nate Sherman's in evening.

March 2

Snowy

We cut wood in forenoon. Aft. it snowed so we did not work. Thurm Warren and Sam Ingraham were up here in afternoon visiting.

March 3

We split wood here by the house all day. I went up to Culver's in the evening.

March 4

Split wood. Cut my hand in the forenoon so did not work any more. Pa went to Schroon to see about sick cow.

March 5

It has been a rainy day

today. About noon Grand
Ma C. Uncle Jim &
Henry, Mr. and Mrs.
Passino and their kid and
Mary came down here and
were here in afternoon.

March 6

Cut wood all day.

March 7

40°   Snow, Blizzard
We sawed little wood in
morning before it began to
snow. Snowed and blowed
hard all day.
I went up to Culver's in
afternoon after medicine
for Ma who is sick. Bashful
day.

March 8

Medicine
The wind blew so we did-
n't get to work till about
ten o'clock. We worked on
wood until Charley
Warren and wife came here
about 2 p.m.
Got 27 eggs today.

March 9

We cut little wood in
morning. Got it all cut.
Snowed hard all forenoon.
In afternoon we drew
wood out of orchard.

March 10

We drew up apple tree wood
from orchard. Aft. we drew
up Uncle Jim W's buckets

and covered up wood with
plank. Went to choir practice.

March 11

Did not do much of any-
thing in forenoon. In
p.m. Pa and I went
down to Uncle Jim's with
his buckets.

March 12

85°
It rained nearly all day.
Grand Ma C, Uncle
Henry and Molly Todd
were down here.

March 13

Pa and I went to Mill
Brook after a load of hay
from Uncle Bish's.

March 14

Pa is not feeling very
well. He has a swelling on
lip. I went to Schroon in
forenoon and afternoon
went to Culvers after
Uncle Jim to help unload
hay. Went up to Emory
Richardson's in evening.

March 15

                          Snow.
Pa has not been out at all
today. I did chores, split
wood, helped women wash,
cleaned out hen roost box
and did not work very
hard either.

March 16

It snowed about four

inches yesterday and last night. Pa awful sick in forenoon. We sent for Dr. Dunn and Emory Whitney's folks. Wind blew hard all day. Went to Lew Richardson's.

March 17

Pa felt little better. I did chores and helped around the house.

March 18

Squally

Pa felt little better. I did not do anything but the chores. Went down to the Post Office after the mail came.

March 19

Rainy

I went up to Culver's and got Aunt Lib. Pa quite sick. We tried to get a Dr. but it rained so hard he did not come. I went to So. Schroon in afternoon after pills.

March 20

Pa took wrong pills and they worked wrong and made him feel worse. Dr. Dunn came in forenoon. Uncle Jim F. and Co. went home. I went to Schroon in afternoon. Pa felt better toward night.

March 21

85°

I kept fire last night. Pa felt better today. Grand ma C. and Molly Todd were down here today.

March 22

Snow some

Continued to act as overseer and foreman of the Whitney ranch. Uncle Henry cut wood for Chan. Emory W. came up a while in a.m..

March 23

4°   Snowy

We telephoned for Dr. Sprague and he came about 10:30. Pa is feeling little better. I took two pills and had to light the candle at 12 last night. It snowed nearly all day. Uncle H. came down in p.m.

March 24

Went down to So. Schroon. Pa felt worse toward night. I went to Schroon after six o'clock. Lew and Martha were up here in afternoon.

March 25

Pa felt worse this morning. Uncle Jim W. came up here. Dr. Dunn came

to see Pa. Uncle Jim C.
went to Mill Brook after
Nora. Pa felt better toward
night. Mr. and Mrs. E.
Whitney here in evening.

March 26

Pa felt little better. Cyrus
and Will K. were up here
to dinner. Arthur Floyd
and Percy Robbins were
here a while in afternoon.
Mary and Uncle Henry
stopped a while too.
Pa got tuckered.

March 27

Shoveled off sugar house
shed. Went to Schroon in
afternoon. Got shoes taken
off horses.
Butter stamp day. Dr.
Dunn here today.

March 28

I carried Mary Whitney
home. It stormed so I did
not work. I went down to
sugar house and looked at
buckets but they didn't
need fixing.
Mary stayed here all night
and Lew Richardson until
one or two in the night
Pa had grip I guess.

March 29

Didn't do much. Rained
most all day or quite all
day and part of the night,
then turned to snow.

Tomorrow was one of
Chans dismal looking
days everything all cov-
ered with snow. See below
for particulars.

March 30

Sqly
Awful windy day. Did
not do much of anything
in a.m. Went up to
Culver's in afternoon.
25-2-4+2-7+2-18-10-19-
16+25-19-20-3-7-
20+14-3-5-8+

March 31

Did nothing much in
forenoon. Uncle Henry,
Grand Ma and Mary
were down here. Aft. Uncle
Henry and I broke sugar
roads and took down part
of buckets.

Saturday, April 1, 1899

Squally too cold for sap
Uncle Henry and I soaked
up buckets. Uncle Jim and
Eliza went to North Hudson.
Doctor came to see Pa
today. Uncle Bish and
Aunt Lucy came over this
forenoon.

April 2

Nora and I went to
Sunday School and
Church.

Mary and Emory W. were up here in evening.

April 3

Went to Schroon. Scattered buckets in p.m.

April 4

Uncle Jim W. worked here. We worked at sugaring.

April 5

We tinkered around sugar house in a.m. Aft. Stub went to Schroon and I fixed few buckets.

April 6

We fixed up things around sugar house. Aft. gathered six barrels sap, but did not boil any.

April 7

29° to 35° Cold, rain, snow I commenced boiling sap about 8 a.m. and boiled till noon. Stub and I gathered two barrels of sap after dinner. It rained so we quit. Boiled sap awhile in afternoon. Got over two buckets of syrup.

SUGAR BUCKET

April 8

It snowed about six inches last night. Stub and I went to Culver's in a.m. In p.m. we emptied snow out of buckets and broke sugar roads. Stub went home.

April 9

Went to Sunday School and Church. Mary, Grand Ma and Uncle Henry stopped here twice en route.

April 10

We tapped few big trees in a.m. p.m. Stub took Nora home. I fixed few buckets. I went up to Culver's. Charley Nichols was there, also George DeL.

April 11

Stub and I worked at sugaring.

April 12

Cld, Rain Stub and I gathered 2 bbls of sap and I began boiling about 9 a.m. Stub gathered 2 bbls. more. We finished boiling about 3:30 p.m. In afternoon, Maude Patreau, Mary and George De Lorme and Uncle Henry inspected our sugar apparatus.

April 13

Went over in Granger's sugar camp after barrel and up to Culver's after ax. We cut sugar wood.

Aft. we lazed around doing nothing except to go to Culver's and to So. S. with double wagon.

April 14
We worked at sugaring after half past ten. Boiled sap till half past seven.

April 15
Got ready to go to Schroon. Went to Culver's after neck yoke. Aft. Stub and I went to Schroon. We broke whiffle-tree and had lots of fun.

April 16
Stub and I went to Sunday School but did not have any church as Mr. Coutois did not come. We went up to Culver's in evening. Leah was there.

April 17
We worked at sugaring. Mary and Leah were down in sugar house in afternoon.

April 18
We filled two straw beds. Fooled around.
Went to Culver's after gun. In afternoon, Stub and I went to Thurman Pond. Went to Culver's in evening.

April 19
We worked at sugaring in forenoon and part of afternoon. Stub and I went up to Culver's after vinegar and then went to Post Office.

April 20
Went to Mill Brook with Stub. Awful bad roads.

April 21
Cleaned out under hen roost.
Mary and Leah were down here and stayed till into the evening.
Pa and I went to choir practice in afternoon.

April 22
We got things ready to go to Schroon and then went in afternoon.

April 23
Went to Sunday School and Church. I played in S. S. Mr. Hunt preached last time.

April 24
Went down to Post Office. Pa and I gathered sap and brought buckets out to the roads.

April 25
I gathered buckets and helped wash after 4 p.m.. Maude Patreau and I went to show at Schroon in evening. Got home at one o'clock.

April 26

We finished sugaring and corded up wood. Went over and saw Granger's water wheel. We moved well house. Ma went up to Culver's.

April 27

Pa and I drew stone until 3 p.m. I went over to Deb Hall's to get him to shear our sheep.

April 28

Drew few stone. We grafted some in afternoon. Deb sheared our sheep.

April 29

Pa and I went to Chester.

April 30

Went up and Uncle Jim cut my hair. Went to Sunday School and Church. Uncle Henry and Mary stopped here twice en route to church. I played in S. S.

Monday, May 1, 1899

We puttered around in forenoon. Pa went to village in afternoon. I took banking away from house.

May 2

Dragged last year's corn ground. Drew stone from front of house. Plowed piece I dragged this forenoon. Went up to Culver's in evening.

May 3

Dragged piece I plowed yesterday. Plowed garden below barn and back of house.

May 4

I plowed all day. Went to choir practice in evening.

May 5

Plowed in forenoon. Aft. drew manure.

May 6

Drew five loads manure. Dragged and sowed upper oat piece. Went over to Jim Wood's after supper to stay all night. Herb and I went to Horseshoe Pond.

May 7

Went to Sunday School and Church. Rev. A. E. Clapper preached first sermon here today.

May 8

Frank Granger and I drew load of manure on to garden and I dragged it. Then we drew stone rest of day. Drew 22 loads. Pa went trout fishing in afternoon. Got 41.

May 9

Pa and I drew manure on to oat pieces and sowed the

oats. Found snake in well. Went to Culver's after jar.

May 10

Finished planting potatoes in forenoon. Aft. Pa and I tinkered around making measuring wheel splicing fish pole etc. Went down to lake fishing after supper. Got 18.

May 11

Whitewashed Chan's room. Worked on measuring wheel. Went fishing in afternoon.

May 12

Pa and I dug stone on corn piece. Tom Cole's house burned up today. Mary and Grand ma were down here. Mary helped paper.

May 13

Pa and I dug stone in forenoon. We had to go up to Tom Cole's about 10 a.m. We dug few rocks off after dinner till it began raining. Sorted over potatoes.

May 14

Went to Sunday School and Baptist Church.

May 15

We dug stone and drew them off. Went down to church in evening.

May 16

We drew few stone. We went to Mary Huntley Smith's funeral down to the church. I helped sing. Went up to Culver's in afternoon. Pa went to Schroon in p.m.

May 17

Pa and I drew 12 loads of manure on to corn ground.

May 18

Rainy

Helped clean my room upstairs. It has rained more or less all day. Pa went down to So Schroon in p.m. I went up to Culver's in p.m. Conversation.

May 19

Went to Culver's after chickens. Helped churn. Hunted wood chucks. Afternoon Pa and I drew manure.

May 20

We drew manure. Plowed little before supper. Showery day but no thunder. Pa and I went to Choir Practice. Uncle Jim and Mary went too.

May 21

Went to Sunday School

and Church and to prayer meeting.

Uncle Henry and Mary were here en route to church. Mary sang in choir and I did in evening.

May 22

Plowed in forenoon. Aft. planted beans and cabbages and went trout fishing. Got 22.

Pa sent to Chester in p. m.

May 23

Plowed on corn piece until I broke bolt about 3:30. Mary and Grand ma were down here. Mary helped Ma paper. I carried her home. Pinky had a worse spell. Helped get Granger's cow out of mud.

May 24

Finished plowing corn piece. Aft. dragged it.

May 25

Pa planted little corn and went to Dorcas Wright's funeral. I helped Uncle Jim Whitney plant corn. Ma went down there with me.

May 26

Pa, Uncle Jim, and Henry and I planted corn all day. Did not get it quite finished.

Heard of the orange trapper.

May 27

Went up to Culver's and helped them a little while in the forenoon. Came home and helped plant squashes in corn field. After dinner. Pa and I went over and helped burn fallow on Culver's. Mary and Uncle Jim started for choir practice but didn't go.

May 28

Went up to Culver's with Ma. She and Uncle Henry went down to Deb Hall's. Went to S. S. and Church.

May 29

Planted corn at Culver's. Had shower in forenoon so did not work for an hour or so.

May 30

Windy

We plowed and drew stones off from new garden. Aft. we planted some sweet corn. Memorial services were held at Schroon today.

May 31

Finished planting garden. Pa and I weeded out beds back of house. Aft. Pa went to Schroon and I helped

Ma clean parlor. Went up to Culver's.

Thursday, June 1, 1899
Went to Culver's. Plowed fodder corn ground, and drew manure and ashes on to it. Aft. Pa and I went to Mill Brook.

June 2
Took Ma up to Culver's but she didn't stay. Grand ma came back with us.
We sowed fodder corn. Aft. Pa and I went to Schroon. Got new wagon. I carried Mary and Grand ma home.

June 3
Hoed 15 rows "taters". Put up crow twine. Went to Dave Hall's after Aunt Sophia. Went to Choir Practice in evening.

June 4
Went to Sunday School and Church. I sang in the choir.

June 5
Planted cucumbers. Pa and I cut, drew up and peeled fence posts in afternoon. Went up and heard a "nigger" preach after supper.

June 6
Set fence posts.

June 7
Made a wire stretcher and put on wire. Pa went to Schroon in afternoon. I fixed dam over by brook and put out tomatoes.

June 8
Hoed potatoes. Went up to Culver's after supper.

June 9
Put paris green on part of potatoes. Worked some in garden. Went to Schroon in p. m.. Had tooth pulled.

June 10
Sprayed 3 rows "tatoes". Weeded garden. We burned part of brush beside road. Hoed corn below barn yard. Went to Choir Practice.

June 11
Went up to Culver's and got my hair shaved off. Mary came down home with me. Went to S. S. and to Church, and to Church again in evening. Mary rode down and back with me. Rev. Pettibon preached.

June 12
Worked over on Culver's fallow planting our potatoes.

June 13

Planted potatoes on Culver's for us.

June 14

Planted potatoes on Culver's for Culver's.

June 15

Went over to fallow and found the sheep. Planted

potatoes down beside road. Burned brush after supper. Went down to Culver's.

June 16

Laid up fence down beside of road. Weeded out onions and turnips. Went fishing in afternoon.
Pa went to Pottersville.

June 17

Cultivated and hoed corn. Went to Choir Practice. Hold.

June 18

Went over on Geo. Rickert's fallow got a few strawberries. Went to Sunday School and our Church and also to Prayer Meeting in evening.

June 19

Finished hoeing corn. Pa and Ma went to Schroon

after we got corn hoed. I went strawberrying and weeded little in garden.

June 20

Went to Post Office. Hoed both gardens. Went up to Culver's little while in p. m. Made two bargains. Pa made gate in front of house.

June 21

I cultivated potatoes while Pa went to fallow looking after sheep. Then we hoed all our potatoes and got through at 5:30.

June 22

We cut maples down beside road and mowed and cut the brush on south side of road from cow bars up to barn.

June 23

Have a hard cold and have not felt very good today. Carried Ma down to Taylor's to go to Mill Brook. Hoed corn below barn.

June 24

Felt better today. Paris greened potatoes.
Went to Schroon in afternoon. G. L.

June 25

Went up to Culver's. Went to Sunday School and

Church.
2-14-+14-2-14-8-0-
12+2-20-2-3-7+14-9-4-
2-21+2-10-14-8-0-2-16-
0-7-20-10-2-12-14+20-
9²-4+14-9

June 26
Bushed peas. Hoed some in
garden. Went over on Lew
Richardson's after straw-
berries. Went to Taylor's
after Ma and to Post Office
after books.

June 27
Went over our potatoes
with Paris green gun.
Went up to Culver's to bug
theirs but wind blew so I
didn't. Went to Schroon
in afternoon.
Pa went to Chester.

June 28
Fixed window curtains.
Pa fixed horse rake.
I put new teeth in bull
rake. It rained nearly all
day.

June 29
Bushed few peas. Pa and I
cut nearly a cord of sugar
wood up by corn piece.
Mary and Grand ma
were down here in p. m.

June 30
We went over our potatoes
and knocked bugs into
pans. Hoed corn. Uncle

David came here in after-
noon. I went up to
Culver's to see him in
evening.

Saturday, July 1, 1899
I churned in morning.
Visited with Uncle David.
Hoed little corn. Afternoon
I went to Schroon.
Had tooth pulled on four
times and he broke it off.
Went to Choir Practice.

July 2
Went up to Culver's after
Uncle David's duffle.
Went to Sunday School
and Church.
Pa and I went to church
again in evening.

July 3
Hoed corn. Visited with
Uncle David. Went up to
Culver's after pictures.

July 4
Churned. Got ready and
went to Taylor's
and to Mill
Brook. Went
down to
lake in
evening to
see fire-
works.

July 5
Went down around Mill

Brook showing my book.
Fooled around in after-
noon and came home on
last boat.

July 6

Worked on road. Had show-
er in afternoon. We all got
wet. Tooth ached hard in
afternoon.

July 7

Worked on road in
forenoon. Aunt Lib and
her boys and Aunt Lucy
and Raymond came over.
Grand ma and Mary
were down. There were sev-
enteen here to dinner.

July 8

Rainy

Uncle David started for
home this morning.
Eddy and I went up to
Culver's in afternoon.
It rained in forenoon.

July 9

Went to Sunday School
and Church. Went up to
Culver's in evening.

July 10

We commenced haying.
Mowed some back of house.

July 11

Went to Taylor's and
then to Culver's. Mowed
back of house.

July 12

Worked at haying. Got in
two loads.

July 13

Pa went to village in
forenoon. Uncle Jim and
Henry helped us get in hay
in afternoon.

July 14

Went to Taylor's. Mowed
up to Culver's.
Machine gave out twice.
Pa mowed there in after-
noon and Uncle J. and H.
helped get in hay here.

July 15

Worked at Culver's. Pa
went to village and
mowed at Culver's after he
got back. Scratch day.

July 16

It rained until about one
o'clock. I went up to
Culver's. Have a sore on
thumb. Went to Church
and to Taylor's in
evening.

July 17

I caught few potato bugs.
We mowed little orchard
and some below lower
barn.
Aft. Pa and Ma went off
and I mowed below barn,
and hoed potatoes beside
road. Got an orange from
Leah.

July 18

Mowed little orchard and

some below barn.

July 19
Hayed it south of road.
Went to Culver's to see
about buttermilk.

July 20
Got in hay east of lane
and mowed some. Helped
Uncle Henry drive his
cows home.

July 21
Hayed it east of barn.

July 22
Cleaned out under hen
roost. Dug potatoes.
Started to go over on
Culver's fallow but it
cleared off so I didn't go.
Pa went to Schroon in
a.m. We got up hay in
afternoon.

July 23
Went to Taylor's twice.
Went to Sunday School
and Baptist Church.

July 24
Picked peas in forenoon.
Aft. Pa, Uncle Jim and
Henry and I mowed
here.

July 25
Went to Taylor's. We
started to get in hay but it
rained so we stopped. Went
up to Culver's.

July 26
Pa and I turned over hay

and in p.m. Uncle Jim
and Henry helped us get
in hay.

July 27
Went to Taylor's. Mowed
south of shade trees.
Got it up in afternoon.

July 28
Pa and I finished our
haying. Mary and
Grand ma were down here
in afternoon.

July 29
Worked for Uncle Jim and
Henry on their fallow.
Went to Choir Practice in
evening.

July 30
Went up to Culver's and
cut Uncle Jim's hair.
Found his keys. Went to
S. S. and Church.

July 31
Worked over on Culver's
fallow.

Tuesday, August 1, 1899
Went to Taylor's. Pa
worked on Culver's. Dug 2
bushels of potatoes.

August 2
Worked in Culver's fallow.

August 3
Went to Taylor's. Pa
worked for Culver's. I dug
two bushels potatoes.

Grand ma and Mary were down here in p.m. Killed hen lice. Went to Culver's after sugar.

August 4
Went to Taylor's. Pa and I went over on Culver's fallow in afternoon. He drew a load of hay home or up there.

August 5
Worked for Uncle J. H. and H. J. on their lower fallow. Got it all done.

August 6
Went to Taylor's twice. Went to S. S. and Church. Charley De Lorme and Culver's folks were here to supper.

August 7
I went to Taylor's and to Culver's after wagon and then to Schroon. Came back across.

August 8
Went to Taylor's. Picked peas. Pa and I mowed one piece of oats in afternoon.

August 9
Gathered up eggs. Cleaned gun. Killed hen lice. Ground scythe. Pa and I went up on John Fey's and fought fire. Twenty-three more fought fire on ledge hill today.

August 10
Went to Taylor's. Went up to Culver's. We traded off my old watch with a peddler for one he had. Gave him $4.00 to even it up. Went to Culver's again in afternoon.

August 11
(no entry)

August 12
Went to Taylor's.

August 13
Went up to Culver's. Mary was off to Church. Went to Sunday School and Church. Went to Taylor's in evening and got back to -5. church. Butter tub night.

August 14
Went to Taylor's twice. We got up our oats and mowed down piece south of potatoes.

August 15
I mowed oats back of barn after I carried Ma down to Fred Ford's. Raked few oats and then we went up to

Emory Richardson's after a cow.
One awful small potato today.

August 16

Went to Taylor's twice. Martha and Myrtle Richardson were up here visiting. Mary and Grand ma were down here. No X. We got in our oats.

August 17

Dry and Fair

I dug potatoes while Pa went to Taylor's. Then we dug all the rest of the day. Got 8 Bushels of good ones. I went up to Culver s after I got the chores all finished. Bushel A No. 1.

August 18

95°   Fair

Went to Taylor's twice. Dug potatoes all day. Awful hot Day. Got awful tired before I got to bed.

August 19

98°   Fair

I went to Schroon with 14 1/2 bushels of Potatoes Got home at 11:10. It was so awful hot we did not do much in afternoon only go over to fallow and dig out bear spring.

August 20

Went to Taylor's twice. Went up to Culver s. Did not go to Church. Mary was down here awhile in afternoon. Show day.

August 21

Went over to fallow. Dug potatoes. Dug out spring. Picked sweet corn. Had shower in evening.

August 22

Went to Taylor's twice. Dug potatoes in forenoon. Pa went to Schroon with them in afternoon. I helped Uncle Jim and Henry rake oats.

August 23

Killed potato bugs. Weeded out strawberries. Wrote church meeting notices. Went to Culver's and got my shoe fixed. Went to Emory Richardson's in evening with horse.

August 24

Went to Taylor's twice. Went into Schroon and had my pretty face put on glass.

August 25

Did not do much of anything in forenoon. Afternoon Pa and I got in oats for Ed Granger.

August 26

(no entry)

August 27

Went to Sunday School

and Church. Went to meeting again in evening. Ma and Mary went too.

August 28
(no entry)

August 29
Went over to fallow looking up sheep. Helped Pa get ready to go to Schroon. Pulled few beans. Went down in sugar works after blackberries. Milked all cows. Mary was here in p.m.

August 30
Went to Taylor's twice. Pa and I went over and looked at our fallow potatoes.

August 31
I did not do much of anything. Went into Culver's in p.m. Picture day. Went to lawn social at Jen Taylor's in evening. Got home at 1:30.

Friday, September 1, 1899
Pa went to Schroon. I went to Taylor's twice. Went up to Culver's little while in p.m.
Helped make out tax list.

September 2
Went to Culver's in forenoon. Helped make out tax list. Afternoon Pa went to church meeting and I did not do much. Went to Choir Practice. Mary rode down with Pa and back with me.

September 3
Went to Church at 10:30. Preaching by Rev. Thomas Smith. Jim Wood and wife were here to dinner. Had light shower just Sunday School time. Went to Jacob Hall's after Mary. Went to Taylor's in evening. Lois rode home.

September 4
Went up and put up notices on school house. Boiled soap. Put box on wagon and went to saw mill for saw dust. Went up to Culver's with Mary cow. Uncle Henry and Grace came home.

September 5
Went to Taylor's twice. Went to Schroon after Grand ma. Got my pictures. Dug potatoes and hunted after sheep.

September 6
Hunted after sheep. Helped unload saw dust. Dug potatoes. Had a sing

after dinner. Mary was here.

September 7
Went to Taylor's. Carried Ma and Grace to Culver's. Dug potatoes.

September 8
Went to Taylor's. Elsie Ford rode up and back with me. Mary and Elsie were here in afternoon. P.P. soft.

September 9
Helped Ed Granger fix fence. Went up to Culver's. Threshed oats to bind corn. Grace, Myrtle and I went to Schroon in afternoon.
Went to Choir Practice.

September 10
Went to Taylor's twice. Went up to Jack Taylor's with Grace. Went to Sunday School and Church and to Church again in evening. Thurm Warren was here in forenoon.

September 11
Went up and got squashes for Grace. Bound up corn and set it up.

September 12
Went to Culver's and from there all over our fallow. Emory, Pa and I fixed sheep pen over to fallow.

September 13
We set bear trap in forenoon. Cut corn below barn and in garden.

September 14
Pa and I dug potatoes. Went to Taylor's.

September 15
Pa and I finished digging potatoes. Anda Floyd came over here. We fixed tax list in afternoon. Anda and I went to Culver's in the evening.

September 16
Took two pills last night so don't feel just right today on that account. Went to Taylor's and to bear trap. Went to Culver's in the afternoon.

September 17
Went to Sunday School and Baptist Church. Mary was here little while before Church time.

September 18
Got up at 4 a.m. and helped Pa get ready to go to Riverside. Went to bear trap. Threshed beans. Went to Granger's spring after water. Went to Culver's. Husked corn below barn.

September 19
Went to bear trap. Did

not do much of anything in forenoon. Pa settled up with Taylor. We drew in corn in afternoon.

September 20

Pa and I husked corn some in forenoon. Afternoon he went to Schroon. I husked corn when I did not visit. Mary was down and Henry C. and Anda in the afternoon.

September 21

Churned in morning. Went up to Culver's. Henry came down with me and stayed the rest of the day. Did not do much. Went to choir meeting in evening.

September 22

Pa and I husked corn all day. Henry C. went home about 11 a.m. Went to first Union Choir Practice. Dog cart night.

September 23

Pa and I dug potatoes on Culver's fallow. Got 7 bushels. Pa stayed over there looking after deer but did not see any. Jim Uncle and Aunt Mary went to North Hudson.

September 24

Went to Sunday School and Church. Had first Union Choir. Pa and I went to bear trap in forenoon.

September 25

Went to Granger's three times after pigs. Drew in corn and pumpkins. Had a shower in afternoon. We gathered apples above house. Pulled carrots, onions and beets.

September 26

It rained hard all last night and a good deal today. About 5 1/2 inches in all. We husked corn. I loaded 27 cartridges for Uncle Henry while he husked.

September 27

Pa and I husked corn.

September 28

Arthur Granger and I went to the fair. I went to Culver's a little while in morning. We met Bert and Marion Dickerson at the fair.

September 29

Went over to bear trap. Husked corn. Pa went to Pottersville in forenoon. We dug potatoes beside of road. Had hard shower in evening.

September 30
Pa and I dug potatoes over on Culver's fallow
Awful cold disagreeable day.
First snow of season.

Sunday, October 1, 1899
Went up to Culver's. Went to Sunday School and Church and to C.E. in evening. Mary and I went to C.E.

October 2
Commenced going to school in Schroon.

October 3
Attended school. Pa and Grand ma went to Chester.

October 4
Attended school.

October 5
Attended school. Commenced studying advanced arithmetic.

October 6
Went to school. Expected a geology in the mail so waited at Schroon but it didn't come.
Went to Choir Practice.

October 7
Churned. Burned brush below lower orchard.
Uncle Jim and Aunt

May were up here visiting. Did not work much in afternoon. Went up to Culver's a little while in evening.

October 8
Went to Sunday School, Church and C.E. in the evening.
Oscar and Lois stopped here to supper and went back to C.E. Lois played organ.

October 9
We went to John Fey's funeral. They practiced music here. Mary rode up and back with me. Wagon drill broke coming home.

October 10
Heated over soap and thinned it. Husked corn. Pa went to Chester.

October 11
We dug our potatoes on Culver's fallow. Had 19 bushels in all. Came home after dinner and worked in orchard.

October 12
Pa and I husked corn. Went to Culver's just before supper and went to surprise party there in evening. I carried Maude Patreau and got home at 1:45 a.m.

October 13
We drew stone out of lower

orchard. Then drew two loads of manure on to it. Cleaned out hen house. Went to Choir Practice.

October 14

Carried soap down cellar. Piled up wood. Churned. Shelled corn. Got tomato dirt. Went up to Culver's. Got poke off Granger's hog.

October 15

Went up to Uncle Jim's and got my hair cut. Went to Sunday School, Church and C.E. in the evening. I played organ in C.E.

October 16

Attended school. Lucy and Mildred Richardson rode up and back with me. Got my new Geology.

October 17

Attended school.

October 18

Went to school.

October 19

Went to school. Addie Stanard rode up and back with me.

October 20

Went to school.

October 21

Pa and I went down to the lead mine. I came back afoot.

October 22

Went to Sunday School and Church. Mary and I went again to C.E. in evening.

October 23

Went to school.

October 24

Attended school. Ma went down to Uncle Jim's visiting.

October 25

Attended school. Aunt L.A. went down to David Hall's.

October 26

Went to school. Aunt L.A. came home.

October 27

It rained all day so I did not go to school. Studied quite a lot. Went up to Culver's in afternoon.

October 28

It rained nearly all day. I studied some. Dug ditch by lower barn.

October 29

Went to Sunday School and Church. Did not go in evening.

October 30

Attended school.

October 31

Attended school. It commenced to rain about

noon so I stayed at Uncle Jim's all night.

Wednesday, November 1, 1899
Went to school. It rained all day so I had to drive home in the rain.

November 2
Went to school. Aunt Sophia came home with me from David Hall's.

November 3
Went to school. Aunt Sophia went back. Went to "sing" in the evening. Came home in the rain.

November 4
Gathered turnips. Banked up house.

November 5
Went to Sunday School and Church and to revival in the evening.

November 6
Attended school.

November 7
Covered our well house and shingled it. Went to Culver's in afternoon a little while. Pa started his singing school enterprise tonight.
Net receipts to date $0.15.

November 8
Helped catch and shear sheep. Studied some.

Aunt Lucy and Uncle Bish came here about noon. I went to Chester about three p.m..

November 9
Took examination in School Law and American History. Looked the shirt or pants factory over.

November 10
Took examination in Arithmetic, Geography, Spelling, Physiology and Hygiene, Composition and Grammar. Came home after I got through.

November 11
Snowy
Churned. Brought in water to wash. Studied some. It snowed most all day but not very hard.
Went up to Uncle Jim's. He was fixing threshing machine.

November 12
Went to Sunday School and Church.

November 13
Went to school.

November 14
Went to school.

November 15
Went to school. Had two passengers up from Rob Shufelt's.

270

November 16
Went to school.
November 17
Went to school.
November 18
We Us & Co. threshed our oats with Uncle J. and H.'s threshing machine. I went up to Culver's to help load sheep for Eddy and Howard.
November 19
Went to S. S. and to Church twice.
November 20
Went to school.
November 21
Went to school.
November 22
Went to school.
November 23
Went to school.
November 24
Went to school. Came down to Emory W's to supper and stayed till choir practice.
November 25
Plowed some. Cleaned out hog pen and beautied up comfort house. Went to Singing School.
November 26
Went up to Culver's and got my hair cut. Went to S. S. and Church. Rev. Contoise preached his

farewell sermon. Went to C.E. meeting. Maude and Mary were here between times.
November 27
Went to school. Had 40-11 errands.
November 28
Went to school.
November 29
Went to school. Ida Hall rode down with me. School was out at 3:15 p.m.
November 30
Pa and I tinkered stable nearly all day. I churned and fixed little fence.

Friday, December 1, 1899
Went to school. Maude Patreau rode up and back with me.
December 2
Churned. Went up to Culver's. Squirted out water pipe. Cut up old boards. Cleaned out hen roost. The folks had a singing school here in evening.
December 3
Went to Sunday School and Church. Had a new organ stool at church. Mary was here a while in forenoon. It began

snowing just at dark.

December 4

It snowed some in forenoon about 8" in all. Did not go to school. Went up to Culver's little while in afternoon.

December 5

Attended school.

December 6

Attended school.

December 7

Attended school.

December 8

Went to school and to choir practice in evening. Went with a cutter.

December 9

Went up and saw Uncle Jim's wood mill. Drew wood into shed. Churned. Singing school here in evening. It adjourned at 11:30 p.m.

December 10

Got up at 8:30 a.m. Finished breakfast at 10 a.m. Went to Sunday School and C.E. in evening. No preaching service.

Ma stayed down to Fred Hard's.

December 11

We killed our old hog and "Mummy" cow. Had bad luck with hog. Got it

hung up and let it fall down again. Jim Wood helped us.

December 12

Attended school.

December 13

Attended school. Ida Hall rode up with me. Took top off old carriage in morning. Pa went to Schroon.

December 14

Went to school. There was a "G.A.R." entertainment at the M.E. Church in p.m. Elsie and Florence rode down with me. It began snowing little in p.m.

December 15

It snowed about 10 inches last night so didn't go to school. Helped churn and ground up sausage meat. Wind blew some.

December 16

We finished drawing wood into shed. I went up to Culver's after saw. Pa went to saw mill after saw dust but did not get any. Banked up water barrel. Singing school here in evening.

December 17

Went to Sunday School and Church. Went to C.E. in evening. I played

organ.
Mary rode down and back
with Pa and I.

December 18

Attended school. Nice road.
Carried up bag of corn and
had it ground.

December 19

I did not go to school as
the road was so bad.
It rained quite a lot and
thawed a lot. Pa went to
Schroon to get horses shod.

December 20

Went to school. Pa and
Ma went to Schroon.

December 21

Went to school. Maude rode
up and back with me.
Carried Grand ma C. home.
Pa and Ma went to Schroon.

December 22

Went up to Culver's. Pa
and Uncle Jim went to
village and stayed nearly
all day. I churned and
broke thermometer and had
a 12-25-3-14+ of a time.

December 23

We commenced cutting
logs up on pasture hill.
We went to Xmas tree in
Schroon in evening.
Mary stopped here and
stayed all night.

December 24

It snowed hard in
forenoon and stopped so we
went to Sunday School.
Did not go down in
evening.

December 25

I churned a long time in
forenoon and went
up and cut wood
a while. We got
ready to go to
Schroon to
Xmas tree in
evening. I went from F.
Ford's in load.

December 26

Pa and I cut wood and
logs up in pasture.
Went to singing school at
Culver's in evening.

December 27

Pa and I cut wood up in
pasture.

December 28

Pa and I cut wood and
logs. Singing school here
in evening.

December 29

Pa and I cut wood in
forenoon. It snowed little
in afternoon so we did not
work more than an hour.
Mrs. Jacob and Charles
Hall were here visiting.
Went to Choir Practice.

December 30

I churned over two hours
in forenoon. Pa went

to Schroon after his teeth.
We cut wood little while in
afternoon. Singing school
here in evening.

December 31
We went to Sunday
School and to Church with
Culver's bobs. Went to P.O.
and back with load. Mary
went with us. Pa, Ma and
I went again in evening.

Funerals and Deaths

F. Olive Whitney Jan. 31
F. Alonzo Bailey Feb. 2
F. Mrs. Lyons Feb. 6
(Mrs. E.J. Dunn's mother)
F. Eleanor Jones Cole Feb. 21
F. Russell Montgomery
March 3
F. Mary Huntley Smith May
16, 1899
D. Thomas Rooney May 15,
'99
D. William Brown April 20,
'99
F. Dorcas Wright. May 25 '99
F. John Fey Oct. 9, 1899
F. Mrs. Fred Bover Nov. 2
1899

The fifth verse of the eleventh
chapter of
Numbers names six kinds of
eatables:
Fish
Cucumbers
Onions
Melons
Garlick

Algebra
Began Radical Quantities
today. Jan. 4

Expense for W. J. Whitney
Jan. 3   This Diary   .45
Jan. 4   Cloth for shirt   1.08
Feb. 23 Rub. boots   .8
"   28 Pr. Rubbers   1.75

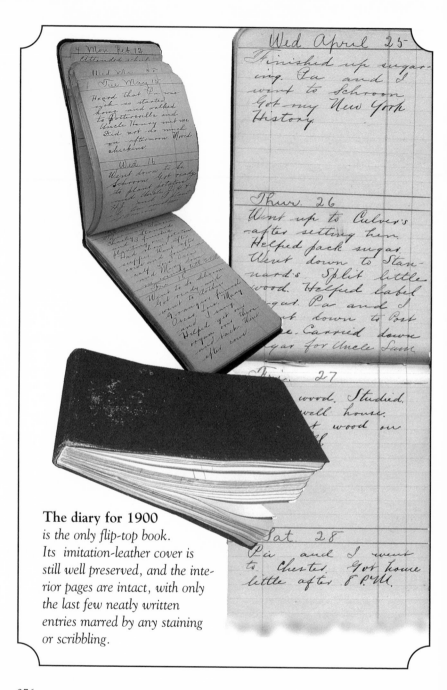

Wed April 25

Finished up sugaring. Pa and I went to Schroon. Got my New York History.

Thur. 26

Went up to Culver's after setting hen. Helped pack sugar. Went down to Stannard's. Split little wood. Helped label sugar. Pa and I went down to Post Office. Carried down sugar for Uncle Sam.

Fri. 27

wood. Studied. well house. got wood on...

Sat. 28

Pa and I went to Chester. Got home little after 8 P.M.

4 Mon Feb 12
Attended school

Wed May

Tue May 15

Heard that Pa was sick so started home and walked to Pottersville and Uncle Harvey met me. Did not do much in afternoon. Hoed chuckins.

Wed 16

Went down to So. Schroon. Got ready to plant potatoes and Chester & ...

The diary for 1900

is the only flip-top book. Its imitation-leather cover is still well preserved, and the interior pages are intact, with only the last few neatly written entries marred by any staining or scribbling.

Main Street, Schroon Lake in 1900

1900 gave rise to the expression, "the turn of the century." One hundred years later, with the turn of another century the term still applies to the change from the 1800s to the 1900s. And why not? It will always be recognized as the beginning of a new era of cultural and social changes.

The world stretched in all directions in 1900. Hawaii became a United States territory, and United States troops traveled halfway around the world and arrived in Peking to help put down the Boxer Rebellion. The United States Navy's first submarine made its debut, and July 2 saw the first flight of Count Von Zeppelin's airship, LZ-1.

On the home front, the United States Post Office issued the first book of postage stamps. Dr. Walter Reed began research that beat yellow fever; and in Connecticut on July 28, Louis Lanssing created hamburger, an idea that has now bridged two centuries and has flourished in its longevity.

Walter makes no direct reference to the November 6 landslide re-election of President McKinley and his running mate, Teddy Roosevelt; but he does record that Ma and Pa went to Schroon on that day as they had on election day in 1896, presumably so Pa could cast his vote. That was one of the rare occasions that Ma, Marion Whitney, went to Schroon. With the exception of visiting relatives and going to church, it appears that Marion's days were filled with home and family, often preparing meals for visiting extended family members, neighborhood men sharing the work of the farm, and anyone passing by at mealtime. Walter recorded that 17 people were to dinner one day.

Marion was not so absorbed in household activity, however, that she did not enjoy a link with the world of fashion and style. In 1894, Marion had her eye on an extension table, a popular and practical design that was frowned on by Edith Wharton, the period novelist and guru of interior design. Its practical aspects won out in spite of the protest; and the extension table became a source of pride in the grand mansions of the elite to accommodate their large dinner parties, as it did in Marion Whitney's kitchen. On January 2, 1900, Pa and Ma went to the Post Office and ordered a fur cape for Ma. Its arrival on January 14 brought visitors with admiring eyes to gaze upon Marion's new fashion.

No mention is made of newspapers in Walter's diaries, but the *Essex County Republican*[2], headquartered in Port Henry, was published weekly and may have been Marion's link to trends of the period. Many of its ads included sure-cure medicines and elixirs such as Swamp Root, "a remedy for kidney problems, an affliction that could make miserable not only men, but women as well." The "cookery" column offered a recipe for "Pickerel a la Hollandaise." Picture ads covered household wares, furniture, farm equipment, and clothing fashion. State news included the governor's praise for the new superintendent of canals for saving 25% expenses over the prior year. It was reported that on Aug. 10, a cyclone raised havoc on the Champlain Valley; and weekly articles chronicled the Boer War in Africa and the Boxer Rebellion in Peking.

Each week a section of the paper was devoted to the news from the towns of Essex County. On July 3, 1900, a South Schroon journalist reported the following:

South Schroon, July 3

- *Hiram King, who has been in employ of W. H. Granberry of NY, is seriously ill with dysentery and inflammation of the bowels. He is in the residence of B. O. Barnes but his home is in Hoffman.*

[2]Essex County Republican, (Port Henry: Article – South Schroon, July 3, 1900.)

- The hay crop in this area will be very light; potatoes are looking finely; oats fair; but corn will have to hurry up to get there before frost comes.
- The Whitney Cottage has five boarders at present.
- Mrs. C. W. Warren is much better.
- Mrs. Sophia Worden has come to stay with her parents, Mr. & Mrs. Orren Murdock, through the summer.
- Miss Grace Traver has been called to Glens Falls to see her uncle who is not expected to live.
- Mrs. Marsden's cottage is being occupied by guests from NY. Among them are eleven crippled children.
- Mr. & Mrs. Aneda Floyd of Newman Falls, St. Lawrence County visited relatives in this place last week.
- E.A. Granger and Mr. Frank Granger made a visit to Chilson last week.
- Howard Floyd is making a short visit in Charley Hill this week."

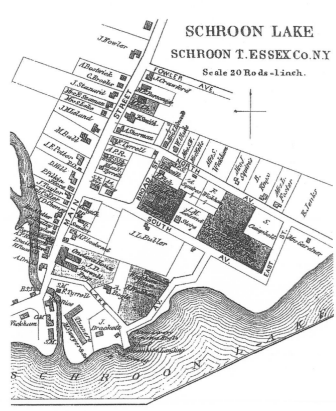

This is a map of the village of Schroon Lake at the turn of the century. It delineates the names of residents and establishments from the bridge at the south end of Main St. to Fowler Ave. at the north end.

1900
Walter J. Whitney
South Schroon
Essex Co. New York
1900

Monday, January 1, 1900
Cleaned out hen house.
Studied some in forenoon.
Pa and Uncle Jim went to village.
I went up to Uncle Henry's in afternoon. churned towards night. Singing school here in evening. Had a good time.

January 2
Did not do much of anything. Mr. and Mrs. Clapper and their girl, Anna, came here about 11 a.m. visiting. It snowed little all day but snow very light. Wrote some. Pa went to P.O. and ordered a fur cape for Ma.

January 3
Pa and I cut wood and logs in forenoon.
I broke my axe helve about 11 a.m. and went to Culver's to borrow a helve but did not get any. Pa went to village in p.m. and Ma went to K.D.

Meeting at Oren Murdock's. I chopped in afternoon and did all the chores.

January 4
Pa and I cut wood and logs. Have 28 pieces already cut and a lot of wood. Had singing school here in evening. Edith, Clara and Will Fairfield came down to hear and see the fun.

January 5
We cut wood and logs. Pa and I went to choir Practice in evening.

January 6
We cut wood and logs. Uncle Henry helped us some. Uncle Jim and Mary went to North Hudson. I went down to Post Office and to Oren Murdock's toward night.

January 7
Went to Sunday School. There was no preaching service. Pa was superintendent. Uncle Jim, Mary and Leah came from North Hudson just dark.
We got ready to go to C.E. but it snowed little so we did not go.

January 8

Went to school. Nice day to go nice sounds. A long way though for Tinker tracks.

January 9

Went to school. Whisper snap day. Wm. Hall rode up with me and Charley Stanard and Mrs. Sherman rode back, she from Uncle Jim Whitney's.

January 10

Went to school. Mary and Leah were here when I got home. Got me a 5¢ collar today.
State Inspector or Truant Officer visited the school.

January 11

Attended school. Grandma went up to David Hall's and stayed during the day. It snowed hard in evening.

January 12

Attended school. It snowed five or six inches last night. Went up to Culver's in evening. Leah D. L was there. A boy arrived at Tom Cole's last night.

January 13

Pa and I skidded logs and drew sugar wood out on top of pasture hill. Edith and Clara Fairfield came here just night. Uncle Jim, Mary and Leah were here in evening.

January 14

Went to Sunday School and Church. Clara, Mary and Leah were here and they went to church with us. Sang lot in evening. I carried parasol coming home from church.

January 15

Went to school. Frank Hall rode up with me.
Mrs. Melinda Tripp died today. Ma's new cape came today.

January 16

Went to school. It snowed four or five inches last night.
Uncle Jim, Mary and Leah were down here in evening to see Ma's new plush cape.

January 17

Went to So. Schroon to Emory Whitney. Did not go to school. Took a pill last night.
Felt rather mean all day.

January 18

Went to school. Went down to Emory's in morning and got his horse to drive.

January 19
Went to school. Went to choir practice.

January 20
It rained nearly all day. We did not do much in forenoon. Pa went to So. Schroon and I went up to Culver's in p. m. Leah was there. We played dominoes.

January 21
Went to Sunday School and to C.E. in evening. Mary and Leah went with us each time. They rode home from here with Oscar.

January 22
Attended the Regents Examination at Schroon. Took Advanced Arithmetic and Advanced English.

January 23
Went to examination in afternoon. Took Physical Geography. Leah rode up with me.

January 24
Went down to Stanard's. Helped unload wood. Went up to Culver's. Mary Whitney and Mabel Cole were up here today. Went to examination in English Composition.

January 25
Went over to Granger's and up to Culver's Eddy and Howard came over. Pa went to Riverside for Uncle Jim.

January 26
The wind blew hard all day. I went to Schroon. Took examination in Geology.

January 27
Pa drew wood for Stanard's folks. I cleaned out granary. Thurman Warren was here quite a while. I churned. Went to Choir Practice.

January 28
Went to Sunday School and Church and to C.E. in evening. Mary went down with Pa and I in evening.

January 29
It snowed last night and the wind blew so I did not go to school. Studied some.

January 30
Attended school. Am going to take up Rhetoric, Civics, 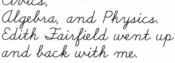 Algebra, and Physics. Edith Fairfield went up and back with me.

There was a social here in evening. 34 here besides "us."

January 31

Attended school.

Thursday, February 1, 1900

Attended school. Wind blew hard some of the way home.

February 2

Did not go to school. 16° below zero in morning. Went over to Mash Pond after logs.
Went up to Culver's in p.m. little while. Studied some.

February 3

Helped load logs. Went down to Emory Whitney's with Fanny. Uncle Jim W. and Aunt Lib came over. I went to Culver's to see them. We intended to go to Mill Brook but Ma gave it up and Mary and I went.
Stayed at Uncle B's.

February 4

Went to Sunday School and Church at Mill Brook. Came home in afternoon. It snowed when we were coming home.

February 5

Attended school.

February 6

Attended school.

February 7

Attended school.

February 8

Attended school. It rained quite a lot today.

February 9

Attended school. Pa and Uncle Jim went to Mill Brook. Mort Stanard gave me three small pickerel.

February 10

Helped load logs. Shelled corn. Made stick on board for Wilson's barn. Cleaned fish. Made rolling pin for Raymond. Mary went to C.P. with Pa and I. Churned.

February 11

We went to Sunday School and Church. Pa and I went again in evening.

February 12

Attended school. Went up and back on the lake. Miss Fountain came up home with me from Fred Ford's. Wm. H. Hall rode to Schroon with me.

February 13

It rained nearly all day. I carried Miss Fountain down to school. Studied some. Pa went to Schroon

in p.m. I went up to
Uncle Jim's a little while.

February 14

Went to school.

February 15

Went to school. Went to
social at Emory Whitney's
in evening. Got home at
12:40.
Mary went down with us
and stayed here all night.

February 16

Went to school.

February 17

Pa and I cut sugar wood
up on pasture hill.
Ma went to Culver's in
afternoon. Pa and I went
to Choir Practice.

February 18

Went to Sunday School.
The kids sang a little at
the close. Quite windy
day.
Mary was here. Had quite a
sing.

February 19

Did not go to school. The
wind blew hard all day.
I studied quite a lot.

February 20

Went to school. Went up
and back on the lake. Mrs.
Wm. Hall rode down with
me.

February 21

Went to school. Mrs. Hall
went back with me. Went
on the lake.

February 22

Attended school.
It stormed some during
the day.

February 23

It snowed some in morn-
ing so I did not start for
school. Pa and I went to
Schroon in afternoon and
I went to school.

February 24

Pa and I cut sugar wood
in forenoon. We went to
Culver's in afternoon to see
them saw wood.

February 25

The wind blew hard all
day and the snow flew. Pa
and I went down to
Sunday School. There
were 25 there. We went up
to Emory's a little while.

February 26

The wind blew hard all
day and it has been the
worst day of the year. I
studied some.
Pa went down to So.
Schroon twice. Have a little cold yet.

February 27

The thermometer was
down to 12° or 13° below
zero. Studied some. Cold
felt good deal better. Went

up home a little while in afternoon. Pa had a cold and Ma likewise.

February 28
Pa and Ma were both dumped up so I did not go to school. It snowed little in p.m. Studied.

Thursday, March 1, 1900
It continued to snow all day about 18 or 20 inches in all. It rained some in evening,
Pa was about half sick. Uncle Henry came down here. No teams went by.

March 2
I went up to Culver's and got them to help break out roads. Hitched up our team and drove to P.O. and back. Pa did not feel quite as well today. Ma got Dick G. to stay here all night.

March 3
Shoveled off sugar house. Went to Schroon after medicine for Pa and to get some other things. Had a pretty blue time. The road was so bad. Uncle Henry helped me do a few chores.

March 4
The road was so bad we did not go to S. S. and Pa would not have gone anyway. Mary was here nearly all day. We printed some for Elsie.

March 5
Helped plow out roads. Shoveled off back shed.

March 6
Helped wash. Mary and Uncle Jim were here. Emory W. was here at dinner. Heard that Raymond Carpenter died this morning. Set up beds upstairs. Uncle H. went to M.B. on snow shoes.

March 7
Went up to Uncle Jim's a little while in forenoon on snow shoes. In afternoon I wrote some and went to Post Office.
Got a letter from "Stub."

March 8
Went to Mill Brook on snow shoes from Walkers. Raymond was buried today. Uncle Henry came home and I stayed at Mill Brook all night.

March 9
Came home. Stopped at Elsie's and to Stannards. Got home at 11 a.m. Shoveled some snow. Churned and studied in

afternoon. Went to Choir Practice.

March 10

Went down to Post Office. Pa and Ma went to Mill Brook in afternoon around the lake.

I went up to Culver's in afternoon and helped saw wood on their mill.

March 11

Slid down hill little. Mary and Grandma came down. Uncle Henry and I went to Sunday School and Church. He was Supt.

We used the new S. S. books first time today. Pa and Ma at Adirondack. Printed in forenoon.

March 12

Studied some. Pa came home from Mill Brook. We went up to Culver's to see their wood mill.

March 13

Uncle Henry and Jim set up their wood mill and sawed a while. It snowed little in middle of day.

March 14

Helped saw wood. Mary was down to help work.

March 15

Helped saw wood. Pa went to Mill Brook after Ma.

Did not get wood quite all cut. Mary Ditto.

March 16

It snowed about 10 inches last night and this forenoon. Studied some. Uncle Henry and Jim were down in afternoon. Pa did not feel very well in afternoon.

Churned. Uncle Henry helpful.

March 17

Plowed out roads. Uncle Henry and Jim plowed it from here up. Went up to Uncle Henry's and got $^1/2$ bu. oats. Pa did not go out any.

March 18

Went up to Culver's. Got my hair frizzed. Mrs. C. F. Taylor was buried today so there was no Sunday School. I went down to Uncle Jim's aft. as he is sick.

March 19

Went up to Culver's after bags. Uncle Jim and I went to village after load of grain.

March 20

Studied some. Pa went down to Uncle Jim's. I emptied middlings and meal and went up to

Culver's little while in afternoon.

March 21

Helped saw wood. Finished our job. Helped set up machine down east of lane. Mary was here.

March 22

Helped Uncle Jim and Henry saw wood. Mary was here

March 23

Helped saw wood. We expected Carl Squires to help but he did not come. Pa went to village.

March 24

Slid down hill east of lane. Split little wood. Churned. Fiddled. Mary and Uncle Jim went to North Hudson. Pa and Ma went down to Uncle Jim's.

March 25

We went to Sunday School and Church. Mr. and Mrs. Samuel Ingraham were on deck.

March 26

Split wood. Helped Uncle J. H. and H. J. sawing their wood. It snowed some in afternoon.

March 27

Went up to Culver's and got my hair cut. Pa, Ma and Uncle Henry started for Mill Brook but met Uncle Bish and Aunt Lucy. Mary and Grandma came down here in p.m.

March 28

Pa and I shoveled around sugar house and shoveled it off. I went to Schroon to examination in afternoon. Took Civics. Stopped to Uncle Jim's awhile.

March 29

Went to examination in forenoon. Took Algebra. Pa and I broke sugar roads in afternoon. Ma went down to Uncle Jim.

March 30

Went to examination. Took Rhetoric and Physics. Uncle Jim very bad today so Ma did not come home.

March 31

Pa went down to Uncle Jim's. I churned for about six weeks. Split wood. Started some hulled corn. Pa and I fired buckets little while.

Sunday, April 1, 1900

Pa went to Uncle Jim's, and to Sunday School. I stayed at home. Mary was

287

here in afternoon.

April 2
We washed buckets some in forenoon and broke sugar roads in p.m.

April 3
Helped Uncle J. & H. get their horse power up home. Split wood. Went up to Culver's to dinner. We scattered buckets in p.m. Went to Culver's after bit brace in evening.

April 4
We tapped trees. Got wet more or less.

April 5
Pa and I tapped big trees in forenoon.
We got things ready and gathered four barrels in afternoon.

April 6
We went over to fallow and tapped few trees and gathered sap. Ed G. helped me gather and make roads in p.m.

April 7
We worked at sugaring. I tapped the trees out in the kitchen and we gathered four barrels in afternoon.

April 8
Pa, Ma, Mary and I went to Sunday School and Church with a wood shod sled. I went into George R's and saw their organ and cornet.

April 9
Pa and I split and piled wood. Went to Emory Richardson's in evening after steel yards.

April 10
Pa and I got ready and carried Uncle Jim Whitney a load of hay. Uncle J. & H. helped us in forenoon. Horses skipped us.

April 11
Split wood. Took off hay rack. Pa and I gathered 8 barrels of sap in afternoon.

April 12
Went to examination in Schroon. Took School Law and History. Went afoot.
Pa boiled sap all day. Frank G. helped him.

April 13
Split wood. Helped sugar off. In p.m. Pa and I swept off bottom of evaporator, cleaned out stove box and gathered 4 bbls of sap.

April 14
Gathered four barrels of sap in a.m.. In p.m. Frank and I gathered 4 bbls and then Pa went to village. I boiled until 6:30 p.m.

April 15

Went up to Culver's. Went to Sunday School afoot. Mary went with Pa. Things went wrong to suit some today.

April 16

Pa and I worked at sugaring. Gathered 14 1/2 barrels. Spot had a masculine.

April 17

I boiled sap in forenoon. Uncle Jim went down to sugar house awhile. I went to Culver's visiting in afternoon. Cleaned gun.

April 18

Pa and I worked at sugar house sweeping off evaporator and shoeing sled. We made a road to spring. He went to Schroon in p.m. I cleaned fish, helped sugar off and split wood.

April 19

Pa and I split wood. Went to Culver's in evening.

April 20

We split wood. Uncle Jim helped us some. I went over to George Rickert's and Clifton Clark's after dinner.

April 21

Pa and I worked at sugaring. Gathered 11 barrels.

April 22

Went to Sunday School. Pa went with big buckboard and carried down a load of meat. Awful bad roads. Stopped into George Richardson's little while.

April 23

Pa and I gathered sap and brought buckets out to roads. We finished boiling and washed few buckets.

April 24

I gathered buckets and washed them. Pa worked down at the church.

April 25

Finished up sugaring. Pa and I went to Schroon. Got my New York History.

April 26

Went up to Culver's after setting hen. Helped pack sugar. Went down to Stannard's. Split little wood. Helped label sugar. Pa and I went down to Post Office. Carried down sugar for Uncle Sam.

April 27

Split wood. Studied. Moved well house. Drew

out wood on top of hill.

April 28

Pa and I went to Chester. Got home little after 8 p.m.

April 29

Went up to Culver's and got my hair cut. Went down to Emory W's and to Sunday School. Came home and did chores and went to C.E. meeting. Came home afoot. Xi K2.

April 30

Drew manure on garden and plowed it. Had little shower and first thunder this afternoon. Went down to Uncle Jim's after Pa. Went to Culver's with two hens.

Tuesday, May 1, 1900

Plowed garden. Drew manure on to strawberry ground and plowed it. Dragged two gardens and potatoe ground. Morley had a morley. Mary and Uncle Henry were down little while in evening.

May 2

Ma and I went to Chester. Had a talk with Mr. Potter.

May 3

Pa and I drew manure. He finished setting out strawberries. We went over to fallow looking after cow. Went up to Culver's in evening. Had quite a visit.

May 4

Pa went to Schroon in a.m. I took some pills last night and did not feel very good. In afternoon I went up to Culver's while Pa and Ma went to Schroon.

May 5

Went up to Culver's and got Mary and Grandma. Did not do much in a.m. Pa and I went over to Clark's brook fishing. Got 10 trout and carried them down to Uncle Jim W's.

May 6

Went to Sunday School and Church. Rev. W. A. Parker preached his first sermon.

May 7

Got ready and went to Chester. Began business at the factory in afternoon.

May 8

Worked in factory. Sorted few shirts and copied bills into sales book.

May 9

Worked in the factory. Mr. Potter went away in forenoon. I worked on in voice record.

Got me a suit of clothes.

May 10

Worked in factory. Did forty eleven different things. Went down to Will's in evening. Thurman C. Warren was over to the factory a while. Mr. Potter away.

May 11

Worked in factory. Helped put shirts in racks quite a lot. Got a pass and practiced on typewriter quite a while.

May 12

Labored in factory. Went down to K's in evening.

May 13

Went to M. E. Church in morning. Went down to K's to dinner and went down south a ways in afternoon. Went to meeting again in evening.

May 14

Worked on the pay roll all day when I did not do something else.

May 15

Heard that Pa was sick so started home and walked to Pottersville and Uncle Henry met me. Did not do much in afternoon. Moved chickens.

May 16

Went down to So. Schroon. Got ready to plant potatoes and Uncle J. H., and J. H. and I planted ten rows in afternoon.

May 17

Thurman Warren, Charley Stanard and I finished planting our potatoes. Had shower after supper. Went after cows and found a calf. Lois, Oscar and Mary down in evening till 12 p.m.

May 18

Went to So. Schroon. Got ready and went to Arthur Granger's funeral. Oscar, Lois, Mary and I sang. Helped get our organ over there and back. Went after cows.

May 19

Went up to Culver's a while in middle of day. Stayed there to dinner. Came home and went over to Dick Hall's. Sowed peas and set out hops. Went to fallow after cows.

May 20

Went up to Uncle Jim's

and got my hair cut.
Mary was away home.
Went to Sunday School
and Church.

May 21
Plowed back of barn and
drew manure. Dragged
and Pa sowed part of the
piece to oats.

May 22
Got ready and Pa and I
went to Chester.
Worked in afternoon.
Went to party in
evening.

May 23
Worked in factory.
Commenced working at the
books at Kettenbach's store
during the evening.

May 24
Worked.

May 25
Worked. Copied all the
books in K store.

May 26
Worked. Copied all books.
Went for a walk.

May 27
Went to Church and
Sunday School. Went
down to Kettenbach's a little while. Came back and
went off west for a walk,
We us and Co.

May 28
Labored in the factory.

Worked on the pay roll.

May 29
Worked.

May 30
Worked. The dam broke so
the machines did not run.

May 31
Worked. The machines did
not run.

Friday, June 1, 1900
Telephoned for Pa to meet
me, and came home as the
factory did not run. Went
up to Culver's in p.m.

June 2
Went to Culver's and
shaved off my moustache.
Pa and I went to
Schroon in afternoon.

June 3
It rained hard nearly all
day. We all stayed home
all day.
Mary and all the
family were down. Had
quite a visit in afternoon.

June 4
Got up about 4 a.m. and
started about 4:45 for
Chester. Worked.

June 5
Worked in factory.

June 6
Buttoned overalls. Worked
little in office. Sorted

shirts. Opened cases of goods.

June 7

Worked in office. Sorted shirts and carried goods downstairs. Cleaned stock room. Opened boxes of cloth. Mopped office.

June 8

Labored.

June 9

Labored.

June 10

Went to the Presbyterian Church in morning and to the M.E. in evening to Children's Day exercises in evening.

June 11

Worked. Got a bicycle at Kettenbach's in evening. Herb Morehouse and Harry Mundy smashed it before I had it half an hour.

June 12

Worked.

June 13

Worked.

June 14

Worked in factory.

June 15

Worked in factory.

June 16

Worked. Went home after 5 p.m. Pa met me on Landon Hill.

June 17

Went up to Culver's. Went to Church and Sunday School. Pa brought me down part way and I walked the rest of the way. Went to the M.E. Church.

June 18

Labored. Mr. Potter went away this morning.

June 19

Labored.

June 20

Worked.

June 21

Worked.

June 22

Worked.

June 23

Worked.

June 24

Went to the Presbyterian Church and Sunday School and to the Methodist in the evening. Fooled around town and went down to Legget's in afternoon.

June 25

Worked in factory.

June 26

Worked in factory. Uncle Bish called here today. Uncle Floyd and his wife came here in afternoon.

June 27

Worked in factory. Have

worked in office nearly all this week so far. Took quite s sweat in the forenoon. It has been awful hot.

June 28

Labored. Worked up stairs quite a lot. Pretty hot day.

June 29

Worked.

June 30

Worked until about four o'clock and went home on my wheel. Pa and Mary went to Pottersville She stayed at our house all night as it rained.

Sunday, July 1, 1900

Went to Sunday School and Church.

July 2

Went to Chester on my wheel from Taylor's. Worked on pay roll.

July 3

Worked in office. Went to Mill Brook on my bicycle.

July 4

We Us & Co. went on Parks Mountain. Went to fire works in evening.

July 5

Worked.

July 6

Worked.

July 7

Worked.

July 8

Went to church twice, to Sunday School to Christian Science meeting and to Epworth League. Pretty dull day.

July 9

Worked.

July 10

Worked.

July 11

Worked.

July 12

Worked.

July 13

Worked. Pa came down and we had quite a long talk.

July 14

Worked. Went home after 6 p.m. Had to fix wheel so did not get to Taylor's until twenty minutes of nine.

July 15

Went up to Culver's and Uncle Jim cut my hair. Aunt Lib, Jimmy and Blanch K. were over. Went to Sunday School and Church.

July 16

Started from home at five a.m. and rode down on my wheel from Taylor's.

July 17
Worked.

July 18
Worked.

July 19
Worked. N. Church buried today. Got a letter from Pa.

July 20
Worked.

July 21
180 @ 12 = 21.60
Worked. Went home with Pa. Rode part of the way on my wheel.

July 22
Went to Church. Went down to Uncle Jim Whitney's in afternoon with Pa.
I took dinner at Fred Ford's.

July 23
Went from home and worked in the factory.

July 24
Worked.

July 25
Worked.

July 26
Worked

July 27
Worked.

July 28
17 x 12 = 204
Worked. Went home after 5:20 p.m.

July 29
Went to Culver's and shaved. Went to Sunday School and Church M.V.B. Knox preached. Very warm day.

July 30
Worked after I rode down on my wheel in the morning.

July 31
Worked.

Wednesday, August 1, 1900
Labored more or less.

August 2
Worked.

August 3
Worked.

August 4
Worked until after 6 p.m.. and got paid up and came home as I learned later for good.

August 5
Went to Sunday School and Cong. Church.
We did not attend the morning service.

August 6
Went to Taylor's with milk.
Went over and worked little at haying on Deb Hults. Seemed different from working in factory.

August 7
Worked on Abel Walker's farm haying for Pa. It rained some so I went fishing and got wet. Went to school meeting. Pa elected trustee.

August 8
Pa and I went to village.

August 9
I went to Taylor's then went to Schroon and to Severance and Alder Meadow.

August 10
Hayed it on Walker's.

August 11
We worked haying on Walker's.

August 12
Went up to Uncle Jim Whitney's on bicycle. Went to Sunday School and Church and to Taylor's in evening.

August 13
It rained quite hard all day. I went to Uncle Jim's and he cut my hair. He and Will Fairfield broke horses and hay racks. I went with milk in the rain in the evening.

August 14
Pa, Deb, Sam and I hayed it on Walker's fallow. I came home and milked.

August 15
Finished haying on Walker's. I went to Schroon on bicycle and came back to Baptist Association in evening. Seven came up to stay all night.

August 16
Went up to Culver's. Went to three sessions of the Baptist Association. Mary rode with us. Stub, Floyd, Eddy and Howard & George Nichols were here to dinner.

August 17
Dug potatoes. Eddy and I went to Walker's after hay wagon etc. Pa and Eddy went to Schroon in afternoon and I picked up little potatoes and milked.

August 18
(no entry)

August 19
Went to Church then went up and stayed with Thurman until afternoon meeting. I played organ in church. Went to Taylor's in evening. Mary went too. Milk can used to a new purpose.

August 20
We dug potatoes, and Pa took them to Schroon in p. m.

August 21
Dug potatoes. The Carpenter and McKee Brigade visited here today. I went to Taylor's in evening.

August 22
Dug potatoes and Pa delivered them in afternoon.

August 23
Pa and I cut our oats on the lower piece and got them up. Had one good load.

August 24
Went to Taylor's. Thurm came home with me and stayed to dinner. Pa went to Schroon in afternoon. I dug potatoes some and Deb helped but it rained so we quit and unloaded oats. Went for a bicycle ride.

August 25
Pa and I dug potatoes, about 15 bushels of good ones. Went to meeting in evening. Mary was down here intending to help paper, but didn't. I worked with my bibs.

August 26
Went down in sugar camp. Went to Church. I went with Ma. Mrs. Frank Cole stopped here in route.

August 27
I went to Taylor's and to Pottersville with Christiania. Pa went to Schroon in afternoon and I went to Taylor's in rain in the evening.

August 28
Mowed few oats. Dug potatoes. Pa carried shingles up to school house.

August 29
We got up our oats. Dug few potatoes.

August 30
Went to Taylor's. Went to Charley Hollow after mowing machine and horse rake. Weeded strawberries in afternoon. Pa worked at school house.

August 31
Dug potatoes. Pa went to Schroon, I went up to Culver's after potatoes. Went to rehearsal at Church in evening.

Saturday, September 1, 1900
I went to Taylor's in evening. Went to Schroon in forenoon with potatoes

for Mrs. Russell. Pa went to Church meeting in afternoon.

September 2
We went to the anniversary of the church dedication.

September 3
Pa and I went to Paradox Lake and to Pyramid Lake. I rode home from Schroon on bicycle.

September 4
Went up to school house. Dug few potatoes. Felt mean all day. Pa went to Schroon in afternoon.

September 5
I felt mean and did not do very much all day.

September 6
Felt better today. Helped kill and pick hens. Accident. Picked up apples.

September 7
Went off hunting sheep in forenoon. Dug potatoes in afternoon.

September 8
Went to Taylor's twice. Dug potatoes. Pa and Ma went to Schroon in afternoon.

September 9
Went to Sunday School and Church. Pa went to

Mrs. Billing's funeral. I went to Taylor's in evening.

September 10
Went to Taylor's. Went to Culver's. Went to Schroon. Mowed few oats.

September 11
Went to Schroon on bicycle for Uncle Jim. Worked on tax list. Carried lamb to Fred Ford's. Lucy and Mildred R. were here visiting.

September 12
Went to Taylor's to have my eyes examined. Helped thresh at Culver's in p.m.

September 13
Picked up apples. Cut corn.

September 14
Cut corn. Loaded and unloaded wood. Dug wood chuck hole.

September 15
We cut corn all day. Went to Culver's as Uncle Jim is sick.

September 16
Went to Culver's. Pa and Ma went to Baptist meeting in forenoon. We all stayed at home in afternoon. Mary was here.

September 17
Began attending school at

Schroon. Went on my
wheel.
Am going to study
Geometry, Latin, Zoology,
and American selections.
September 18
Attended school.
September 19
Went to school.
September 20
Went to school. Uncle Jim
Culver and Mrs. Clara
Fairfield were married here
today. Went to school with
a horse as it was rainy.
September 21
Attended school. Went up
to Culver's in evening.
September 22
Pa and I went over on
George Fey's and dug two
bu. of potatoes. Uncle Jim
Whitney and Bird R. were
up. Visited with them and
churned. Mary, Leah, and
Uncle Henry called in
evening.
September 23
Bird, Us & Co. went to
Sunday School and M.E.
Church. Uncle Henry,
Mary and Leah were here
to supper.
September 24
Attended school.
September 25
Attended school.

September 26
Attended school.
September 27
Mary and I went to the
fair with Uncle Jim's buck
carriage. Had a big time.
September 28
Went to school. School out
at half past three.
September 29
Pa and I drew in one load
of corn. Then I wrote a
letter and went to post
office. Churned.
It rained in afternoon
some so I finished read-
ing "The last of the
Mohicans."
September 30
Went to Sunday School
and Lewis church. I
played organ in both.
Went to Fred Squires
in evening.

Monday, October 1, 1900
Attended school.
October 2
Attended School. Mary
finished working at
Culver's and came down
here to stay a few days.
October 3
Attended school.
October 4
Attended school. Caught

coon in corn field last
night.

October 5

Attended school. Mary
went home today.

October 6

Pa and I went over to
Deb's and got load hay
and took it down to Sam
Ingrahams.

October 7

Went to Church. Bird
went down to Uncle Jim's
after Grandma in
evening.

October 8

Went to school.

October 9

Attended school.

October 10

Attended school.

October 11

Attended school.

October 12

Attended school. Mary
rode down with me.

October 13

Pa and I went over to
Deb Hall's after hay.
I picked a barrel of apples
for Mrs. Russell.
Pa went to Schroon in
p.m. with wood. I covered
over wood pile.
Mary and Uncle Henry
went to Mill Brook.

October 14

It rained all day so we
all stayed at home. Aunt
Sophia was here.

October 15

Went to school.

October 16

Went to school.

October 17

Went to school.

October 18

Went to school. It rained
some.

October 19

Attended school.

October 20

Pa and I gathered apples.
Bird went to the Branch.

October 21

Went to Church. Sarah W.
stayed here all night.

October 22

Attended school.

October 23

Attended school.

October 24

Attended school.

October 25

Went to school.

October 26

Attended school.

October 27

Pa and I intended to go to
Ti to hear Depew but it
rained in a.m. so we
didn't go and in the afternoon it cleared off.

Churned. Husked corn.
Went to post office.

October 28

Went to S. S. and
Church.

October 29

Attended school.

October 30

Attended school.

October 31

Attended school. Had a surprise party here in
evening. Had a big time
until one o'clock.

Thursday, November 1, 1900

Attended school.
A Miss Seaman visited
here today.

November 2

Attended school.

November 3

Pa and I picked up apples
over on Abe Walker's. Got
50 bushels.

November 4

Went up and Uncle Jim
cut my hair.
We went to Sunday
School and M.E. Church.
Mary was over.

November 5

Attended school. Mr. Lewis
visited the school awhile in
the afternoon.
Stopped and helped Elsie do

a few examples.

November 6

Helped unload sawdust. Pa
and Ma went to Schroon.
I husked corn. Bird printed quite a lot of pictures.

November 7

Went to school. It rained
quite a lot.

November 8

Went to school. Pa went
up on auditor business and
did not get home until
after I had done the chores.
It was cloudy and rained
some. I did not get home
until after dark.

November 9

It rained and snowed so
I did not go to school. The
wind blew hard all day.
I studied quite a lot.

November 10

Went to the cider mill and
got our barrel of cider.
Churned. Pa tinkered up to
the school house.

November 11

Went to Church and S. S.
We saw a bear Arthur
Brucer killed on Ledge
Hill. Edith and Will were
here in morning.

November 12

Attended school.

November 13

Attended school.

301

November 14
Attended school.

November 15
Attended school.

November 16
Attended school.

November 17
We threshed here. Had 50 bushels of oats. I went to Mill Brook in afternoon.

November 18
Went to Sunday School and Church at Mill Brook. Visited etc. Came home towards night.

November 19
Attended school.

November 20
Attended school. Went with bicycle.

November 21
Attended school.

November 22
Attended school. Had terrible wind here last night.

November 23
Attended school. Finished circles in Geometry. Finished ophidia in Zoology. Had declension of audan felix amans and prudens in Latin, Class in American Selections reading the "Present Crisis" by Lowell.

November 24
I set up a leach and started soap. Helped Pa tinker back shed.
Went to So. Schroon, Studied quite a lot.

November 25
It snowed 6 or 8 inches last night, and nearly all day rather slowly. Pa and I went down to Emory Whitney's. Bird's Freddie had a run-away.

November 26
It snowed more last night and rained nearly all day so I did not go to school. Went up after Bird. Studied and helped fix cow stable.

November 27
It snowed nearly all the forenoon.
I studied and helped fix cow stable and went to school house twice.

November 28
Attended school.

November 29
Did not do any very great things. Mary and Uncle Bish were over. Fixed Bird's erasers.

November 30
Attended school.

Saturday, December 1, 1900
Puttered with soap. Helped

fix cow stable.

December 2

Attended church.

December 3

Attended school.

December 4

Went to school.

December 5

It snowed about a foot last night so I did not go to school. Helped Pa get ready to go to Schoon. Studied. Churned.

December 6

Went to school.

December 7

Went to school.

December 8

Shoveled off sugar house. Tinkered in hen house. My jaw is swollen quite badly.
Pa and Bird went to Schroon.

December 9

Went to Sunday School and Church. Rev. Mr. Pettibone preached last time today.

December 10

Attended school. My jaw busted in evening.
Pa and Ma went to social for Mr. Pettibone at Emory's in evening.

December 11

Went scholar.

December 12

Went scholar.

December 13

Attended school. They U.S & Granger killed hogs.

December 14

Attended school. Bessie Holden came home with me.

December 15

Picked up potatoes and carried them down to Don Bailey. The Charley Hill kids were here in evening to practice. Will Fairfield had tip over.

December 16

We went to Sunday School and Church. Bess and Bird went.

December 17

Attended school. Bessie Holden went home.

December 18

Attended school. Miss Brown came down with me to stay over night.

December 19

Attended school.

December 20

Attended school. Harry Bailey rode down with me. Via bono et. Epistula puero erat.

December 21

I wrote some letters, and went to the P.O.
Went up on hill to prac-

tice Christmas in after-
noon and To So. Schroon
in evening.
Got my violin bow.

December 22
Pa, Ma, Achsah and I
went to Schroon. Bird
stayed up.

December 23
Went to Sunday School.
There was no church.
The kids practiced some
after Sunday School.
Mary came over from
Adirondack to spend
Christmas.

December 24
We went down to the
church to help fix the
Christmas tree. Mary and
I took dinner at Emory
Whitney's.
Went to the come off in the
evening. I played violin
on voluntary.
Aunt Lib and
the boys were
over.

December 25
Went up
and helped fix the Charley
Hill tree. Fixed up a tater
and went to the tree in the
evening. Played both
organ and violin.

December 26
We went up and helped

clean school house.
Pa and Miss Jones went
to Schroon in p.m.
I churned and fixed gate.
Began helping Mary in
arithmetic.

December 27
Wrote some letters and
went to Post Office.
Studied quite a lot. Helped
get middlings to the barn.
Helped Mary on
Percentage.

December 28
Studied quite a lot in
forenoon. In Afternoon
Pa and I went over to Abe
Walker's barn and got in
a load of our hay.

December 29
Pa and I drew two loads
of hay. Studied some and
helped Mary on examples.

December 30
We all went to Sunday
School and Methodist
Church.

December 31
Pa and I drew two loads
of hay. Got Frank
Granger to help us unload
one load. Studied some.
Churned toward night.

Ther.   TUES. JAN. 1, 1901   Wea.
Fair.

Drew wood into the shed.
Pa and Ma went down
to Uncle Jim Whitney's.
Miss Jones, Mary and I
stayed at home.

Ther.   WEDNESDAY 2   Wea.
Clr. Cold.

Pa and I drew hay
from Walker's. Drew little
wood into shed. Had
picture taken in morning
and we developed it
in evening.

Ther.   THURSDAY 3   Wea.
12°

Drew little wood into shed.
Helped Mary in Arithmetic.
Pa and I cut little
wood down in woods.
Mary went home.

1901, Walter's last diary, *is
the smallest of all the diaries,
only 4 ³⁄₄" long,
and in perhaps the worst
condition of them all.
On December 26 of this year,
Walter wrote his last,
sad entry in a handwriting that
is small and wavering,
as he describes how sick
he is feeling.*

The Windsor Hotel, Schroon Lake

1901 "Tuesday, January 1. Fair Weather," so states Walter's first diary entry. The preface to this year's diary does not, however, convey a fair-weather feeling. There seems to be an element of foreshadowing of what we know is the inevitable. Considering that and all we have learned about Walter, this year bears witness to his finest moment. The studying and exam-taking paid off, and he became a teacher. He had as many as ten students at a time and traveled as much as thirty miles a day, by carriage or cutter, bicycle or foot, to present his lessons.

In spite of his busy schedule, however, Walter took time to enjoy a social life and often visited the Windsor Hotel in Schroon Lake.

Judging from Walter's generally gentle demeanor, one can assume that he was a compassionate teacher. One has to believe that he excused Harry Bradley for not having his homework done, due to the delivery of a new calf the evening before. Don't you suppose that he asked Horace Wilson to comfort and see to his little sister Janette when she fell during recess and hurt her arm? It is certain that Mr. & Mrs. Gregory welcomed him to take dinner and stay the night many times during the frigid winter months. Can you imagine the pride on Florence McCalom's face, as well as Walter's, when he presented her with the gold pin for "leaving off ahead?" Think of the excitement of Clarice Reid and Elinor Bradley and the satisfaction for Walter when they completed the five-times tables. One hopes that Norris Kingsley eventually came to understand the importance of books and learning and to admire and appreciate his teacher, Mr. Whitney.

*We assume this is a picture of Walter and his class
as it was found in the box with the diaries.*

One wonders what things must have been written in Walter's lesson-plan book. It's certain there was a current-events section. Walter grew to know the importance of things happening in the world and would assuredly help his students to grow in this regard as well. One can almost hear the sensitivity in his voice when he announced to his class at the Alder Meadow School on Monday, September 9, that the President had been shot and the Vice-President was standing by. How hard it must have been for him to tell them a week later that President McKinley died on September 14 from infection due to the assassin's bullet and that Theodore Roosevelt was now President of the United States. The only thing like it in Walter's life was the rumored Lagoy murder at the bridge in Schroon Lake in 1897. So the assassination of the President was a rude awakening, not only for his students, but for Walter, as well.

One has to wonder if Walter was able to adequately explain to his students the meaning of Teddy Roosevelt's quote, "Speak softly and carry a big stick?" Oh, but foreign policy could wait. More important things were on the agenda for these students. The sugar had peaked. The hay needed raking, and potatoes were ready to be dug. The house had to be banked. The old cat had kittens, and it didn't matter much that the Queen of England died and the new King was Edward VII. The important things were family, home, and community; and as Walter taught us all, "get lessons" and try to live so that each day becomes a legacy for the future.

Good bye, Old Year.

THE POTTERSVILLE FAIR

Walter and his father enjoyed trips to the famous Pottersville Fair, a favorite with farming and town families in the North Country. It was held in late September, after the hay had been harvested. While the Whitneys had only a short way to travel, others came considerable distances. Some stayed at the Pottersville Hotel, today known as the Wells House. The fair was held on a broad, flat section just north of the center of town and west of today's Route 9, across from the Glendale Road which leads to Adirondack and around Schroon Lake. Later, in the mid-20th century the site was occupied by Glendale, a popular dance hall and roller skating rink.

Unlike the county fairs in the region, the Pottersville Fair was privately operated. It appears to have been started in the early 19th century as the Glendale Union Agricultural Society, a display area for livestock and farm produce. It was especially well known for its floral displays, and for its half-mile racetrack for sulky and mounted racing. One newspaper estimated the fair was attracting 3,000 visitors per day. By Walter's time the fair had become more commercial and there was a greater emphasis on entertainment on a midway.

Seneca Ray Stoddard, the photographer and writer of guidebooks, made the mistake of visiting the fair in 1906. Appalled by what he saw, he wrote a scathing article for his magazine the *Northern Monthly*. Stoddard encountered a midway full of, to him, bizarre attractions. He saw a strong man lifting a barrel of water by his teeth, a palm reader named Mme. Freda, and all sorts of games designed to fleece the farmers. Looking for a place to sit, Stoddard found himself in a tent full of painted women and lecherous men, all the worse for drink.

But for many generations of hard-working North Country folk, the fair was just plain fun, an event to be anticipated during the long winters and pressured times of spring planting and summer cultivation. To them the fair offered cosmopolitan entertainment and an opportunity to mingle with people from other towns.

Diary   1901
For Identification:
My Name is Walter J.
Whitney
My Address is South
Schroon, New York

In case of accident
or serious illness please
notify
L. W. Whitney
South Schroon, N. Y.

Things to be Remembered:
The make of my Bicycle
is Newport Special
The number on the case of
my Watch is 1617433
The number of the works is
90064.

Size of my Hat 7
" " Shirt 154
" " Collar 18¹/2
" " Shoes 8

January 1, 1901
Drew wood into the shed.
Pa and Ma went down to
Uncle Jim Whitney's.
Miss Jones, Mary and I
stayed at home.
January 2
Clr. Cold
Pa and I drew hay from
Walker's. Drew little wood
into shed. Had picture
taken in morning and we
developed it in evening.
January 3
12°
Drew little wood into shed.
Helped Mary in
Arithmetic. Pa and I cut
little wood down in woods,
Mary went home.
January 4
Cold
Pa and I went to
Pottersville to have my
tooth pulled. Nora Floyd
came over here with Uncle
Henry.
January 5
My face was so sore and
ached so I didn't work
much.
Helped Pa load few logs in
p.m. Studied some. Face
and bunch ached quite
hard in evening.
January 6
We all went to S. S. and
Church. The reorganization
took place after the S. S.
January 7
Snowy
Pa and I went to
Schroon. I saw the Dr.
about my face.

Studied some in P.J.

January 8

Fair

Poulticed my face so did not go out much. Printed pictures. Some were of the cat. Studied.

January 9

Studied. Made some pictures.

Pa and I went to Pottersville to see about my jaw.

January 10

Finished reading Reveries of a Bachelor. My jaw busted in evening. Did not do much work.

January 11

29 31   Cld

Drew wood into shed. Helped do work in house. Ma and Nora visited at Culver's. We unloaded lumber.

January 12

Pa and I drew wood into shed. He went to P.O. in afternoon. Bird went to Schroon.

January 13

Attended Sunday School and Church. I was elected S. S. Tres. and Secty. Elsie came up after church. Lew R. and wife were here in evening.

January 14

Did some correspondence. Studied some. Puttered at pictures. Miss Jones packed up some of her duffle.

January 15

Attended school. Bird packed up and went to Schroon with me.

January 16

Rain

Attended school. Addie Stunard rode up and back.

January 17

Attended school. Mary Whitney came up home with me. Got Posy shod.

January 18

Attended school. Cold day.

January 19

-16°

It was so cold we did not do very much. Fixed plow to plow out road. Went to Post Office. Studied.

January 20

-16°

Went to Sunday School. Mr. Lewis preached.

January 21

Did not do very much in forenoon. Pa went to P.O. In p.m. we plowed out road over to wood and Pa and I drew two loads.

January 22

Went to examination.

Took a.m. Selections. Ate
dinner at Mr. Parker's.
Did not get around to do
much in afternoon.
Studied.

January 23
Went to examination.
Took Zoology and
Economics in afternoon.
Got through at 5:30 and
home at 7.

January 24
Went to Culver's. Helped
draw wood. Cut wood some
in afternoon.

January 25
Pa went to Riverside. I
cut some wood. Churned.

January 26
Pa and I cut a birch tree
for sled runners and cut
up part of the top for wood.
Ma and Uncle Henry
went to Mill Brook.

January 27
Attended Sunday School
and Church. Ma got home.

January 28
Attended school. There were
few regular classes, as the
last term was begun. Had
fun etc.

January 29
Attended school.

January 30
Attended school. Went to
prayer meeting in

evening afoot.

January 31
Attended school. Came
home about 2 p.m.

February 1, 1901
Attended school. Three visitors were at school in
afternoon. Went to choir
practice in evening. Aunt
Lucy came over.

February 2
Pa and I cut wood. Nice
day as ever was.

February 3
We went to Sunday
School. No church.

February 4
It snowed some nearly all
day. I did not go to
school. Studied. Churned.
Pa visited at South
Schroon. Uncle Henry
and Will cut wood for
Aunt Lu.

February 5
The wind blew so hard I
stayed in the house nearly
all day. Studied.

February 6
Felt rather mean in
morning. Was chilly and
sick to my stomach. Took
a sweat and felt very
mean all day.

February 7
Felt better today. Studied

quite a lot. Uncle Bish came over after Aunt Lucy. Cold day.

February 8
Pa did not feel good in a.m. and felt worse toward night. I did chores at night. Uncle H. and Will down in the evening. Uncle H. to stay all night.

February 9,
Pa felt little better. Ma improving too. Studied and did chores.

February 10
We all stayed at home. Emory and Mary came up in evening. Found Ma was sick.

February 11
Cared for the property. Folks on the gain on an average. Went to P.O.

February 12
Did chores. Folks not any better. Uncle Bish and Mary came over. She stayed over. Studied.

February 13
Wind blew hard all day. Did not do anything but chores and wait on women.

February 14
Another windy day. Did the same old thing. Helped

wash. Helped break out roads.

February 15
Uncle Henry and I went down to P.O. Wind blew hard all day. Will F. and I went to P.O. Did chores etc.

February 16
Dr. Dunn came up to see Pa. Mary went home. Did chores etc.

February 17
Went to Sunday School and did not stay to Church. Went up to Uncle Jim Whitney a little while.

February 18
Went to Schroon with corn to have ground. Got lot of merchandise and so on. Lew and Martha were up in p.m.

February 19
Pa had a bad headache and did not feel as well today. The Dr. was up again. Did chores.

February 20
Chored around in a.m.. and went to Schroon in p.m.

February 21
Chored around and did not work very hard either. Pa felt better.

February 22
Did the same old things.
Went to Post Office.
February 23
Uncle Henry and I went
to Mill Brook. Got home
just night. Aunt Lib and
Eddy were at Chester.
February 24
Uncle Henry and I went
to Sunday School and
Church. Pa feeling better.
February 25
Sawed little wood. Helped
wash. Emey Whitney up
in forenoon.
February 26
Sawed quite a lot of wood.
Went down in woods to see
Charles S. and I.C.W. Pa
did not work much but
did lot of chores.
Studied some.
February 27
Went up to Alder Meadow
to see about school. Studied
Sawed wood. Went to
prayer meeting in
evening.
February 28
Went to Post Office twice.
Laura Sherman came up
here. Sawed wood some.

———

Friday, March 1, 1901
Sawed wood and studied.

Went to Choir Practice.
March 2
Sawed wood and studied.
March 3
Went up to Culver's and
borrowed a cutter for the
folks. In afternoon I
drove to Schroon and
Elizabeth and I went for a
ride.
March 4
Sawed wood and studied.
March 5
Pa and I attended town
meeting. C. C. Whitney
elected supervisor against
C. L. Weeks.
March 6
Sawed wood awhile. Went
to Pottersville to have tooth
pulled.
Will Fairfield here in p.m.
while Pa and Ma went to
Quaker meeting. Composed
a new tune.
March 7
Sawed wood. Studied. Pa
drove away the dog that
followed me home yester-
day. Pa went to Schroon
in afternoon.
March 8
We sawed quite a lot of
wood. Studied. Pa went to
P.O. in a.m. and I went
down at night after my
mail.

March 9
Helped women some. Sawed wood. Heard that George Whitney died this morning at Lake Placid.

March 10
Pa and I went to Sunday School and meeting. Ma stayed at home with Grandma and Chase.

March 11
It rained and hailed so we did not saw wood. I studied a lot.

March 12
Sawed wood and studied, Martha and Myrtle Richardson were up here in afternoon. Went up to Schroon in evening and went for a drive and visit.

March 13
Sawed wood. Aunt Lib and Eddy were over. Went to P.O. in a.m. and Pa and I went to prayer meeting in evening.

March 14
Sawed quite a lot of wood then hitched up Posy and Uncle Henry and I went to Schroon. Called a few minutes at the Windsor. Visited the school and studied some.

March 15
Snowy

Copied music. Studied. Helped wash. Sawed wood. Shaved ladder rungs.

March 16
We finished cutting up our wood pile. Went to the Windsor in the evening.

March 17
Got nearly ready for Sunday School but Uncle Bish, Aunt Lucy and Mary came over so we did not go. I went to Schroon after Bird.

March 18
Went to Schroon and back home and got ready to go and went up to Jerper Gregory's to begin school.

March 19
Cloudy

Began teaching school today. Had five scholars Howard and Morgan Gregory, Norris Kingsley, and Harry and Georgi Heriman.

March 20
Cld

Had 5 scholars again today. Went down to Severance after school.

March 21
Rain Clr

Taught school. Had a new scholar – Willie Gregory.

March 22

Taught. Let out school. Started home at 3:30. Stopped at Schroon in route.

March 23

Rode bicycle on snow crust. Shoveled off sugar house, and we got down few buckets in p.m.

March 24

Went to Culver's and got barbered and went to Church and Sunday School, and from there to Alder Meadow. Stopped at S. in route.

March 25

Taught. Had 3 new scholars.

March 26

Taught. Had 2 new scholars, making ten present today.

March 27

Went down to Schroon to the examination in Geometry, but guess I failed. Howard G. carried me down. Called at the Windsor.

March 28

Taught. It went pretty well today.

March 29

Taught. Walked to school and rode home with Will Fairfield. Called at the Windsor.

March 30

Wrote some letters and went to Post Office. Churned and helped saw some wood in afternoon. Catted Bird in evening.

March 31

Went to Sunday School but did not stay at Church. Went to P.O. Jim W. came up in p.m.

Monday, April 1, 1901

Pa carried me up to the school in morning.

April 2

Taught.

April 3

Taught. It snowed some today. Had five scholars.

April 4

Taught.

April 5

Taught. Rode to Schroon with Frank Garfield and down to Uncle Jim's with him and then came home afoot.

April 6

Studied and visited with Bird. Ate sugar.

April 7

It rained nearly all day.

Stayed at home. Bird was there and we read, visited etc.

April 8

Taught. Pa brought me clear up as the water was way over the road.

April 9

Taught.

April 10

Taught. Came down to Schroon and stayed at Pell Jones'.
Bird came down and we studied some.

April 11

Went to Teacher's Examination. Took Drawing, Current Topics and English Composition. Lizzie came up to Jones' in the evening.

April 12

Went to examination. Took History and Spelling in a.m. Went for a sun bath. Took Reading, Civil Govt and Methods in p.m. Came home.

April 13

Helped churn. Worked in sugaring. We boiled until half past ten at night.

April 14

Went to Sunday School and Church. Lizzie and

Eunice came up with Bird and I rode back with them. Intended to go to Alder Meadow but didn't. Ha! Ha!

April 15

Walked up to a.m. in morning and taught school.

April 16

Taught. Very fine day.

April 17

Taught. Mary Wallace visited us after the afternoon recess. Stayed at the school house writing until after 5 p.m.

April 18

Helped saw wood in morning.

April 19

Helped saw wood in morning. Taught and let school out at 3:30. Rode down with Mr. Gregory. Lizzie and I went to show in evening. Pa went too.

April 20

Tinkered number machine, globe and bicycle. Drove up sheep. Cleaned hay pen.

April 21

Attended Sunday School and Church. I played the organ in both. Bird rode down with Mr. Parker. It

rained in afternoon.
April 22,
Pa carried me up to school.
Taught. Cloudy and
rainy.
April 23
Taught. Cloudy and
rainy.
April 24
Taught.   Cloudy
April 25
Taught. Sawed wood in
morning and after supper.
April 26
Taught. Let out at 3:30
and Mr. Gregory brought
me down to Schroon via
Paradox.
Rode home with Pa.
April 27
Pa and I picked up stone.
Blabbed with Bird.
Went to Choir Practice.
April 28
Went up and cut Uncle
Jim's hair. Got ready and
went down on my wheel
to Uncle Jim W.'s to din-
ner, and then to George
Whitney's to funeral.
Went to church in
Schroon in evening.
April 29
Stayed at Jones' and rode
up to Alder Meadow in
morning and taught.
Shook up a kid.

April 30
Taught school. Changed
my room last night.
Cloudy and rainy. Called
at Wilson's after school.

Wednesday, May 1, 1901
Taught. Fixed Lennie
Wilson's violin at noon.
Went down to Geo.
Shaw's after supper, and
stopped at Wilson's a few
minutes.
May 2
Taught.   Rainy
May 3
Taught in forenoon and
in afternoon took or had
our pictures taken. Had
short Arbor Day exercise
and went home.
May 4
Helped clean Bird's bicy-
cle. Churned. Set up leach.
Pa and I went over
beyond Marsh Pond.
Shot twice at a wood
chuck. Went to Schroon
in evening.
May 5
Uncle Henry and I
intended to go to Mill
Brook but we couldn't get
a boat. Visited I.C.W.
before church. Attended S.
S. and church.

May 6

Taught. We went sucker-
ing after school.

May 7

Taught. Took supper with
Eva Wilson.

May 8

Came home in morning as
Uncle David came yester-
day. Aunt Lucy, Uncle
Bish, Mary, Grace and the
company all came.

May 9

Went up to Uncle Jim's
in morning. We went up
there to dinner. Visited
Bird's school. Planted few
potatoes. Sung.

May 10

My wheel gave out so I
had to have Pa carry me
up a ways toward school.
Taught. Came down afoot
to Uncle Jim W's and
stayed. Called at Windsor.

May 11

Tinkered bicycle. Churned.
Helped wash carpet. Pa,
Bird and I went to
Schroon in evening.
Went north for a little
drive.

May 12

Pa and I went to John
Crawford's funeral. I
stayed up and called here
and there.

May 13

Went up from Jones afoot
and taught.
It rained in morning
some.

May 14

Taught.

May 15

Taught. Called at Jimmy
Bradley's and Dennis
Bradley's after school.

May 16

Taught.

May 17

Taught. Walked down as
far as Uncle Jim W's and
rode home with Pa.

May 18

Helped clean house. Did
not do a very great lot. It
rained nearly all day.

May 19

It rained early all day so
we did not go to Sunday
School. Went down to
Fred Ford's after Mary
towards night.

May 20

Pa carried me up to the
village and then we went
in a load to Crown Point
to Institute.
I. C. Warren and I
roomed together. We went
down to the Lake House.

May 21

Attended Institute. Went

down to the station. Wrote a letter.

May 22
Attended Institute. Went to the last end of a ball game. Went to Vermont. Went to Lake House again until 11 p.m.

May 23
Attended Institute. Went shopping in p.m. after Institute. Peeked in at the dance window.

May 24
Attended Institute in forenoon. We came home in p.m. Called at The Windsor. Bird came up home with Pa and I.

May 25
Tinkered bicycle. Slept up some that I lost during the week. I. C. Warren called in the p.m.

May 26
Went to Schroon to Memorial service on my wheel. Took dinner at Uncle Jim Whitney's. Lizzie and I visited more or less.

May 27
Pa brought Mary and I up to Schroon and I went to school from there with my bicycle. Taught.

May 28
Taught. It rained quite a lot.

May 29
Taught. Finished reading "Pioneers". Went home after school.

May 30
It rained quite a lot today. I painted wood-work.

May 31
Took Pinkey and went to Alder Meadow and taught and went home.

Saturday, June 1
Churned. Helped fix Bird's bicycle. Helped draw manure. Planted citrons, beans, cucumbers, melons etc. Talked bicycle trade.

June 2
Went up to Uncle Jim's. Aunt Lucy and Uncle Bish came over. Went to S.S. and Church. Went to Alder Meadow, Called at the Windsor.

June 3
Taught. Went to Schroon after school.

June 4
Taught. Morgan and I went fishing after school. Got 19. My bicycle tire sprung a leak.

June 5

Taught. Tinkered bicycle.

June 6

Taught. Hot. Started for home after school but it rained so I had to stay at Uncle Jim W's.

June 7

Taught. Went home.

June 8

Tinkered bicycle. Went fishing in afternoon. Got 32 trout.

June 9

Attended Church. Had no Sunday School. Herb Wood went down with Bird and I.

June 10

Went up to school and taught. Came down to Schroon and made a few calls.

June 11

Taught. Tinkered bedroom window.

June 12

Taught. Very warm.

June 13

Taught. Came home after school.

June 14

Taught. Went up and back with horse.

June 15

George and I cultivated and hoed potatoes.

I churned and help set up stove after dinner. Bird and I went to Commencement at Schroon.

June 16

Attended Sunday School and Church.

June 17

Went to school and back with a horse which I got shod at night.

June 18

Ditto

June 19

Went up with bicycle. Taught and went up to Carey's to stay as Mr. Gregory's people moved up there. Norris got hurt.

June 20

Showery

Taught.

June 21

Taught. Nice day after it cleared off about 8 a.m. Went home.

June 22

Pa, George, Uncle Henry and Jim and I cleared off fallow over on Merrill's Hill. Very warm.

June 23

Attended Sunday School and Church. Wrote a letter.

June 24

Rode up from home and

taught and then came back to Schroon to get my wheel fixed. Fred Sawyer did it. Went back to Alder Meadow.

June 25
Taught. Very warm.

June 26
Taught. Warmer.

June 27
90°
Taught. Went home. They got the cat out of the well today.

June 28
Pa and I went up to Alder Meadow. I taught and he led a new cow home and I drove home at night. Miss Fountain was up.

June 29
Tinkered bicycle. Picked strawberries. Hoed sweet corn. Bird and I went to market with our berries.

June 30
We all attended Sunday School and Church.

Monday, July 1, 1901
Tinkered bicycle in morning and then went up to school. Roscoe Carey and I went fishing and got none.

July 2
Taught. Warm.

July 3
Taught. Went home after school.

July 4
Picked strawberries. Pa and I went over and looked at Abe Walker's hay. Bird and I intended to go to Schroon but it rained.

July 5
Went up to school with a horse. Took some berries to the village.

July 6
Set out cabbages. Hoed gardens. Went to Schroon in evening. Had quite a visit. Met someone coming home.

July 7
We all stayed at home all day except when Bird and I went to the P.O. It rained about church time. Mr. Havens buried at 2 p.m. We had our picture taken.

July 8
Went up to school. Norris and I had a little understanding in afternoon. A new hired girl came to Carey's to work.

July 9
Taught. Went up to Wilson's at noon.

July 10
Taught.

July 11
Taught. Mr. George Smith came up and stayed at Mr. Carey's all night.

July 12
Taught. Went home.

July 13
Helped Paris green potatoes. Worked at haying. Went to Taylor's.

July 14
Went to Sunday School and Church.

July 15
Drove up to school and finished up. Went up to Carey's to supper. Called at Windsor in evening.

July 16
Hayed it. Quite a change too.

July 17
Hayed it some. Had big rain in p.m.

July 18
Hayed it.

July 19
Hayed it.

July 20
Mowed little. Machine broke. Weeded gardens. Helped Uncle Jim and Henry hay it in p.m. Uncle Sam came up.

July 21
Did not do much of anything. Uncle Sam and Jim here. Eddy. Rupert Johnson and Rev. Vodra here to dinner. W. to I.

July 22
Worked haying west. of house. Went to Emory Richardson's in morning.

July 23
Hayed it. Uncle Sam around here.

July 24
Hayed it. Got in 3 loads. Caught 2 wood chucks. Aunt Sophia came up with Pa from Taylor's.

July 25
We mowed back of barn and got in some. We mowed yesterday. Uncle Sam helped us some. W 2 I.

July 26
Pa and I went to Schroon in a.m. Hayed it some in p.m. I went over and looked at our taters. Sold chickens. W. to I.

July 27
Finished haying in the orchard.

July 28
Went to the church but Mr. Parker did not come.

July 29

It rained so I did not work very hard. Chopped brush beside road. Weeded strawberries.

July 30

Uncle Jim, Henry and I wed out our fallow potatoes. Went to Schroon in evening.

July 31

Hayed it east of barn. W. to I.

Thursday, August 1, 1901

Hayed it. Machine broke in a.m. and Pa went to Page's after a new wheel.

August 2

We finished haying here.

August 3

Ma and I went to Schroon. I went again after supper on my bicycle.

August 4

Went to S. S. and Church.

August 5

Hayed it on Walker's after we moved over there.

August 6

Hayed on Walker's.

August 7

Did lot of tinkering on bicycle and went on it to Chester in p.m.

August 8

Rode to Warrensburgh. Took examination in p.m. Stayed down at Dickinson's.

August 9

Went to Caldwell and to Glens Falls. Took examination in p.m. We went over to Rob Hall's in evening.

August 10

Came home from Warrensburgh. Very muddy roads.

August 11

Went to S. S. and Church. Uncle Sam went.

August 12

George and I mowed down south fallow on Walker's.

August 13

Hayed it on Walker's George Bruce tipped over.

August 14

We hayed it on Walker's. Grandmother died at 4:45 in p.m.

August 15

Went berrying, fishing and berrying. Pa and Ma went to Schroon.

August 16

W. to I. Went to Fred Ford's after wagon.

Helped get our organ to Culver's. Grandmother's funeral at 2 in p. m.

August 17

Dug potatoes. Charley Stanard helped me in a. m. and Uncle Henry in p. m.

August 18

W. to I. Went to Mrs. Jim Carey's funeral at Schroon in afternoon.

August 19

W. to I. Pa started to Buffalo. Went to Schroon with potatoes.

August 20

Dug potatoes. Poked cows. W. to I.

August 21

Eddy and I dug potatoes in a. m. In p. m. we went berrying. W. to I.

August 22

W. to I. Went to Schroon with potatoes and dug in p. m. Eddy and I.

August 23

Dug potatoes and went to Schroon with them. W. to I.

August 24

Went to Taylor's and Riverside after Pa. Paid Clayton Griswold $1.25.

August 25

Went to S. S. and

Church. W. to I.

August 26

We dug potatoes and I went to Schroon with load in afternoon. Music catalogue came.

August 27

W. to I. Mowed oats. Emory W. helped us.

August 28

We worked getting up oats. Went to lawn social at Emory W.'s in evening.

August 29

Finished our oats. Puttered around in p. m. while Pa went to village.

August 30

Got up at 3 a. m. Lew Richardson, Charley Stanard, and Thurman Warren and I went to Burlington.

August 31

Got home at 4:30 a. m. Slept some. Went to Schroon in p. m. and enjoyed a school.

Sunday, September 1, 1901

It rained nearly all day. W. to I. We all stayed at home.

September 2

Dug potatoes. Pa went with them in the after-

noon. Posy fell down.
Tinkered bicycle.

September 3

Dug potatoes. Pa delivered
them. Pulled weeds. Chased
the cows out of the corn.

September 4

Dug potatoes. We unloaded
oats. Went berrying. Pa
and Ma went to
Pottersville.

September 5

We dug few potatoes.
Cleaned hen house.
Went to Mill Brook in
p. m. Heard Rev. C. M.
Tower preach in evening.

September 6

Visited in Mill Brook in
a. m. Came home in p. m.
We got in out scatterings.
Went to I. and to Choir
Practice. Heard McKinley
was shot. Got stung.

September 7

Went up and put up col-
lector's notices.
We dug 6 bu. potatoes. Pa
went to church meeting in
p. m. and I worked on
cash book.
Have a hard cold.

September 8

Attended Church and
Sunday School. Rode
home with Herb Wood. He
stayed till evening.

September 9

Began teaching at Alder
Meadow. Drove up and
back.

September 10

Taught.

September 11

Taught.

September 12

Taught.

September 13

Taught. Bird Jones came
up home with Pa.

September 14

Cut corn. Visited with
Bird. President McKinley
died this morning.

September 15

Bird was here. It rained so
we did not go to Sunday
School. I went to
Taylor's in evening

September 16

Drove to school and back.
Got Pinky shod.

September 17

Drove up and back and
taught.

September 18

Drove up and taught and
drove back. Got Posy shod.

September 19

Taught till 3 p. m.
McKinley day. Drove up
and back. Copied tax list.

September 20

Taught. Came home on

my wheel. Went up on it too.

September 21
Went on a cow trip to Granger's.
Finished cutting corn.
Took Ma to Taylor's.
Visited with I.C. Warren.
Went to Church meeting.
Went to Fred Ford's.

September 22,
Went to S. S. and Church

September 23
Taught.

September 24
Taught.

September 25
Taught. Came home for the fair.

September 26
Went to the fair. Pa and Ma went too. Fell off my wheel.

September 27
Uncle Henry and I went to the fair.

September 28
Had toothache so I could not work in forenoon. Went down and Will Hall pulled 2 in p.m. Helped draw in corn.

September 29
Went to Sunday School. No Church.

September 30
Went up and back with the horse.

———

Tuesday, October 1, 1901
Taught. Went up on my wheel.

October 2
Taught.

October 3
Taught.

October 4
Taught. Came home.

October 5
Pa and I husked corn in the field all day 22 bushels.

October 6
Went to S. S. and Church.
Wrote some in the evening.

October 7
Drove up and back. Got two shoes set on Posy.

October 8
Went up on wheel. Taught school.

October 9
Taught.
Began boarding at Mrs. Wilson's tonight.

October 10
Taught.

October 11
Taught. Came home after school.

October 12
Pa and I dug potatoes.

October 13
Rainy. Did not do much of anything.

October 14
Drove up and back with Pinky.

October 15
Went up and taught.

October 16
Taught.

October 17
Taught.

October 18
Taught. Came home. Snowed little today.

October 19
Went to P.O. Helped make line fence by muck bed. Bird Jones came up in a.m. I churned and gathered apples in p.m.

October 20
Attended S. S. and Church

October 21
Went up and taught.

October 22
Taught.

October 23
Taught.

October 24
Taught.

October 25
Taught.

October 26
Drew sawdust and load of leaves. Pa not feeling very

well as he was sick during week.

October 27
Went to funeral of George Blinn.

October 28
Taught.

October 29
Taught.

October 30
Taught.

October 31
Taught.

Friday, November 1, 1901
Taught. Came home.

November 2
Churned. Ma and I went to Schroon in afternoon.

November 3
Went to Sunday School and to Church in evening.

November 4
Drove horse up and back to school.

November 5
Went down around S. S. selling soap. Wrote for Star. Churned. Went to meeting in evening.

November 6
Taught.

November 7
Taught.

November 8
Taught and came home.

Sold soap some. Went to meeting in evening. Played organ.

November 9,
Banked up house. Churned. Carried Pa's dinner up to him. Drew leaves in p. m. Went down to South Schroon.

November 10
Went to meeting in evening Ma and I. We all stayed at home and did not go to S. S.

November 11
Went up and taught. Sent after soap, cards and books.

November 12
Taught.

November 13
Taught.

November 14
Taught. Cloudy squally day.

November 15
Taught. It snowed 2 or 3 inches last night. Came on bicycle through snow down to Jim Whitney's where Pa met me.

November 16
Cleaned hen house. Went over to W. Person's and to P. O. Churned.

November 17
Went to S. S. and Church. Eddy and Uncle Henry over from Mill Brook.

November 18
Pa carried me up to Lee Garfield's and I rode my wheel what I could from there. Taught.

November 19
Taught.

November 20
Taught.

November 21
Taught.

November 22
Taught. Came home on bicycle.

November 23
Painted fancy things with gold paint. Went up and piled up little sugar wood. Picked up 10 bu. potatoes. Pa went to Pottersville.

November 24
We all stayed at home all day and never saw only one man. It snowed some nearly all day.

November 25
Drove up and back with Posy.

November 26
Drove up and came back to Uncle Jim Whitney's. Pretty windy night.

November 27
5°
Drove up from Uncle Jim's and came back home

at night.

November 28

Went down and got my soap and desk. Drove around and delivered soap.

November 29

We drove two rigs to Schroon and then Pa carried me up and I walked back at night.
He got horses shod.

November 30

We Us and Co. butchered. Went down to S. S. with half a ham for Frank Hall. Bird rode back with me.

Sunday, December 1, 1901

Went to Sunday School and Church. Uncle Henry and Aunt Lucy came over.

December 2

Drove to Alder Meadow and back

December 3

Drove up and back. Was cloudy and rained a little in morning.

December 4

Drove up and back.

December 5

Drove up and back.

December 6

-7°
Drove to school and back. Cold in morning.

December 7

Pa and I cut brush beside road in forenoon.
In p. m. I went down around the burgh selling butter, soap and books.

December 8

Went to Sunday School.

December 9

Drove up to school and back. They closed the school for a time because of measles. I have a hard cold.

December 10

Did not feel very well. Stayed in house. Studied. Pa and W. Ford worked down by Alder Brook tomorrow and not today.

December 11

Chopped some beside road. Studied.

December 12

Pa, Walter Ford and I skidded and cut logs down by Alder Brook. I rolled them about 72.

December 13

We cut and burned brush beside road. Went to social at George Richardson's in evening.

December 14

Churned. Helped burn brush. Fixed wagon. It

rained some and wind blew terribly from the south.

December 15
It commenced growing cold in morning and continued thus all day. Went to Sunday School and Church.

December 16
Pa carried me up by way of Paradox and the river flats were flooded. Began at 10 a.m.. Quite cold day.

December 17
Taught.

December 18
Taught. Felt rather out of sorts all day.

December 19
I had the wheezes so I did not sleep much last night and my lungs felt mean so I came home. Did not feel good a bit in p.m.. Dosed and doctored. Harry Thayer died today.

December 20
Felt some better today. Did not go out any. Read Burke's Speech on Conciliation through. Pa went to Schroon.

December 21
Pa and Ma went to Schroon. I studied and composed a Xmas piece of music. Uncle Jim was here a while in p.m.

December 22
Went to Sunday School They practiced for Christmas quite a while after.

December 23
Lazed around. Did not go out very much. Cold is on my lungs quite bad. Went down to church in evening.

December 24
Studied. Pa went to village. Did not feel very well.

December 25
Did not feel very well especially towards night. The rest went to the Xmas tree and Chase Grandma and I stayed at home. Coughed quite hard.

December 26
Guess I have the measles. Coughed awful hard all day. Went to bed in evening and began to sweat and foam.

Memorandum

In the storms of life,
When you need an umbrella
May you have to hold it,
A handsome young fellow.

Perhaps at some time,
we must part,
And Oh! It is
with an earnest heart,
That I ask thee,
while in glee,
Or in sorrow, to
" Remember me."

When the name
that I write here
is dim on the page,
And the leaves
of your album
are yellow with age,
Still think of me kindly,
And do not forget,
That wherever I am,
I remember you yet.

EPILOGUE

Two weeks after his last diary entry, Walter died on January 9, 1902. His gravesite and tombstone can be found in the South Schroon Cemetery.

Walter's mother, Marion, was born March 20, 1855, and died February 9, 1940. Walter's father, Lewis, was born March 21, 1852, and died October 22, 1926.

Walter never mentioned any brothers or sisters in his diaries. He is also the only child buried with his parents. However, it was known that Lewis and Marion adopted a girl, probably after Walter's death. This daughter is mentioned as Mrs. George Dupree in her mother's funeral notice (see page 344). The granddaughter, Miss Ruby Dupree, was known to some of the older residents still living in the Schroon Lake area.

Charlotte Rowe, who still lives in Schroon Lake, was a Cole before marriage and lived as a child in the house pictured on page 241 of this book. Charlotte's grandfather on her mother's side was one of Lewis Whitney's brothers. Charlotte is also pictured on her grandmother's lap in the Family Album (see page 348).

Many of the people mentioned in these diaries are buried in the South Schroon Cemetery, which can be found on the Old Schroon Road just north of Exit 27 on the Northway.

It is also interesting to note that Maude Patreau, who apparently dated Walter, later married Charles Holden, who was two years younger than Walter. Charles wrote his memoirs of life in Schroon Lake as the son of the miller who had a grist mill at the bridge in the Town of Schroon. The Holden memoirs are available in the Schroon-North Hudson Historical Society Museum.

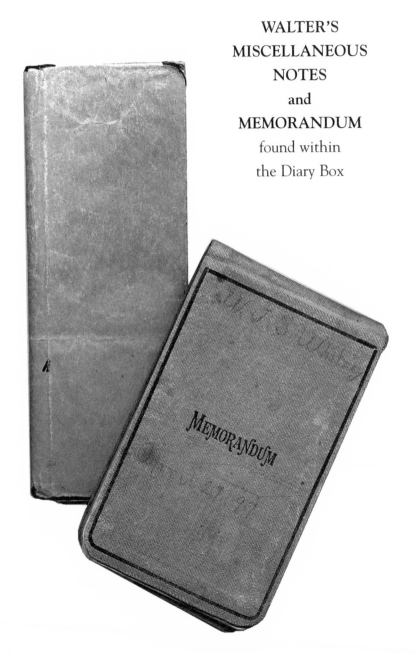

WALTER'S
MISCELLANEOUS
NOTES
and
MEMORANDUM
found within
the Diary Box

1901

W. J. Whitney
(page 8)
South Schroon, N.Y.
Cash Receipts.

Oct. 1	Pencils	.02
		.04
2		.01
8		.01
10		.01
		.01
	Laura Sher	.83
Nov.10	School Dist.	1.50
10	F. Sawyer	.25
27	F. McCalvin	.02
28	Laura Sherman	1.78
27	Mrs. J. Bradley	1.50
Dec. 1	Brad Jones	1.50
9	Dist. No 11	35.00

Cash Payments   (PAGE 10)

Aug. 30	Fare to Burlington	
		1.50
	Expense there	.50
Sept. 2	Postage N.R.S.R.	.18
	Envelopes	.22
5	Boat fare	.10
10		.10
	Postage E.J.D.	.02
	Envelopes P & S	.06
Sept. 2	tablets P & S	.10
13	Postage M.D.	.02
	Cookies W.P.& Co	.05
16	Postage Ref.	.02

17	R.R.&Co.	.02
18	Candy D.C.B.B	.05
17	Stamp M.E.D.	.02
18	Peppermint P.& S.	.13
20	Rhubarb Dr. P.	.15
25	Legal	
	Cap	.05
26	Fair Fare	.25
	Bananas	.05
	Candy	.01
	Check Bicycle	.01
	Peaches	.10
27	Fare to Fair	.25
	Expense	.15
Sept	Brot Over	4.40
30	Postage L.A.C.S	.01
	Pencils	.10
	Paper	.10
4	Cement	.15
7	Prospectus	.25
	Postage	.02
	Pen & Holder	.02
	Physiology	.50
	Envelopes	.22
	Ball	.10
	Pamphlet	.05
18	Envelopes	.03
21	Tape	.10
	Tablet	.05
29	Postage Star	.03
1	Saleratus	.08
2	Candy	.05
2	Middlings	2.70
11	Soap	10.00
	Cards	.25
	Books	1.50
		20.78

Nov.	16 Brot over	20.78
"	" Postage & Fee	.15
"	18 Postage Rep.	.03
"	" Postage on Books	.48
"	" Postage	.02
"	" Pen	.01
"	23 Varnish	.10
"	25 Middlings	2.70
"	26 Board Wilson	11.00

Dec.	9 Board Greg	7.00
"	7 Will Hall	.25
"	14 Social	.25
"	19 Gregory for W.O.	.25
"	" Burke's speech	.10

James Expectorant

Syrup squills	2 oz.
Tincture tolu	12 drams
" "	1 dram
" "	2 drams
laudanum	4 grains
powdered ipaca	4 grains

Mix.

School Enrolled
1901

Morgan Gregory	12/22	10
Willie Gregory	2/25	7
Harry Bradley	2/17	8
Horace Wilson	3/25	8
Clar(ice?)	Rec'd	6
Howard Gregory	5/8	
Norris Kingsley	12/27	13
Florence McCalom	11/6	12
Elinor Bradley	3/1	7
Jannette Wilson	5/16	6

FAMILY NAMES
MENTIONED IN THE DIARIES

Allen
Babe
Bailey
Barnes
Barney
Billings
Bishop
Blanchard
Blinn
Bradley
Brooks
Brown
Bump
Burbank
Careys
Carpenter
Church
Clapper
Clark
Cole
Cornell
Coutois
Crawford
Culver
Cyrus
Day
DeLorma
Dickinson
Dunn
Fairfield

Fey
Ferguson
Floyd
Ford
Foster
Fountain
Garfield
Geame
Granger
Grant
Green
Gregory
Griswold
Hall
Havens
Heriman
Holden
Howe
Hunt
Huntley
Hurd
Ingraham
Johnson
Jones
Kennenbach
Kingsley
Knox
Landing
Leland
Lewis

Lynn
Maxim
McAllister
McKee
McKinley
Morehouse
Mundy
Murdock
Nichols
Noble
O'Neal
Page
Palmer
Parker
Parsell
Pascos
Passino
Patreau
Persons
Pettibone
Pierce
Prouty
Rice
Richardson
Rickert
Robbins
Rounds
Russell
Sawyer
Schneider

Seaman
Shaw
Sherman
Silverman
Smith
Sprague
Squires
Stanard
Stone
Stowell
Taylor
Thayer
Todd
Torins
Tower
Traver
Tripp
Tyrrell
Walker
Wallace
Warren
Warrington
Watson
Wilson
Wood
Wright
Young

WHITNEY FAMILY GENEALOGY
THOMAS AND MARY (BRAY) WHITNEY
Westminster, England

JOHN WHITNEY *b.* 1589   *d.* 1673   *m.*   Elinor   *d.* May 11, 1659
m.   Judith Clement

John and wife Elinor left England April 1635 and arrived in Watertown, MA June 1635

John   Richard   Thomas   Jonathan   JOSHUA (first born in America)

JOSHUA, Deacon   *m.*   (#1 Lydia) (#2 Mary) (#3 Abigail Tarbell)

Cornelius *b.* 1680   *m.*   Sarah Shepherd

Sarah   Abigail   **Matthias**   Mary   Joshua   Lydia   Sarah

Matthias *b.* May 26, 1720   *m.*   Alice

Matthias *b.* February 22, 1749 *d.* Killingly, CT c. 1800   *m.*   Elizabeth Vaughn

George   Aaron   Martha   Elizabeth   Sarah   Selah (female)   Achsah (female)

George *b.* March 10, 1775 Killingly CT/Foster, RI *d.* Oct. 1856, Schroon Lake, NY *m.* Lillis Graves *b.* 1777 *d.* 1861

Eseck   Cyrus   Ira   Delila   Celia   **CHAUNCEY**   Marcia Ann   Betsey Lansford   **GEORGE M.**   Edward F.

GEORGE M. *b.* April 5, 1817, Schroon Lake, NY *d.* April 26, 1901   *m.*   Olive Baker *c.* 1845

Charles C.   Halsey B.   Celia Ann   Elizabeth

Charles C. *b.* 1847 Schroon Lake, NY *d.* May, 1915 Schroon Lake, NY *m.* Celeste P. Root November 12, 1872

Male infant *b.* May 14, 1875 *d.* May 16, 1875   **Clarence R.**

Clarence R. *b.* July 7, 1876 Schroon Lake, NY   *m.*   **Kate B. Tyrrell**, October 16, 1906
d. March 13, 1924, Schroon Lake, NY

Charles T. *b.* June 3, 1909 Schroon Lake, NY *d.* June 16, 1990, Glens Falls, NY   *m.*   Winnifred Reaffel

Rutheda Elizabeth (Burke)   Clarence Charles   Kathryn Jane (Batt)

Chauncey *b.* 1804 *d.* 1884   *m.*   Lucy Barnes *b.* 1806 *d.* 1891

Lewis   Emory

Lewis *b.* 1852 *d.* 1926   *m.*   Marion Culver *b.* 1856 *d.* 1940

WALTER *b.* 1882 *d.* 1902   Beth *m.* Dupree
(author of diaries)

Ruby

Emory *b.* 1847 *d.* 1917   *m.*   Mary Richardson *b.* 1852 *d.* 1926

Mabel *b.* 1880 *d.* 1952   Jesse Cole *b.* 1875 *d.* 1962

Charlotte Rowe   Racheal McGinn

A
Whitney
Family
Album

Walter's mother's
obituary

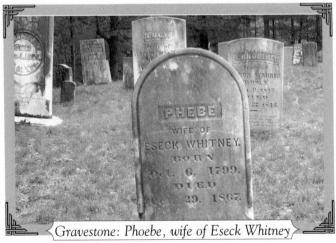

Gravestone: Phoebe, wife of Eseck Whitney

Henry Culver

Scaroon Manor Group

Chums at Taylor House – 1899

Taylor's on Schroon – Circa 1880

Emory Whitney

Mary Richardson Whitney

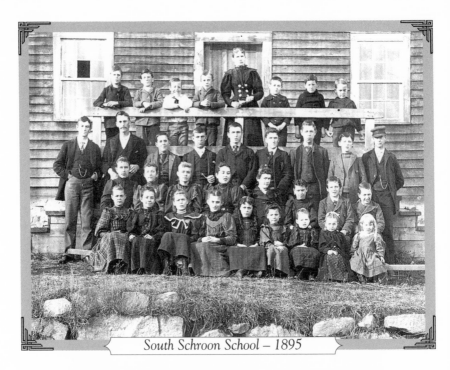

South Schroon School – 1895

Mary Whitney (1921) and
Charlotte Rowe (5 years)

Chauncey Whitney

Lucy Barnes Whitney

Taylor House – 1898

BIBLIOGRAPHY

Aiken, Conrad, *Comprehensive Anthology of American Poetry*, New York: Random House, 1944.

Bernstein, Burton, *The Sticks, New York:* Dodd, Mead & Co., 1972.

Gilborn, Craig, *Durant, Blue Mountain Lake, New York:* Adirondack Museum, 1981.

MacColl, Gain and Wallace, Carol McD., *To Marry an English Lord*, New York: Workmen Publishing, 1989.

Metcalfe, Ann Breen, *The Leland House: An Adirondack Innovator*, Elizabethtown, New York: Essex County Historical Museum, 1994.

Metcalfe, Ann Breen, *The Schroon River*, Lake George, New York: Warren County Historical Society 2000.

Murphy, Eloise Cronin, *Theodore Roosevelt's Night Ride to the Presidency*, Blue Mountain Lake, New York: Adirondack Museum, 1977.

Sloane, Eric, *Our Vanishing Landscape*. New York: Funk & Wagnalls, 1955.

ELECTRONIC SOURCES

Internet: Google; www.ScopeSys.com/today/

INTERVIEWS

Jim Williford, Jean Williford, Gertrude Beswick, Phyllis Bogle (Town of Chester Historian).

LECTURE

Godine, Amy, "Adirondackers Anonymous: Lost Worlds and Hidden Heroes in Northern New York." Alice T. Minor Museum, Chazy, New York, 2000.

PICTURES AND POSTCARDS

Archives of Schroon-North Hudson Historical Society Museum.

Book design, Cover Design, and Special Photographics by Nadine McLaughlin.

Picture collections of Virginia Fish and Charlotte Rowe.

Original line illustrations by John Osolin and Bob Borquist.

PRIMARY SOURCES

"South Schroon," *Essex County Republican*, 3 July 1900. Brewster Library, Essex County Historical Society, Adirondack History Center Museum.

Historical Archives of Essex County, Essex County Historical Society, Adirondack History Center Museum.

Historical Archives of Schroon and North Hudson, Schroon-North Hudson Historical Society Museum.

Gray, O.W and Son, *Topographical Atlas of Essex County New York*, Philadelphia, 1876.

Smith, H.P., ed. *History of Essex County*, 1885.

Smith, *History of Warren County*.

Adirondack Museum Library.

References

Conklin, Henry, *Through Poverty's Vale*. 1832–1862.

Jones, Clarence, *When Does A Twig Become A Limb?* 1988.